Arnold Jacobs:
Song and Wind

Brian Frederiksen
Edited by John Taylor

WindSong
Press
Limited

The following trademarks appear throughout this book:
Inspirx®
Voldyne® is manufactured by Sherwood Medical of St. Louis .

Portions reprinted from the following sources:
Atlanta Brass Society Journal, copyright 1995.Used with permission.
Billboard. ©1949, 1954 BPI Communications Inc. Used with permission from *Billboard*.
Ron Bishop and *TUBA Journal*. Used with permission.
Brass Bulletin. ©1981 by Roger Bobo and Brass Bulletin (Jean-Pierre Mathez,). Used with permission.
David Brubeck and *TUBA Journal*. Used with permission.
Chicago Reader. Copyright ©1984 Chicago Reader, Inc. Used with permission.
Chicago Symphony Programs. Copyright ©1995 by The Orchestral Association. Used with permission.
Chicago Tribune. © Copyright Chicago Tribune Company. All rights reserved. Used with permission.
Charles Daellenbach and The Canadian Brass. Used with permission.
Jeff Funderburk and *TUBA Journal*. Used with permission.
Hal Leonard Corporation. Used with permission.
Paul Haugan and *TUBA Journal*. Used with permission.
The Horn Call. Used with permission.
International Trumpet Guild Journal. Used with permission.
Journal of the International Trombone Association. Used with permission.
Daniel Kohut and *TUBA Journal*. Used with permission.
Charles Lipp. Used with Permission
Musical America. Reprinted with permission of K-III Directory Corporation.
Ravinia Festival. Used with permission.
Softkey International. Used with permission.
William Trusheim. Used with permission.
Simon & Schuster, Inc., from *Season with Solti: A Year in the Life of the Chicago Symphony* by
          William Barry Furlong. Copyright ©1974 by William Barry Furlong. Used with permission.
Mayo Clinic Family Health Book. Copyright ©1993, IVI Publishing, Inc. All rights reserved. ©1993 by Mayo
          Foundation for Medical Education and Research. Reprinted with permission, all rights reserved.
Richard Schneider and Fritz Reiner Society Newsletter. Used with permission.
Smithsonian. ©1995 by *Smithsonian*. Used with permission.
Sony Classical. Used with Permission.
Dee Stewart and *TUBA Journal*. Used with permission.
Cover photo © John Taylor. Used with permission.
TUBA Journal. Used with permission.
WFMT-FM. Used with permission.
Ed Whitfield and *TUBA Journal*. Used with permission.

First Printing 1996
Second Printing 1996
Third Printing 1998
Fourth Printing 2000
Fifth Printing 2002
10th Anniversary / Sixth Printing 2006
Seventh Printing 2010

ISBN: 0-9652489-0-9
Library of Congress Card Number: 96-60508
WindSong Press Limited

To Arnold (1915-1998),
Gizella (1911-1999),
and my mother,
Mary Grundset (1926-1996)

Arnold Jacobs:
Song and Wind

Table of Contents

Arnold Jacobs, Dale Clevenger and Adolph Herseth on the cover of the Chicago Tribune
Sunday Magazine, *January 27, 1985*

Foreword by Adolph Herseth

I cannot think of anyone in our exotic world of music, and particularly, of course in the world of brass players, who has made such a contribution to so many facets of our art. Having Jake as a personal friend and colleague for all these years has been a marvelous experience, not just for me, but for everyone who had the good fortune to be associated with him—both on stage and off stage.

Keep it up, Jake!!

i

Foreword by Dale Clevenger

High School was for me most memorable because of my activities in the music department. The director of the bands at Chattanooga "City" High School was for many years A.R. Casavant. He is probably known for his expertise in the marching realm however, he was equally wonderful in the concert band field. One of his methods of inspiration for us was to play recordings at lunch time, before and after school.

Most often we heard the Chicago Symphony recordings because "Cass" considered the CSO and its famous brass section as the best in the world. The foundation of this great brass group was, of course, Arnold Jacobs, a legend in his own time.

Very early on, I dreamed of being a professional musician and naturally, playing with the CSO was a primary goal. In February 1966, I realized my ambition and was engaged as Principal Horn (Gulp!!). I found myself actually sitting near Arnold Jacobs every day. It was unbelievable!! For over twenty years Jake was my colleague, my friend, my mentor and yes, even my teacher.

While we spent hours on stage playing rehearsals and concerts, off stage we conversed about many subjects. During the rehearsals, I was treated, nearly daily, to Arnie's beautiful tone and his lovely phrasing. To this day, it is often Arnie's natural sense of music making that motivates me, and I try to emulate.

Off stage among the subjects were music, teaching, philosophy of teaching, medicine and just life in general. Literally, every subject imaginable! I recall the information this dear gentleman imparted to me, in daily life and at critical times. I am touched at just how he was able to enrich and influence me. When it comes to teaching, a most important part of any musician's life, not one lesson that I teach passes that is not replete with Arnold Jacobs' wonderful and profound ideas. Also, as a teacher I am forever indebted to him.

Freely and graciously he shared his whole self to me. He helped me immeasurably with the horn, my artistic ideas and my teaching. My friend, Arnie, was for me a musical angel.

Preface

Growing up in the Chicago area, my mother would often take me to Chicago Symphony Orchestra concerts. Here I was first exposed to great music even before I had played a note on an instrument. Afterwards, I began playing the trumpet, later switching to tuba.

A few years later, while I was a student at Interlochen, Michigan, we were playing Bartok's *Concerto for Orchestra*. For the first time, I really heard the magnificent sounds of Mr. Jacobs while listening to the Chicago Symphony recording with Fritz Reiner conducting. I have never been the same player since.

In 1974, I had my first lesson with Mr. Jacobs. It was the most remarkable lesson I have ever had! He had recently moved his studio to the fourth floor of the Fine Arts Building. Later that year I enrolled at the American Conservatory of Music, at that time located on the fourth and fifth floors of the Fine Arts Building. I was constantly at his studio while studying with him until 1978.

During this time I saw the steady flow of students come into his studio. They played all wind instruments and would travel from all parts of the world to improve their skills with the master. As is his custom, he would always introduce them to me.

By the time I was in graduate school at Northwestern University (1978-80), Mr. Jacobs had retired [from Northwestern, for the first time], but his legacy was there as it always should be. Starting in the summer of 1981, he gave the first of his week-long master classes at Northwestern.

With a legendary teacher such as Mr. Jacobs, once you are a student, you are always a student. When he gave a master class, I would show up whenever possible.

During 1986, I began assisting him and video taping his sessions at Northwestern. Starting in 1991, I began traveling with both Mr. and Mrs. Jacobs throughout the country for all master classes. I always made a point of packing a video camera in my luggage to preserve his lectures.

For years, Mr. Jacobs has constantly been asked "When are you going to write a book?" In 1987, Dee Stewart compiled *Arnold Jacobs The Legacy of a Master* {see: Acknowledgments}[1] that primarily consisted of tributes from many of his students and colleagues. As years passed, Mr. Jacobs' eyesight was failing and arthritis was taking its toll. Obviously he was not physically able to write a book. It was something that had to be done.

Arnold and Gizella Jacobs with Brian Frederiksen

Starting in January 1992, I gathered all the information that I could find about him. It was scanned into the computer and created a large but unorganized document. Next, through much editing, an outline for the book was created. On the next trip with him, in my luggage was another tool—a laptop computer. After each session, I would enter the day's notes. Additional research was done for background material. Many of his colleagues and past students were consulted, portions of master class tapes were transcribed and he granted me interviews that I had transcribed. After final writing and editing, the long-overdue book emerged.

This book tells about Mr. Jacobs' life as a performer and teacher. There are several lists including colleagues and recordings. Although his teachings make up more than half the book, it is neither a "how to" nor a medical book. There is no discussion of the therapeutic treatment of diseases.

I have included many quotes from Mr. Jacobs' spoken statements. They were not intended to be transcribed, but to communicate with an audience (or individual) to best get a message across, and often has a casual flow. I wanted the reader to imagine themselves in the audience being personally addressed, and have not tidied up his speech for grammatik perfection. I hope no one will find fault with this, and if they do, my apologies.

Also, Arnold Jacobs nearly always refers to the student as being of the male gender, "he". The reason for this is that the reference most often originates with the tuba population, which, until very recently, were almost always men. Mr. Jacobs has had many wonderful women students, and his master classes appear to be evenly mixed with men and women.

In June 1995 a draft of this book was presented to Mr. Jacobs in honor of his 80th birthday. It is an overdue present from myself and many of his friends. To Mr. Jacobs:

Happy 80th birthday, and we hope that you have many more!

Brian Frederiksen

Acknowledgments

Creating a book about Arnold Jacobs is an impossible job for one person to do alone. A group of his students and colleagues pooled information to make this a reality. All shared the vision that a comprehensive book documenting Mr. Jacobs' career was needed. They gave up their valuable time and were more than helpful.

John Taylor studied the tuba with Mr. Jacobs from 1962-66 before his career in both the Buffalo and Quebec Symphony Orchestras. Later he was a member of the United States Army Band (Pershing's Own). During this time he was also involved in photography and journalism. Upon his retirement from The Army Band, he became the editor of the *TUBA Journal (1994-98)*. John was a perfect choice as editor of *Arnold Jacobs: Song and Wind* as he brings experience from two worlds, journalism and music. John is also a professional photographer and provided many photos including the cover photo.

David Fedderly was a student of Mr. Jacobs from 1973 to 1983. Later he became the tubist of the Baltimore Symphony Orchestra. As a teacher, he has taught in the Chicago area and is currently on the faculty of the Peabody Conservatory and the University of Maryland. He has been enthusiastic from the moment he first heard about this book and was especially helpful working with the discography.

Richard Nelson, M.D. is a member of the Illinois Brass Band where he is a part of the tenor horn section. He received his training at Stanford University, the University of Chicago, University of New Castle upon Tyne, and University College - London. He is currently a surgeon and professor at the University of Illinois at Chicago College of Medicine. As a horn player and physician, he has had an interest in the physical requirements of brass playing. As a medical consultant, Dr. Nelson helped explain the complexities of physiology.

Roger Rocco is a Chicago native who studied with Mr. Jacobs in the late 1960s. He was a member of the Honolulu and Seattle Symphonies before his return to Chicago where he has taught at the VanderCook School of Music and Northwestern University. Roger has written many articles inspired by Mr. Jacobs' teachings.

Robert Rusk was the tubist of the Milwaukee Symphony for twenty-five years. He has taught at the University of Wisconsin-Milwaukee and Northwestern University. In addition to being a performer, he is the designer of the Canadian Brass and Getzen tubas and euphonium. Bob provided much information on the York tuba and was the chief proofreader of the book.

v

In June 1995, during the International Tuba Euphonium Conference, an 80th birthday celebration occurred with many who contributed to Arnold Jacobs: Song and Wind. *From left to right are: Bob Rusk, Brian Frederiksen, Gizella Jacobs, Arnold Jacobs and Dr. Richard Nelson. Also present were David Fedderly and John Taylor.*

Norman Schweikert has been a member of the Chicago Symphony Orchestra horn section from 1971-98. He is working on his own book, *Bio-Bibliographical Index of Symphony and Opera Musicians in the Major U.S. Organizations, 1842-1992.* He has provided much background information on members of the CSO and other colleagues of Mr. Jacobs.

For those few questions that Norman could not answer, Brenda Nelson-Strauss at the Chicago Symphony Archives provided information. Many photographs of the CSO and its members came from the Archives. Resources used in this book will be given to the Archives.

For over thirty years, Harvey Phillips has been *the* driving force behind the acceptance of the tuba. When approached with the idea of a book about Arnold Jacobs, Harvey offered his support including the resources of the Harvey Phillips Foundation. Although retired from Indiana University, he offered support to me as if I were a doctoral student. His advice was invaluable.

This is not the first book about Mr. Jacobs and hopefully will not be the last. To help those in the future who would like to continue research, Carole Nowicke provided expertise on the bibliography. A tuba player, she is working on a doctorate in library sciences at Indiana University.

One of Mr. Jacobs' earliest students was Abe Torchinsky, the former tubist of the NBC Symphony, Philadelphia Orchestra and professor at the University of Michigan. He brought a perspective of Arnold Jacobs beginning in the 1930s.

Several colleagues have offered tributes in recognition of their years of having the privilege of knowing Mr. Jacobs. Those colleagues include Dale Clevenger, Adolph Herseth, Edward Kleinhammer, Gene Pokorny, Charles Vernon and CSO Executive Director, Henry Fogel.

In the preparation of this book a wide variety of institutions and individuals were contacted requesting the use of previously published materials for direct quotes and as background material. The *Instrumentalist* magazine has, over the years, published several articles about Arnold Jacobs, and The Instrumentalist Company is the publisher of *Arnold Jacobs The Legacy Of A Master*[1] by M. Dee Stewart. Unfortunately, The Instrumentalist Company has not granted permission for the use of any materials published by them. However, the author wishes to thank Dee Stewart for granting permission for the use of materials authored by him, but published other than by The Instrumentalist Company.

Those organizations and individuals who have graciously granted permission to reprint material include: Mike Moore, *Atlanta Brass Journal*; Ron Bishop; Susan Kaplan, *BPI Communications*; Jean-Pierre Mathez, *Brass Bulletin*; David Brubeck; Tom Teranova, *Chicago Reader*; Sandy Spikes, *Chicago Tribune*; Charles Daellenbach; Jeff Funderburk; Brenda Cline, *Hal Leonard Corporation*; Paul Haugan; John Pherigo, editor, *The Horn Call*; Vern Kagarice, Editor, *Journal of the International Trombone Association*; Anne Hardin, editor, *International Trumpet Guild Journal*; Rod Richards, *IVI Publishing*; Stephanie Challener, *K-III Directory Corporation*; Daniel Kohut; Denise Wagner, *The Orchestral Association*; Jack Zimmerman, *Ravinia Festival*; Doug Gillespie, *Simon & Schuster*; Jim Doherty, *Smithsonian Magazine*; Joe Seward, *Softkey International*; Warren Wernick, *Sony Classical*; William Trusheim; Karen Cotton, Ed Goldstein, *TUBA Journal*; Lois Baum, *WFMT-FM*; and Ed Whitfield.

Starting in 1991, I traveled with Mr. and Mrs. Jacobs across the country for his master classes. This gave me valuable time with him resulting in much of the data that went into this book. Those who organized master classes during this time were: Col. John Bourgeois and Captain Frank Byrne, *United States Marine Band*; Paul Ebbers, *Florida State University*; Richard Frazier, *University of Oregon*; Jeff Funderburk, *University of Northern Iowa*; Art Jennings, *University of Florida*; Doug Klein and Steve La France, *University of Arizona*; Ed Livingston, *Illinois State University*; David Hickman, *Summit Brass-International Brassfest*; Rex Martin, *International Tuba Euphonium Conference (ITEC)*; Jim Moore, *Northwestern University School of Music*; Don Owens, *University of South Florida, Playing Less Hurt*; Harvey Phillips, *Indiana University*; Charles Schuchat, *Northern Illinois University*; Alan Siebert and Steven Gross, *University of Cincinnati*; and Susan Slaughter and Becky Staub, *First International Women's Brass Conference.*

Many individuals provided information or technical assistance. Included are: Franco Albion; *Baltimore Symphony Music Library*; Daniel Corrigan, *Indianapolis Symphony*; David Dahl; Richard Frazier, *University of Oregon*; Mark Frederiksen; Ed Goldstein, *Towson State University*; Mike Goode; Genevieve Grosbaum; Charles Guse, *Chicago Federation of Musicians*; Dr. Edwin Heilakka, *Curator - Stokowski Collection, Curtis Institute*; Wally Horban, *Chicago Symphony Music Library*; Jim Howarth; Dallas and Dorothy Jacobs; Roger Janssen; Michael Johnson; Sheldon Kirshner; Charles Lipp; Donald Little, *North Texas State University*; Rex Martin, *Northwestern University*; Margaret McGregor, *Discount Music*; *Northwestern University Music Library*; William Scarlett, *Chicago Symphony Orchestra*; Paul Schmidt, *Heavy Metal Music*; Richard Schneider; Pat Sheridan; Becky Smith; and Bob Tucci, *Bavarian State Opera.*

Assistance came from other members of the *Illinois Brass Band* besides Dr. Nelson. Others included George Foster, Colin Holman, Ian Robinson, Laura Smith and Jim Sobacki.

Once the research, writing, and layout were concluded, it was time to go to print. This was done by Thomson-Shore located in Dexter, Michigan. Their assistance and expertise were invaluable. While their entire staff was helpful, those individuals who were of assistance included Jim Holefka, Bill Campbell, Diane Nourse, Laurie Briegel and Sue Campbell.

During the early 1980s the TUBA Chapter in the Chicagoland area was the Metropolitan Chicago Area Tuba Society [*Metrocats*]. The group later disbanded but left funds for education. These funds were transferred through the Harvey Phillips Foundation and used to partially defray production costs of this book.

While writing this book, I worked with Art Morganstein as a consultant for audio-video systems. He always allowed me to take time off to work with Mr. Jacobs both in Chicago and on the road.

One day, I was working in the home of Irwin Schneider. He had recently moved and had an overstock of cameras and video equipment. It did not take me long to explain that I needed some to preserve the teachings of a great musician. He generously gave me all the equipment with the hope that I could put to it good use. Being an opera lover, Irwin has indirectly benefitted by listening to those who have studied with Mr. Jacobs.

From the beginning of this project, my mother, Mary Grundset has put up with a lot of grief! I would disappear while she would need things done. She was the person who was mainly responsible for transcribing tapes. Being both a flutist and a nurse, she transcribed some of the complex terminology with which others had difficulty.

Finally, Gizella Jacobs. She took care of Arnold for over sixty years allowing him to continue making music.

Musicians everywhere thank you for this.

Arnold and Gizella Jacobs during their sixtieth anniversery celebration, December 1997

Early Years (1915-1930)

Arnold Maurice Jacobs was born in Philadelphia on June 11, 1915, the youngest of Albert and Mary Jacobs' four children. His sister Agnes was six years older than Arnold, brother William five years and sister Charlotte fifteen months.

His father, Albert A. Jacobs was an accountant, who had earlier studied medicine but never practiced. Within six months of Arnold's birth, Albert moved his family to Long Beach, California, where he worked as a shipyard paymaster.[2] Later, the family moved to other towns in southern California including Los Angeles, Long Beach, Santa Monica and Willow Brook, a small town, population 400, on the edge of the desert.

Arnold's mother, Mary Singer Jacobs, was, according to Arnold, "A very fine professional pianist." She had studied as a concert pianist, and had performed on the Pantages Circuit of Vaudeville. She later provided piano and organ music for early silent films on the California movie lots. Mary was a second-generation musician, as her father was a violinist. The household was filled with music, with Mary playing the piano many hours a day, and the family singing along with her.

Arnold's father, Albert Jacobs in a portrait painted by Gizella Jacobs

Arnold was not the only third-generation musician of the family. His brother, William played bass, and his sister Charlotte played piano. His cousin, the late Joseph Singer, also had a distinguished musical career.

Joseph Singer began his career in 1927 as a violist with the Detroit Symphony. In 1931 he began playing in the horn section, and in 1933 assumed the position of third horn. In 1937 he was a member of the Boston Symphony Orchestra horn section. In 1943 Singer became principal horn of the New York Philharmonic, moving to associate principal in 1944, and, in 1967, again became principal horn until his retirement in September 1974. One of his many students was Dale

Clevenger, current principal horn of the Chicago Symphony and a colleague of Jacobs' for many years. Joseph Singer passed away on September 1, 1978.[3]

Arnold Jacobs' first performance was not in the concert hall, but in the movies. During the silent-picture era, the studios would send people into the neighborhoods looking for extras. In 1920, when he was five years old, he lived in Los Angeles near Studio Lodge. One day someone knocked on the door looking for children to appear as extras in a Mary Pickford film.[4]

Mary Pickford was Hollywood's first female superstar and was called "America's Sweetheart." During her career, Pickford won an Academy Award for her first sound motion picture, the 1929 production *Coquette,* and a special Academy Award in 1976 for lifetime achievement. In 1920, Pickford made *Pollyanna*, an adaptation of Eleanor Porter's book about the "glad girl." Her second film of 1920 was *Suds* in which Pickford was a laundrywoman. These are considered her two classic silent movies.[5]

Jacobs remembers his mother telling him that he was paid $5 to eat an ice cream cone. Viewing both films, there is no scene with a child eating an ice cream cone, but there are several scenes with children used as extras. The closing scene of *Pollyanna* has Mary Pickford holding a little blond boy on her lap in a trolley car. Jacobs has viewed this and has stated that it may be him.

When Arnold was four years old, his mother taught him piano for about a year. He has often said, "She was my first, and perhaps, one of my finest music teachers."[6]

Several years later, when he was ten or eleven, he wanted a bugle, which his parents purchased. Willow Brook had no brass teacher at the time, so his mother played the various bugle calls on the piano, and by listening as his mother played, he learned to play the bugle by ear. He then began walking about the neighborhood practicing, much to the consternation of his neighbors.

He became an instant success with the local Boy Scout troop, which needed a bugler. The minimum age to be a Scout was twelve, and he was only eleven, but they put him into uniform anyway. In a Boy Scout competition, Jacobs later won a silver-plated bugle.[7]

Arnold (right) with sister Charlotte
Photo from collection of Arnold Jacobs

His father then bought Arnold a Wurlitzer trumpet, but no instruction book. Although he did not approve of a music career for Arnold, he agreed that if music was to be studied, it should be done on a good instrument. Arnold figured out the valve positions by listening to the pitch his mother would play on the piano, imitating it and writing down the fingerings. His connection was directly from the ear to the brain, such as the Suzuki method developed many years later.

At this point, Arnold's mother would bring home music, and she would play the piano with Arnold playing the melody line. Jacobs states, "I played many difficult things but no one told me about the difficulty."[8] It was later, in grade school, that he played in his first orchestra, as their lone trumpet player.

On the wall in his room, he had a picture of Saul Caston, then principal trumpet of the Philadelphia Orchestra. He would practice in front of a mirror imitating his embouchure. At the same time, the nearby Long Beach Municipal Band was led by the famous cornetist of the Sousa Band, Herbert L. Clarke, who quickly became Jacobs' idol.

During this time, he was working on the *Carnival of Venice,* and won a school competition when he performed it. However, he became discouraged with the trumpet. He was disappointed because other trumpet players in the school had silver instruments—his was brass. Then his father heard a recording of Herbert L. Clarke and told Arnold, "You don't sound like he does. You're not doing so well." Arnold recalls, "To a little fellow, it was more than a little discouraging," and he drifted away from the trumpet.[9]

When he was about twelve or thirteen, Arnold had a job as a theater usher, the only non-musical job he ever had. Part of the job involved changing the lettering on the theater's marquee, which he hated, since it meant going up a ladder. However, he took part of the money he earned and bought an old trombone for $10 from a pawn shop. It was a silver-plated Philadelphia Keefer with a gold bell, and held together with string and tape.

He had the same problem with his trombone that he had with the trumpet, "I did not have a book, so I worked it out by knowledge of partials—like the bugle system. As a kid, I became a pretty good trombone player—I loved the instrument."

He planned to play the trombone in the junior high school band, but his relationship with the trombone was short-lived. While traveling through the mountains of west Texas with his family in their 1927 Hudson, the trombone, which was strapped to the running board, fell off and was lost forever.

When he returned to junior high school in Santa Monica, he had ideas of playing a school trombone, but the bandmaster told him that he had no trombone for him to play. However, he did have a new King sousaphone, and no one to play it. The mouthpiece was a King *Equa-tru*, a large mouthpiece that, to him, felt like a "coffee cup."[10]

3

Since he had learned the *Carnival of Venice* on the trumpet, he started to play it on the sousaphone with much success and rapidly became first tuba in his school band. A local newspaper sponsored a newsboys' band and they lent him a tuba on which to practice. It was at this point that he had his first teacher. Jacobs stayed with the tuba because they made it so attractive. His career as a tubist started like so many other tuba players—he fell into it.

"I knew a great deal about music from my mother who was a fine, master musician. She taught me a great deal and accompanied me. I was having a ball playing, while I did not have proper teaching [as a brass musician], I was challenged to interpret music at a very early age."

By this time, Arnold was in high school, attending Los Angeles' Manual Arts High School. He was having continuing success with the tuba, and grown to five feet ten inches and all of 135 pounds.[11] In 1929, the Jacobs family moved back to Philadelphia.

Arnold's mother passed away in 1936, at the age of forty-six, his father, Albert, lived well into his nineties passing away in the mid 1970s.

4

The Curtis Institute (1930-1937)

The Curtis Institute of Music in Philadelphia is one of the major music conservatories in the United States. Founded by Mary Louise Curtis Bok, the school provides full-tuition scholarships to all of its students.[12] One of Jacobs' teachers at John Adams Junior High School in Santa Monica was a graduate of the Curtis Institute, and he suggested that when he moved back to Philadelphia that he audition for the Curtis Institute.[13]

For his audition, Jacobs played a four-valve Conn E♭ tuba, which he played as a BB♭ tuba by tying the fourth valve down and pulling the slides sufficiently to allow him to play in tune.[14] He played the *Carnival of Venice*, with all variations, and Herbert Clarke's *Stars in a Velvety Sky*. The audition panel consisted of Josef Hoffman, director of the school; Philip Donatelli, tubist of the Philadelphia Orchestra and the Curtis Institute's tuba teacher; and the concertmaster of the Philadelphia Orchestra.

Next, they asked him to play the tuba part of the overture to Wagner's *The Flying Dutchman*. It was the first time he had seen a high C. He did not think he could hit the note and brought it down to a B♭.

Excerpt from the tuba part of Wagner's The Flying Dutchman

He remembers saying to the panel, "'I cannot play that, it is too high for the tuba!' I was a fifteen-year-old playing on a little E♭ tuba.
"They asked, 'Why do you say that?'
"I said, 'It's a C. The highest note on the tuba, according to the [Otto Langley] book, is B♭, that's what I was told.'
"They just laughed and said, 'Well, try it again.'
"I tried it and missed it.
"They said, 'Try it again.'
"I tried it again, and played it perfectly. I played the rest of the music without a problem."

Finally they asked him to play Wagner's *Rienzi* Overture.

Recalling that audition, Jacobs said, "Can you imagine that little E♭ horn with a valve taped down. I was doing Wagner operas and all sorts of music on it. They liked me very much. I had a very fine audition."

Having passed his audition, he was rejected because he was underweight. His father, realizing the value of a full scholarship in depression-ravaged America, took him to the soda fountain for milk shakes and egg creams to put on weight. He gained about ten pounds in two weeks. Finally he was admitted as a fifteen-year-old-scholarship student.

Being in college at age fifteen was more than a challenge as he was thrust into college level courses without finishing high school.[15] He graduated from the Curtis Institute in 1936, but remained there until 1937.

Faculty

At that time, the Director of the Curtis Institute was Josef Hoffman who helped found the school in 1924, and taught piano. In 1927, he was appointed director until his retirement in 1938 to devote full time to concertizing and radio performances. During it's fiftieth anniversary, The Curtis Institute wrote about Hoffman, "His genius was unique not only as a performer and teacher, but also as an analyst of the talents and abilities of others."[16] As part of the audition panel, Hoffman must have realized the talent that Jacobs possessed in order to admit him to the Curtis Institute as a fifteen-year-old.

The faculty of the Curtis Institute was formed of teachers from all aspects of music, composition, harmony and counterpoint, solfege, music history, all orchestral instruments, piano and voice. Additionally, the school's faculty had members who taught foreign languages and diction, and had two academic tutors.[17]

The instrumental faculty consisted primarily of members of the Philadelphia Orchestra. The brass faculty during Jacobs' term at the Curtis Institute consisted of Saul Caston, trumpet (1924-42); Anton Horner, horn (1924-42); Charles Gerhard, trombone (1931-42) and Philip Donatelli, tuba (1928-42). The wind department was closed for portions of World War II starting in 1942.[18]

When asked about his most influential teachers, Jacobs mentioned his mother and these teachers from the Curtis Institute:[19]

Philip Donatelli, Tuba

Philip Donatelli was the tubist of the Philadelphia Orchestra from 1923 to 1948 and the tuba instructor at the Curtis Institute from 1928-42. He was born in 1885, and later began playing the tuba in his hometown of Roseto, Italy. He played in several bands in Europe before coming to the United States at the age of twenty.

Philip Donatelli
Autographed "To my good friend Arnold Jacob"
Photo From the collection of Arnold Jacobs

Before his appointment to the Philadelphia Orchestra, he played in many famous American bands including Pryor's, Conway's and Vesella's. He died in Ardmore Park, Pennsylvania, on April 5, 1954.[20]

Jacobs has always referred to Donatelli as a fine musician with a beautiful sound, but Donatelli was also a strict disciplinarian. If Jacobs missed a note or made a mistake during a lesson, Donatelli would have him repeat the entire work for the next lesson. Jacobs said, "He did not say much or play much in lessons, but I did hear him play at concerts, and that taught me a great deal."[21]

During this era, the solo repertoire for the tuba consisted mostly of mediocre works. Jacobs, therefore, appropriated material from other instruments such as the horn concertos of Mozart and Richard Strauss. He also found a great deal of vocal material suitable for the tuba. He often commented that violinists and pianists would practice works from the great masters, yet tuba players had only pieces such as *Solo Pomposo*.

During his first years at the Curtis Institute, Jacobs played on the school's Italian-made CC tuba, which was not a good instrument. One day, Donatelli brought him to the Academy of Music [the home of the Philadelphia Orchestra] to show him a tuba that was specifically made for the Philadelphia Orchestra. Unfortunately, Donatelli, a corpulent man, could not use the instrument because each time he took a breath, the mouthpiece would move away from his lips. It was in 1933 that Jacobs bought his York tuba from Donatelli for $175 {see: York Tuba}, an instrument he would play throughout his career.[22]

In 1948, Donatelli was forced to retire from the Philadelphia Orchestra due to it's mandatory retirement age of sixty-five, a policy since changed.

Renee Longy-Miquelle, Solfege

During his entire time at the Curtis Institute, Jacobs studied solfege, repeating the course every year. He has stated, "Solfege is one of the finest studies a brass player can undertake. By assigning a name to a note, a concept of pitch is created in the brain." Therefore, it is not surprising that he would say that Renee Longy-Miquelle was an influential teacher.[23]

Madam Longy arrived in the United States from France in 1914. One year later, in 1915, she formed the Longy School of Music in Boston, with her father, Georges Longy (1868-1930) who was principal oboe of the Boston Symphony from 1898 to 1925.

During this time she taught at the New England Conservatory of Music and, in 1925, wrote a book on music theory.[24] She then taught at the Curtis Institute (1926-41) and later The Juilliard School, Peabody Conservatory and the University of Miami. She died May 10, 1979, at the age of eighty-one.[25]

Fritz Reiner, Conductor

Jacobs' long relationship with Fritz Reiner began at the Curtis Institute where Reiner was the conductor of the Curtis orchestra from 1931 to 1941. Reiner was forty-two and Jacobs was fifteen. Later, they would be reunited in the Pittsburgh and Chicago Symphonies {see: Conductors: Reiner}. During his career, Jacobs felt that he "Saw more of Reiner than of my own father." Reiner was not part of Jacobs' audition at the Curtis Institute, and had never met or heard him play until the start of school.

With the exception of grade school [where he played the trumpet], the Curtis Institute Orchestra was the first orchestra with which Jacobs had ever performed, and he continued with Reiner and the orchestra his entire time at the Curtis Institute.

Years later, Paul Haugan asked, "Was Reiner's approach to the student orchestra at the Curtis Institute different in any way from his approach to professional orchestra?"

Jacobs replied, "Very, very slightly. He did not particularly like to teach. He was a very severe taskmaster with a young group. But he had proficient musicians and very high standards. Actually, there was a philosophy on his part that you were already musicians. Of course, he allowed us time to develop our parts—we did not have to sight read perfectly—but were allowed to take our parts home and develop them. However, at rehearsals he demanded fine performance, and he received excellent performances."[26]

After Jacobs bought his York tuba from Donatelli, he brought it to the Curtis Orchestra rehearsal. They were playing an arrangement of Bach's *Toccata and Fugue in D Minor*, which was perfect for a large tuba. When he played his first note, the difference in tone from the school's tuba was so noticeable that Reiner's head jerked up, and he stared straight at Jacobs. During the break, Reiner asked him to play his York tuba at all rehearsals. Jacobs brought the tuba to school on the trolley every day, until, once, when the trolley driver slammed on the brakes, a large woman in front of him fell—and landed right in the bell of his new tuba! Although the woman was not injured, the rim of the bell was bent. Jacobs told Reiner that it was too difficult bringing the tuba to rehearsals on the trolley. Reiner agreed, but still wanted the sound of that tuba.

In response, Reiner sent his personal car and chauffeur to Jacobs' house every rehearsal day. The chauffeur brought him and his tuba to Casimir Hall for rehearsal and at the end of the day, he would drive Jacobs and his tuba home. This continued for several years![27]

Jacobs has said, "With the York tuba, which is a tubist's version of a Stradivarius, and with a conductor like Fritz Reiner, I had a tremendous start for a career."

Marcel Tabuteau, Phrasing

The Curtis Institute required all wind players to take a class on phrasing taught by Marcel Tabuteau, then principal oboist of the Philadelphia Orchestra. Jacobs said, "All wind players would be in one class as a group, and we would study his concepts of phrasing and play exercises to develop control of the instrument so that we could develop phrasing. I rarely played tuba parts in Tabuteau's class, because, in order to get the greatest benefit from the class, I had to be exposed to a wide variety of music that would require all types of phrasing. I found it one of the most rewarding classes I had at the school."[28] Although the school required only one year in Tabuteau's class, he spent three years.[29]

Tabuteau was born July 2, 1887, in Compiegne, France, and studied oboe with Georges Gillet at the Paris Conservatory. In 1905, he came to the United States and played in the New York Symphony Orchestra. He joined the Metropolitan Opera Orchestra in 1908, then under the direction of Arturo Toscanini. In 1915, he joined the Philadelphia Orchestra during the Leopold Stokowski era. He remained with Philadelphia for thirty-nine years, and became one of the most familiar figures in the orchestra. Tabuteau retired in 1954, another victim of the Philadelphia Orchestra's mandatory retirement age of sixty-five.

Tabuteau taught at the Curtis Institute from 1925 to 1942, and again from 1943 until his retirement in 1954. The Curtis Institute awarded him an honorary doctorate, and the French government awarded him the Red Ribbon of a Chevalier of the Legion of Honor, in recognition of his eminence as an artist, and his services to music. He died in Nice, France on January 4, 1966.[30]

Many of Jacobs' theories of teaching have roots with Tabuteau. In 1942, Tabuteau wrote:[31]

♦ "Each student must be treated as an individual problem. How often have I had the experience of teaching a class of three or four, of correcting one student with a certain observation, and finding myself called upon to say the exact opposite to the next one."

♦ "A fine oboist can produce as many as fifty different tone colors on one note, just as a singer can vary the colorings of the voice in an infinite number of ways. Therefore, the oboist must think vocally."

♦ "A thorough preliminary training in music is especially important to the young oboist. He should study solfege, piano, theory and voice in his early years. When he has reached the age of thirteen or fourteen, he is ready to begin with the oboe itself."

♦ "I always tell my students that if they think beautifully they will play beautifully. For it is what you have to say in music that determines the quality of your performance."

♦ "The greatest problem for an orchestral player is not to perform his own part, but to adjust himself to the others. He must know the score and sense his own position in the music as a whole."

Jacobs said, "Tabuteau formalized the concept of controlling phrasing and dynamics by a numbering system. Each dynamic would have its own level, depending on the instrument. During the class, Tabuteau would have us play at various dynamics by asking for 'oboe, number five' or 'tuba, number three.' It was magnificent training."

John Krell offers a simplified version of Tabuteau's system. "Marcel Tabuteau preferred to describe the scaling of impulse and intensity more explicitly in terms of numbers. Each note [in a phrase] was assigned a number indicating the degree of intensity and dynamic with which it was to be played. Any change of the same number implied a change of bow or impulse. One of his great talents was the imaginative contouring and assigning of these numbers."[32]

Fellow Students

Since its founding in the 1920s, there has never been a lack of talent at the Curtis Institute. During Jacobs' first years, he was not the only tuba student. Ross Wyre, graduating in 1934, was the other tubist. Wyre did not play with the Curtis Institute Orchestra.[33]

Other brass players during Jacobs' years at the Curtis Institute included [year of graduation is in parentheses followed by known professional experience]:[34]

The Curtis Institute class of 1936.
Arnold Jacobs is in the third row on the left
Photo from the collection of Arnold Jacobs

Trumpet:	John Harmaala (1936) - Pittsburgh Symphony [with Jacobs]
	Melvin Headman (1935)
	Samuel Krauss (1935) - Philadelphia Orchestra
	Carmen Parlante (1938)
	Leopold Podder (1934)
	Arthur Statter (1935)
Trombone:	Ralph Binz (1935)
	Guy Boswell (1935) -Indianapolis Symphony (1937-39) [with Jacobs]
	John Burkhart (1936)
	John Coffey - Boston Symphony.
	William Gibson (1939) - Boston Symphony

Robert Harper -Indianapolis Symphony (1938-42) [with Jacobs],
Philadelphia Orchestra (1943-81)
Gordon Pulis - Philadelphia Orchestra, NBC Symphony,
Toronto Symphony, New York Philharmonic,
Metropolitan Opera
Harvey Wilson (1938)
Gerald Woerner (1934)

Tuba: Ross Wyre (1934)
Horn: Ernani Angelucci (1936) - Cleveland Orchestra
Mason Jones - Philadelphia Orchestra
Herman Watkins (1936)
Henry Cowles Whitehead (1937)

Other students included:

Julius Baker, Flute (1937) - Played with Jacobs in the Pittsburgh
(1941-43) and Chicago (1951-53) Symphonies prior to
becoming principal of the New York Philharmonic (1965-83)[35]
Samuel Barber, Composition (1934) - Pulitzer Prize winning composer[36]
Harold Bennett, Flute (1936) -Pittsburgh Symphony 1938-40
[with Jacobs]. Philadelphia Orchestra 1940-44,
Metropolitan Opera 1944-65
David Frisina - Los Angeles Philharmonic: first violin 1937-43,
concertmaster 1943-73, concertmaster emeritus 1973-78
Frank Miller, cello (1931) - NBC Symphony, Minneapolis Symphony,
Chicago Symphony
Gian Carlo Menotti, composition (1934) - Pulitzer Prize winning
composer [37]
Vincent Persichetti, conducting (1939) - Composer
Bernard Portnoy, clarinet - Pittsburgh Symphony (1939-40) [with Jacobs]
Oskar Shumsky, violin (1936) - Juilliard Quartet
Frank Sinatra, percussion (1936) - National Symphony
Leonard Treash - Voice & Opera Dept., Eastman School of Music
Leon Zawisza, violin - Indianapolis Symphony (1938-39)[with Jacobs]

Voice Scholarship

Jacobs also studied voice at the Curtis Institute, and was offered a
scholarship as a voice major.

"The voice teacher had me forcing my voice so that I could not sing. I was
constantly losing my voice through sore throats, and he kept telling me to support
my tone.

"I was called into the office at Curtis when they offered me the
scholarship. They said, 'You can now put your tuba away and stay with us as a

12

singer.' I thought of the sore throats, plus the fact that I used to like to go out and play jobs on string bass or tuba, sometimes on trumpet or trombone or whatever in those days. I was having fun! So, I turned it down, but I continued to be interested in singing and this was what later motivated me to work a bit on the study of breath. I wondered, why I was so comfortable playing the tuba and so miserable when I was singing?"

Another factor in his decision to turn down the scholarship was, "I figured it would mean another six years of study."[38]

Freelancing in Philadelphia

In his second or third year at the Curtis Institute, Jacobs began playing professionally in Philadelphia. He played in dance bands and other groups at shows, theaters, parties, and other functions. Besides playing the tuba, he doubled on trumpet and trombone, but his days of doubling did not last long. "Some of the Curtis faculty members were at a job that I was playing and they mentioned it around the school. I was called in and told I had to specialize on tuba."[39]

Jacobs interpreted specializing to mean that he could play different styles of music, but only on the tuba. "In those days they used tuba a great deal in Dixieland jazz. They were not using the string bass because the old carbon mikes would not pick them up. I would play Wagner and Brahms in the daytime, and *Tiger Rag* at night. It was a very rewarding experience for me."[40]

He played with orchestras lead by Howard Lannon and Meyer Davis. After suffering exhaustion from classes during the day and jobbing at night, his doctor prescribed some time off. During the winter of 1933, he took leave from the Curtis Institute and went to Miami. There he played tuba in a three-month show with Charlie Kerr's big band.

When technology improved microphones, Jacobs began playing string bass. "I got a bass and taped a chart on its fingerboard to locate the notes. Fortunately, I did not have many to play. From keeping at it, and later studying with a teacher at Curtis, I eventually improved."[41] He began playing with a group called *Three Blue Blazers* that consisted of violin, guitar, and string bass. One of their regular jobs was playing for several variety shows on radio station WPEN in Philadelphia.[42] Jacobs continued playing bass until 1959 {see: Professional Experience: Freelancing in Chicago}.

One evening, the station's producer asked Jacobs to sing in a quartet on a show. The producers liked his voice as a singer and speaker so much that he almost started a different career. During one summer they hired him as an announcer, later offering him a full-time position. "It appealed to me very much, but of course this was in the days before they paid big money," he said. "It was one of those crossroads in life." Should he give up his scholarship at Curtis, and go into full-time announcing? He declined. "With that scholarship at Curtis, I decided I did not want to branch out."[43]

Arnold Jacobs

Photo from the collection of Arnold Jacobs

Gizella Jacobs

Photo from the collection of Arnold Jacobs

Gizella Jacobs and Family

One night in Philadelphia, Arnold Jacobs met a dancer from the show he was playing.[44]

Arnold Jacobs: *Song and Wind*

Gizella Valfy [b. January 9, 1911] had been dancing for several years on the Vaudeville circuit, working shows with many big bands. Gizella and her dance partner performed such dances as the *Adagio* and *Bolero*, wearing costumes she designed and made for herself and other dancers.

Gizella remembers about those early days when she met Arnold, "He was so handsome—and such a gentleman!" Arnold moved to Indianapolis when he became a member of the Indianapolis Symphony, {see: Professional Experience: Indianapolis Symphony Orchestra} but traveled to Gizella's hometown of Chicago during the Christmas break. On Christmas Eve, Gizella and Arnold were married and have been together since. They celebrated their sixtieth wedding anniversary December 24, 1997.

Gizella and Arnold Jacobs
Photo from the collection of Arnold Jacobs

Although her dancing career diminished at the time of her marriage, she still performed and taught dancing for many years. She was an active member of the local school's P.T.A. Gizella passed away on November 26, 1999.

Arnold and Gizella's son, Arnold Dallas Jacobs was born in Philadelphia on July 30, 1939. During college, he studied marine biology at the University of

The Jacobs family. Dallas, Gizella and Arnold (1992)
Photo by Author

Miami. He currently lives in Sarasota, Florida with his wife, Dorothy where they own and operate a restaurant.

Part of a musical family, Dallas has performed on the guitar and his son, Robin Arnold Jacobs [b. November 16, 1963] is a musician currently living and working in the San Francisco area.

16

Gizella's mother, Tereza Valfy, was well known to the students who traveled to their Normal Avenue home for lessons. She was born in Budapest, Hungary, and was married to the late Geza Valfy who was, himself, involved in the arts. She is best remembered as greeting students at the door and talking to them while awaiting their lessons. John Taylor remembers, "Mrs. Valfy was a nice lady who always offered coffee and made much to do about their little dog Schwepps [and later Trouble]. She also did most of the cooking in the Jacobs' house." Mrs. Valfy passed away on December 27, 1985, at the age of ninety-five.[45]

Jacobs said that she was a very smart person and would listen to him teaching. On occasion she would remember a student's last lesson and when talking with them before a lesson, she would ask them if they remembered to practice this or that.

Mrs. Tereza Valfy (1933)
Photo from the collection of Arnold Jacobs

The Valfys lived in the house on Normal Avenue, Gizella's girlhood home. Eventually, Arnold and Gizella bought it from Mrs. Valfy, and lived in this house until 1982, when they moved to their current residence on Maplewood Avenue.

Professional Experience (1937-1949)

Rapidly, Jacobs became known as a highly competent musician and job offers were frequent.

In 1933, at age eighteen, Jacobs was offered a position with the Boston Symphony Orchestra by Serge Koussevitsky. At this time, the Boston Symphony was non-union. Koussevitsky wanted him to start in the middle of the season and, because of Jacobs' age, with no contract, but with the potential of a contract for the next season.[46]

"At the time I was working a nightclub in Philadelphia and between salary and tips I was making about $90 a week. Koussevitsky offered me $90 a week to go with the Boston Symphony. I would have gone except that I heard how tough he was—that he was hard to please—and I was so afraid that if I did not satisfy him, I would be tossed out of the orchestra. I would have been out of the [Philadelphia] union automatically for joining the [non-union] Boston Symphony at that time. So I turned it down."[47]

Photo from the collection of Arnold Jacobs

In 1936, Eugene Ormandy offered Jacobs the tuba position with the Philadelphia Orchestra, replacing his teacher, Philip Donatelli. Out of loyalty to Donatelli, he declined.

Later in 1936, he was offered a contract by the St. Louis Symphony. He quit his job in the Philadelphia night club, and had purchased concert dress clothes preparing for the move to St. Louis. About two weeks before his departure, he received a telegram from the St. Louis musician's union. They were not accepting Jacobs' transfer, because they had a local musician, John Bambridge, who was capable of filling the job. Rather than fight, he remained in Philadelphia.

Many years later the St. Louis musician's union was in a similar situation, and called Jacobs, who, by then was well established in Chicago, for advice. Bambridge had left the orchestra, and there was a local player that the union wanted Jacobs to evaluate. The musician in question was not capable and the position eventually went to John McEnulty. The union told him, "In 1936, there was a tuba player from out east that we turned down in favor of a local person and it worked out quite well." He never told them that he was the person who they would not allow into the local.[48]

Indianapolis Symphony Orchestra (1937-1939)

For many years, the Indianapolis Symphony Orchestra was an amateur orchestra, but in the 1937-38 season, the orchestra engaged Fabian Sevitsky {see: Conductors: Sevitsky}, who began hiring professional musicians.

Sevitsky auditioned players at the Curtis Institute and one of the Portnoy brothers [Bernie or Harry] was given the assignment of asking the players to audition. "I was one of those asked, and I had a very interesting audition. Sevitsky liked my playing very much," Jacobs said.

The Indianapolis season consisted of twenty pairs of Friday and Saturday concerts, three young people's concerts and a tour of fifteen concerts, primarily through the state of Indiana.[49] "It was like going to school, but with a small salary. It was a learning situation for us, and it gave us a chance to play professionally and get a very modest salary. It was a stepping stone."

During his tenure with Indianapolis, Jacobs was featured as a soloist once. At a popular concert on December 11, 1938, he performed Arcady Dubensky's *Fantasy on a Popular Folk Song for Tuba and Symphony Orchestra*.

Dubensky was born in Viatka, Russia, October 3, 1890, and, in 1923, joined the New York Symphony Orchestra as a first violinist who continued with the merged orchestra [the New York Philharmonic-Symphony Orchestra] from 1928 to 1953. He died in Tenafly, New Jersey, October 14, 1966.[50]

The program notes described the work. "Like most American composers, native-born or not, Dubensky has been interested in the folk songs of the Negro, which, together with the cowboy ballads, comprise our largest body of traditional melody.

"The idea of writing this Fantasy came to Mr. Dubensky through Vincenzo Vanni, the tuba player of the New York Philharmonic Symphony Orchestra (1923-1943). He gave the theme to Mr. Dubensky, and Mr. Dubensky made the Fantasy of it. This is the first performance anywhere of this work."[51]

Dubensky's best known work for tuba is his *Concerto Grosso for Three Trombones and Tuba*, written shortly before his death for the low brass section of the New York Philharmonic.

Other Curtis Institute students hired that first season were, Guy [Duffy] Boswell, trombone and Max Woodbury, trumpet {see: Appendix B: Brass Personnel}. The next season they were joined by fellow Curtis Institute students, Robert Harper, trombone [who would eventually be a member of the Philadelphia Orchestra] and Leon Zawisza, Concertmaster. During Jacobs' final year the low brass section was dominated by graduates of the Curtis Institute Guy Boswell, Robert Harper and Jacobs. Charles Payne played second trombone and later became the conductor of the Long Beach Municipal Band, Long Beach, California.

19

Frank Brouk commuted between Indianapolis and Chicago where he was also playing with the Chicago Symphony Orchestra's training orchestra, the Chicago Civic Orchestra. He would later play in the Chicago Symphony with Jacobs {see: Chicago Symphony Orchestra: Horn Section: Others}. Those who also played with Jacobs in Indianapolis and Chicago were the Siegel twins, Harold and Ray, who both played bass.

Several members of the Indianapolis Symphony, including Jacobs, occasionally traveled to Cincinnati to perform with the Armco Band. The regular tuba player in the band was Bill Bell who was then playing with the NBC Symphony in New York. Whenever Bell could not play, Jacobs substituted for him.

Although Jacobs gained professional orchestral experience, he did not make much money in Indianapolis. "When Gizella and I were there, we never made enough money to live on. So, during the summer I had to go back to Philadelphia and work. I then had to call them [Indianapolis Symphony] to send money so we would have enough to get back to Indianapolis. So by the second year, I was already indebted to them."

Jacobs was in Philadelphia for the summer playing in clubs. By this time, Fritz Reiner became the conductor of the Pittsburgh Symphony Orchestra (1938-48).[52] Reiner sent John Harmaala, a trumpet player and graduate of the Curtis Institute, to ask him to audition for the Pittsburgh Symphony. Jacobs told him, "I am under contract to the Indianapolis Symphony and owe them money—I am not available."

A few weeks later, Harmaala came back to Jacobs' house trying to persuade him again to audition. At that time, one of Jacobs' students was planning to drive to Steinway Hall in New York to audition. Jacobs finally relented, and said, "All right, I'll drive up with my student," and went to the audition.

There were about twenty-five to thirty tubists auditioning. Jacobs recalls, "Reiner knew my work. I had been with him for about seven years at Curtis, so he did not need to audition me, but he made me play for about three-quarters of an hour. Then he offered me the job. I said, 'I am already contracted for in Indianapolis.'[53] Reiner said he would take care of it.

"I did not hear anything further from him until two weeks before the season was to start in both Indianapolis and Pittsburgh. We were packing, but we still had know idea where we were going. We got a contract from the Pittsburgh Symphony with a note saying they traded their first cellist to Sevitsky [in Indianapolis] for me. It was like a baseball team, they traded a cellist and I went to Pittsburgh."

To say that Fritz Reiner was known to go through many players throughout his career is an understatement. In Pittsburgh, from the 1938-39 season to the 1939-40 season, thirty-six members of the orchestra were replaced including two cellists. Comparing the personnel of the Pittsburgh Symphony for the 1938-39 season with the Indianapolis Symphony roster of 1939-40, there is no member of the Pittsburgh Symphony that joined the Indianapolis Symphony.[54] Although both orchestras seasons were twenty weeks, the pay in Indianapolis must have been lower than in Pittsburgh at the time, a major disadvantage. There seems to be a mystery whether this trade actually occurred or if it was just talked about.

Pittsburgh Symphony Orchestra (1939-44)

Jacobs joined conductor Fritz Reiner and the Pittsburgh Symphony Orchestra at the beginning of the 1939 season. The low brass section had undergone a major change when Reiner replaced three of its four members from the previous season. Joining the orchestra with Jacobs were trombonists Donato Cerilli and Howard Cole {see: Appendix B: Brass Personnel}. Cole later played with Jacobs in the All-American Youth Orchestra and later was a member of the Philadelphia Orchestra.

Principal trombonist Neal Di Biase, who later became a member of the NBC Symphony, was starting his second season with the orchestra. Jacobs considered him to be a fine player. Di Biase and Jacobs' relationship within the orchestra grew, and Jacobs was Di Biase's best man at his wedding.

It was in Pittsburgh that he made his first recordings {see: Appendix A: Arnold Jacobs Discography}.

With the advent of World War II, members of all the nation's orchestras, including Pittsburgh, entered the armed forces. However, Jacobs was exempt from the military, due to health {see: Retirement}. He often stated that he would have loved playing in one of the premier service bands in Washington, D.C., but, "I was 4-F."

Reiner, realizing Jacobs' artistry, wanted to keep him, and sought ways to increase his paycheck by finding other positions for him. At the beginning of the 1942-43 season, Reiner appointed Jacobs Personnel Manager of the Pittsburgh Symphony.[55] He was not excited with the job and hated getting phone calls from fellow orchestra members complaining of their stand partner's odor.

The final straw came when the strings were rehearsing Mozart and members of the brass section were rolling dice against the back of the orchestra shell. Reiner ordered Jacobs to break it up. Jacobs told them to move it downstairs, but Neal Di Biase took him by the collar and told him to "get lost." It was then that Jacobs decided he would rather keep his friends than be Personnel Manager.

When he took the Personnel Manager's position, he stipulated that he could quit at any time without jeopardizing his position as tubist. When he did quit, Reiner said, "That's okay, you weren't a very good Personnel Manager anyway." His career as Personnel Manager lasted seven weeks.

Later, Reiner offered him an additional position as part-time bassist.[56] "I got to the point that I could play Beethoven's Fifth Symphony on the bass."

All-American Youth Orchestra (1941)

Leopold Stokowski organized the All-American Youth Orchestra in the summer of 1940 for a tour of the United States and South America. The orchestra had an age limit of twenty-seven and was under the auspices of the National Youth Administration.[57] Jacobs joined the orchestra for the 1941 season.

Stokowski said about the orchestra, "I would not exchange this orchestra for any other orchestra in the world. These young people are phenomenal. Technically, they are the equals of any musicians. And they have the enthusiasm of youth. They are so sensitive, so quick. With them, the playing of music is not just a job. They have a love for it," he said, explaining his own position, "I have a debt to America that I want to repay. America has been wonderful to me. Now I can do something for America, in giving all of these fine youngsters from all over the country a chance to play in a fine symphony. I receive no payment whatsoever for this work. This is not a commercial venture."[58]

Beginning in April of 1941, the orchestra's three-month tour took them to fifty-six cities across the country. They played in civic auditoriums, state fair pavilions, coliseums, baseball parks, stadiums and in concert halls. Stokowski had designed an acoustical shell, carried with the orchestra, and had a special seating arrangement for the orchestra members. American composers were commissioned and their works were performed at every concert.

The initial concert was on Sunday, May 11, 1941, in the ballroom of Atlantic City's Convention Hall. The orchestra traveled along the east coast from Washington, D.C. to Boston, then to Toronto, Canada, followed by concerts in the Midwest. To complete the tour, a final series covered the Pacific coast from Seattle, Washington, to Los Angeles, California. The

On tour with the All-American Youth Orchestra (1941)
Photo from the collection of Arnold Jacobs

final concert was played before 15,000 people at the Rose Bowl in Pasadena, California. After the tour, the orchestra recorded for Columbia Records in Hollywood from July 3 to July 11, 1941 {see: Appendix A: Arnold Jacobs Discography}.

Playing bass trombone during the first season's orchestra [1940] was Edward Kleinhammer whom Jacobs would later play with in the Chicago Symphony {see: Chicago Symphony Orchestra: Trombone Section: Edward Kleinhammer}.[59] In 1941, the low brass section consisted of Charles Gusikoff [whom Jacobs would later play with on a tour with the Philadelphia Orchestra], Robert Marsteller, and repeating from the previous year, Howard Cole [who played alongside Jacobs in the Pittsburgh Symphony].

The trumpet section included Saul Caston who was also the orchestra's assistant conductor. He was the trumpet instructor at the Curtis Institute during

Jacobs' student years. Completing the section were John Clyman and Lloyd Geisler.

Included in the horn section was Helen Kotas, who was principal horn of the Chicago Symphony when Jacobs arrived in 1944 {see: Appendix B: Brass Personnel}.

With the outbreak of World War II and institution of the military draft, combined

Brass section of the All-American Youth Orchestra
Photo from the collection of Arnold Jacobs

with a lack of funding, the All-American Youth Orchestra, which existed for two summers, ceased to exist.[60]

Freelancing in Chicago

Beginning in 1940, during the off season in Pittsburgh, Jacobs freelanced in Chicago. His wife, Gizella, was from Chicago, and there was more work available there than in either Philadelphia or Pittsburgh.

At first he worked at the Blackstone Hotel with Neil Bonshue. "Another funny situation, they asked me to come in and hold the bass and look busy. Their regular bass player had to leave suddenly for California because his mother was ill. Then they found out that I could play," Jacobs said.

He played with Lou Diamond who used to play all the off nights at the hotels and night clubs. Monday at the Palmer House, Tuesday night at the Hilton, and Wednesday at Chez Paris. He played in cocktail lounges, bars, clubs, and hotels. For ten years, he played the noon style shows at Marshall Field's.

During the baseball season, Jacobs played at Wrigley Field between innings for Chicago Cubs games with a group lead by Lou Diamond. He used to take his son, Dallas, with him to those games. He recalls, "I came from Philadelphia to Chicago, and both teams were bad. I really didn't know which team to root for."

In 1942, Jacobs was called to substitute for a tuba player at CBS in Chicago. "I was playing the tuba, but there were some string bass parts in the music, and there was a bass sitting there. I also played the bass parts, and there was a lot of pretty good jazz. They hired me on staff right away, because I could play bass."

In 1943 CBS was located in the Wrigley Building on North Michigan Avenue. For many years, he would play at CBS providing background music for radio and television shows. The leader of the group at CBS was Ceasar Petrillo, brother of then Chicago musician's union president James Petrillo. After Jacobs joined the Chicago Symphony in 1944, Ceasar Petrillo tried to talk him into quitting the symphony and working more at CBS. In addition, Jacobs occasionally worked for NBC in Chicago.

Playing the bass (1942)
Photo from the collection of Arnold Jacobs

Later, as a member of the Chicago Symphony, he continued to play many outside jobs. "I loved to play bass, and I did not stop until 1959, when everything just got too busy, and I decided to stick the tuba."

More Job Offers

Jacobs has been offered jobs from nearly every top orchestra in the country.

While freelancing in Chicago, Jacobs played several jobs with members of the Chicago Symphony who mentioned his name to the CSO's personnel manager. In 1943, the orchestra performed Berlioz's *Symphonie Fantastique*, which requires two tubas. The CSO called Jacobs. As would be expected, the CSO's tubist, George Hamburg, played the first part, and Jacobs, the second.

After the performance, Milton Preves and John Weicher [at that time the orchestra's principal violist and concertmaster, respectively] went up to the Music Director, Desire Defauw, and said, "You'd better hire this guy."[61] The CSO's tubist, George Hamburg, was suffering some physical problems {see: Chicago Symphony Orchestra: Other Tubists of the CSO}, and they were searching for a replacement.

"I played for them [*Symphonie Fantastique*], and they came back and offered me the job. I told them that I was already signed up for Pittsburgh, but they said 'We will hold it for you, and you can come with us next season.'"

In the meantime, he had other offers.

"I said that I would consider it, but when we had to make the choice I chose the Chicago Symphony because Gizella liked it the best. Well, we were *from*

Chicago. Gizella's home was there, and I had been doing very well working summers. There was a lot of work in Chicago."

At Ravinia the following summer, the orchestra again played *Symphonie Fantastique,* but, this time, Hamburg asked Jacobs to play the first part.

During Jacobs' final year in Pittsburgh, Serge Koussevitsky, conductor of the Boston Symphony, came to Pittsburgh and Jacobs played for him. "He tried hard to get me, but his management would never pay enough money. I told him I could not afford to go to Boston for what they were offering."

This was not the first time the Boston Symphony tried to get him nor would it be the last. "The first four or five years I was with the Chicago Symphony, the Boston Symphony contacted me every year to try to take me away to Boston. Our manager, George Kuyper, used to be Assistant Manager in Boston, and knew about the offers before I did. I had a very enjoyable situation when he would call me and say, 'Well, Arnold, what's it gonna' cost us to keep you here?' And he let me name my price."[62]

Years later, when Kilton Vinal Smith retired, the Boston Symphony again offered Jacobs the job. Again, this final time, he turned it down.

In 1943, the late Bill Bell was the tubist with the NBC Symphony, having been there since its formation in 1937, but was now leaving to join the New York Philharmonic. "Bell was negotiating a contract with the New York Philharmonic so they contacted me in case he turned it down. They said they could import me into New York [the American Federation of Musicians allowed principals to be imported to the New York Philharmonic]."[63]

In fact, both the NBC Symphony *and* the New York Philharmonic were watching the situation with Bell. NBC planned to offer Jacobs the job if Bell left to go to the Philharmonic. But, unlike the Philharmonic, NBC could not import players and Jacobs would have to wait six months to become a member of the New York local.

Years later, when Bell's mother was ill, and Bell needed to be with her, Jacobs substituted for Bell for a short time with the New York Philharmonic.

These were not the only offers Jacobs received. In Los Angeles, while with the All-American Youth Orchestra, he was offered work in the recording studios. While he was with the Chicago Symphony, Josef Krips offered him a position with the San Francisco Symphony, and George Szell repeatedly tried to get him to join the Cleveland Orchestra.

On Loan to the Philadelphia Orchestra (1949)

In 1943, after Jacobs was promised the job in Chicago, Ormandy again offered the job in the Philadelphia Orchestra. Jacobs declined.

Abe Torchinsky relates events in 1947. "When I was playing with the NBC Symphony [replacing Bill Bell], I received a call from the personnel manager of the Philadelphia Orchestra asking if I could come down to substitute for Mr. Donatelli, who was ill. I came down and played a week, and was then asked to stay another week, which I could not do. I was asked if I would be interested in coming to Philadelphia, and my answer was no."

In 1948, with the retirement of Philip Donatelli [at the Philadelphia Orchestra's mandatory retirement age of sixty-five] Ormandy offered Jacobs the job, and Jacobs turned it down. But Ormandy needed a tuba player as the Philadelphia Orchestra was to leave on a tour of England and Scotland on May 13, 1949. Ormandy hired Clarence Karella. However, Karella's career with the Philadelphia Orchestra was unfortunately short lived as the March 19, 1949, edition of *Billboard* explained:

"A strike by members of the Philadelphia Orchestra over the hiring of a tuba player from another city was averted when the local musicians' union and symphony orchestra management reached an arbitration agreement last week before Judge Nochem S. Winnet of Municipal Court. The agreement provides that Clarence Karella, a tuba player from Chicago, be dismissed at the end of the season here, to be replaced by a local oomp-paher acceptable to both the symphony's musical director and the local union.

"The strike threat was the climax of year-old dispute begun when the symphony 'retired' a tuba player who had been twenty-five years with the orchestra. The union objected and refused the orchestra's request to hold auditions for a new player, saying 'no vacancy exists.' Thereupon the orchestra hired Karella out of Chicago. The local union refused to honor Karella's transfer card and ruled that no members could play with him after March 7. However, all parties concerned finally agreed to arbitration and the matter was thrashed out in the judge's chambers. Karella will carry on until the final concert of the season on April 23, when a member of the local union now playing in another city's symphony, will 'become available.'"[64]

Jacobs recalled, "Ormandy asked me to go to Europe with them on their tour in 1949, and then he tried to get me to join the Philadelphia Orchestra. In fact, he went so far at one of our [Chicago Symphony] board receptions as to talk to one of our board of trustees to try to get them to transfer me back to Philadelphia for his orchestra, because I was a member of the Philadelphia local of the union."[65]

Abe Torchinsky tells of his start with the Philadelphia Orchestra. "They approached me again and at that time, since Donatelli was gone, I asked Ormandy if there was any chance that Mr. Donatelli could come back, and his answer was, 'No.' I then accepted the job, but told them I could not start until the following September. I do not know what happened, but in the middle of the season, I started

getting calls to come sooner. Finally, they wanted me to come on March 7, 1949, to finish the season, and go on the English tour. I told Ormandy I could not because my wife was having a baby. They said 'It's your position so it's up to you to get Mr. Jacobs to substitute for you on the tour.' The day my daughter was born, I was in a phone booth in Jamaica Hospital, New York (with $20 in quarters), pleading with Arnold to go."

The Chicago Symphony allowed Jacobs to go on tour with the Philadelphia Orchestra, with Abe Torchinsky playing the first week of the American portion of the tour, and Jacobs joining the orchestra in New Orleans, finishing the remainder of the American tour. Jacobs and the Philadelphia Orchestra left on May 13,

Photo from the collection of Arnold Jacobs

1949, for twenty-eight concerts in England and Scotland in twenty-seven days.[66]

In the Philadelphia trombone section were principal Charles Gusikoff [who was with Jacobs in the All-American Youth Orchestra] and assistant principal Robert Lambert [who would later play in Chicago with Jacobs]. On second trombone was an old friend, Howard Cole [who played in Pittsburgh with Jacobs and the All-American Youth Orchestra]. Another friend was bass trombonist, Robert Harper [who was at the Curtis Institute and the Indianapolis Symphony with Jacobs]. The trumpets were Samuel Krauss, first; Seymour Rosenfeld, second; Harold Rehrig was third, and Sigmund Hering, fourth.[67]

The tour opened May 22, 1949, in Birmingham, England and later the orchestra performed in Royal Albert Hall before members of the royal family. During the tour, the noted British conductor Sir Thomas Beecham also directed the orchestra.[68]

Chicago Symphony Orchestra (1944-1988)

The Chicago Symphony Orchestra [CSO] is the third oldest symphony orchestra in the United States and is managed by the Orchestral Association of Chicago. The CSO was organized in 1891, by it's first conductor, Theodore Thomas. In 1905, Frederick Stock succeeded Thomas as conductor, and remained with the orchestra until 1942.

Chicago Symphony Orchestra, Desire Defauw, conductor (October 12, 1944)
From CSO Archives

Jacobs joined the Chicago Symphony in the fall of 1944 during the second year of the orchestra's third conductor, Desire Defauw (1943-47). He has also served in the CSO under the direction of Arthur Rodzinski (1947-48), Raphael Kubelik (1950-53), Fritz Reiner (1953-63), Jean Martinon (1963-68) and Sir Georg Solti (1969-1991). Daniel Barenboim (1991-2006) was a frequent guest conductor while Jacobs was with the orchestra. Current conductor Ricardo Muti (2010-) first appeared at Ravinia in 1973 with Jacobs and the CSO {see: Conductors: Music Directors of the Chicago Symphony}.[69]

Other Tubists of the CSO

Jacobs was the Chicago Symphony's sixth principal tubist.

The original tubist of the Chicago Orchestra, later renamed the Chicago Symphony Orchestra, was August Helleberg Sr. Born in Denmark on March 7, 1861. He was with the Chicago Orchestra from 1891-95.

Tuba players will instantly recognize the Helleberg name from his famous mouthpiece designs. Legend says whenever Helleberg bought a tuba, he would custom design a mouthpiece for it, and when he sold the tuba, the mouthpiece went with it. Since then, many manufacturers have reproduced these mouthpieces, all retaining the Helleberg name. Most present day American tubists, including Jacobs, have played on a Helleberg-style mouthpiece.

Helleberg was not only a mouthpiece designer, but probably one of the greatest tubists of his era. Besides the tuba, Helleberg also played the bass. A listing of Helleberg's known professional experience includes Philharmonic Society of Brooklyn, Theodore Thomas, Conductor, April 19, 1889; Theodore Thomas Orchestra of New York, Thomas Testimonial Tour, October 9 - November 9, 1889; Theodore Thomas Orchestra Mayfest Concert, Cincinnati, Ohio, May 22-24, 1890; Philharmonic Society of Brooklyn Orchestra, Theodore Thomas, Conductor, 1890-91; Theodore Thomas Orchestra, Indianapolis - Third Annual Mayfest, May 26-28, 1891; Theodore Thomas Orchestra, Nashville, Tennessee, May 4-7, 1891; Chicago Orchestra, 1891-95; Orchestra of the Columbian Exposition [Chicago], 1893; New York Philharmonic Society, November 26, 1897 - April 3, 1908 [bass section, 1888-90, principal tuba, 1888-91 and 1897-1908]; Metropolitan Opera Orchestra, 1909-1912 [He possibly was in this orchestra as early as 1896, but this has not been verified.]; Sousa Band - 1900 to 1904; World Tour with the Sousa Band - departed New York December 24, 1910; Edwin F. Goldman's Metropolitan Sextet, 1911; New York Military Band - Edwin F. Goldman, conductor, June 9-August 1919; Goldman Concert Band - June 7- September 3, 1920; Goldman Concert Band - Summer Season, 1921.

Helleberg played in several orchestras organized and directed by Theodore Thomas in various cities. When Thomas formed the Chicago Orchestra, he, therefore, hired Helleberg as the CSO's original tubist. Later Helleberg played with the Sousa Band and in 1904, was joined in the tuba section by his two sons, August Jr. and John. He died in Newark, New Jersey on November 17, 1936.[70]

Frederick Otte played both tuba and bass with the orchestra. He appears on the personnel roster in the bass section from 1895-98 and 1901-14, and as principal tuba, 1895 -1914. Otte was born in Germany in April 1855, and died in Chicago on October 8, 1914.[71]

Born in Germany in 1873, the first known professional experience for Emil Gatterfeld was as principal bass of the Cincinnati Symphony Orchestra from 1906 to 1907. From 1907 thru 1908, he was in the bass section of the New York Symphony Orchestra, [not to be confused with the New York Philharmonic Orchestra with which it merged in 1928]. In the CSO, he was a bass player from 1911-19 and principal tuba from 1914-17. He was in the bass section of the Chicago Civic Opera in 1923-24. Gatterfeld died April 21, 1948.[72]

Another tubist who also played bass, William Dietrichs was principal tuba from 1917-20, and in the bass section from 1919-20. Previously, he was with the St. Louis Symphony Orchestra as a bass player from 1913-16 and principal tuba from 1913 to 1917.

Jacobs' predecessor, George Hamburg was born in Chicago on February 22, 1886, and was the CSO's principal tuba from 1920-44.
Edward Kleinhammer joined the symphony during the 1940-41 season, the final years of Hamburg's career. He remembers Hamburg as a very nice man and recalls that Hamburg knew of Jacobs by reputation prior to 1942.
While Jacobs' contact with him was limited, when asked about Hamburg, he stated, "He was a very nice man. I got so embarrassed, because I called him Mr. Hamburger when he called me one time, and I'll never forget that. He laughed—he had been called that before.
"I think he was having some sort of health problem and had to leave. I'm not sure. He may have had surgery due to cancer. I remember going up to see him, and he asked me to buy his Alexander tubas, which I did."
Hamburg died in Chicago on February 6, 1963.

At one point, the CSO had two tuba players. Fred Boos was listed in the personnel roster on bass, 1932-45, second tuba, 1938-45, and as a librarian, 1938-56. He was born May 29, 1881, in Joliet, Illinois and died July 25, 1967 in Chicago. It was Fred Boos who built Jacobs' mute, which he used nearly his entire career with the CSO.

At the time of Jacobs' retirement in 1988, the reputation of the Chicago Symphony had grown to be recognized as one of the finest orchestras in the world. The auditions for the coveted tuba position attracted applicants worldwide.
The one who emerged from the auditions was Gene Pokorny. Pokorny recalls being told the news. "I walked into a little room and there sat Sir Georg Solti, Arnold Jacobs and several others. Sir Georg told me I had won the job. I don't know exactly what I said, but I knew I had the presence of mind to say in so many words that several people could play the position of principal tuba in the CSO but *nobody* replaces Arnold Jacobs."
Pokorny was born in Los Angeles on May 15, 1953 and attended the University of Redlands and the University of Southern California, from which he

received his Bachelor of Music degree cum laude. From 1975 to 1989 he was a member of various orchestras including the Israel Philharmonic, Utah Symphony, and Saint Louis Symphony Orchestra. He is a founding member of the Summit Brass, and is also a proud member of the Three Stooges Fan Club.[73]

Prior to his appointment to the CSO, Pokorny has passed through Jacobs' studio often. He tells about his current relationship with Jacobs."Our relationship is more of a friendship than a student/teacher relationship though I feel very comfortable when I call him on the phone and ask about some aspect of playing. It is easy to take on that student role when I am making an inquiry. I feel very privileged to ask him about some aspects of survival on the job that nobody has experienced unless one has had the opportunity to sit in the tuba chair in the CSO. Although he has a respect for players, conductors, soloists and orchestra hierarchy, he is exceedingly perceptive in separating the wheat from the chaff.

"Mr. Jacobs has an overwhelming confidence—a knowledge of his abilities and a knowledge of himself that knows its scope and range. A person of lesser qualities would have difficulties listening to a new player sitting in the old position without the former player not making critical comments. Mr. Jacobs has never once told me after a performance (and he and Mrs. Jacobs come to many on the Thursday night series) that I should have played a part this or that way. He has not made any comment even remotely insinuating that.

"Mr. Jacobs and I enjoy a very good relationship. I appreciate his good humor, sharp mind and genuine strong feelings that seem to inspire people into being all they can be in terms of quality."

During the 1992-93 season, Pokorny took a leave of absence from the CSO and performed the season with the Los Angeles Philharmonic. According to Pokorny, "I left for the Los Angeles Philharmonic job because L.A. was home. It was where I was born, and I have a tremendous friendship with Jeff Reynolds, the Los Angeles Philharmonic's bass trombonist. I also have an innate appreciation for places that support human life forms in the winter." Replacing him that season was Floyd Cooley who, similarly, took a leave of absence from the San Francisco Symphony {see: York Tuba: Copies}.

As a tribute to his predecessor, Arnold Jacobs, Gene Pokorny writes, "For me Mr. Jacobs started off as a legend, turned into a hero, evolved into a person and has become a friend. I regard him in the way that I regard another very, very important person in my life, Tommy Johnson. They are both exquisitely gifted with the unique abilities of being warm, caring human beings who happen to be world class musicians and who happen to be tuba players. My life has been richly rewarded by each of them in their own unique ways. I hope that I can have the influence on others as those two gentlemen have had on my life. Their roles have been both powerful and inspirational. I am fortunate to have had such close contact in my life with these two people."

Chicago Symphony Orchestra, Fritz Reiner, conductor (April 25, 1958)
From CSO Archives

Performances

Throughout his career, Jacobs has played thousands of performances at home and throughout the world. Over the years, audiences could be measured in the millions of people ranging from school children to royalty, Presidents and the Pope.

One performance that stands out with Jacobs and several other members of the CSO occurred on October 14, 1958, in Symphony Hall, Boston, with Fritz Reiner conducting. The program for the concert was Berlioz's *Corsair Overture*, Brahms' *Symphony No. 3*, and Strauss' *Ein Heldenleben*. Many consider this the only "perfect" concert given where no one made a mistake. Jacobs thought that this was his greatest musical experience with Fritz Reiner. "Reiner said that it was the concert he waited for all his life."[74]

Orchestra Hall

The home of the Chicago Symphony is Orchestra Hall, located at 220 South Michigan Avenue. It was designed by the famous Chicago architect, Daniel H. Burnham and built at a cost of $750,000. The dedicatory concert was played December 14, 1904. The stage is a shallow half-circle under a high arch, with walls that curve in two directions to encircle the orchestra below, and to rise to the peak of the arch like a huge scallop shell.

In 1966, the hall was renovated by Chicago architect Harry Weese for $3 million. Air conditioning was added and most of the plaster ceilings of the auditorium were replaced with perforated aluminum panels to provide air circulation. The pipe organ was replaced with an electronic organ. Seats were reupholstered in deep red mohair and seating was reduced from 2,581 to 2,566.

Orchestra Hall (1966)
From CSO Archives

Lounges and offices were also expanded. Overall, the project was not successful in terms of the acoustical environment.

To fix problems from the 1966 restoration, the architectural firm of Skidmore, Owings, and Merrill restored the hall again in 1982. All the seats were rebuilt to decrease the sound absorption by replacing the upholstery on the seats with a different fabric and removing it altogether from the back of the seats. Seating in the hall is now 2,574. The electronic organ was replaced by a Moeller pipe organ that has seventy-four ranks and approximately 4,000 pipes. Total cost of the renovation project, including installation of the new organ, was approximately $3.4 million

Ground was broken in May 1995 for further renovation and expansion totaling $105 million. Two adjacent buildings were demolished. The firm of Skidmore, Owings, and Merrill designed a rotunda and arcade with increased spaces for rehearsals, practice rooms, an education c enter a nd in creased a dministrative o ffices. T he h all w as modified including an enlarged stage, reconfigured seating and the ceiling was raised ten feet. Renamed Symphony Center, dedication was in September 1997.[75]

Jacobs thought that perhaps part of the reason that the CSO sounds so good is that acoustically, Orchestra Hall is not the greatest concert hall in the world, even with the various restorations. On the stage, it is difficult to hear other sections of the orchestra, requiring close attention to the conductor. "The orchestra was especially successful on tour in halls that they could actually hear each other [Carnegie Hall, Boston's Symphony Hall, the Musikvereinsaal in Vienna and others].

"Where the conductor stands, he cannot hear a strong brass section sound, instead, he hears a strong sound from the string section and little brass, even though in the hall [and especially the gallery] the brass is dominant. When Reiner discovered this, he told the brass section to 'Play like you were in a bubble—don't dominate.' Two hours later Reiner was asking for more brass and the brass section responded, playing like they always did."

Ravinia Festival

The summer home of the Chicago Symphony is the Ravinia Festival, located in Highland Park, Illinois, approximately thirty miles north of downtown

Chicago. The festival is managed by the Ravinia Festival Association, a separate entity from the Orchestral Association that produces the concerts of the Chicago Symphony the remaining nine months of the year.

Today, the railroad is a nuisance to many as trains always seem to pass through the park during the softest sections of the music, but it was because of the railroads that Ravinia Park was developed. The Chicago & Milwaukee Electric Railroad developed the park in 1904 to profit from the transportation of those who attended concerts from Chicago, and from as far north as Milwaukee. In 1916, the railroad was sold and renamed the Chicago, North Shore & Milwaukee. Since 1963, when the North Shore Line ceased operation, the park has been served by the Chicago and North Western (later operated by Metra), using diesel locomotives.

On May 14, 1949, the old Pavilion was destroyed by fire. A new stage and orchestra shell was constructed with an improvised roof that had once been a tent-style hangar for World War II bombers. The present-day Pavilion was built in 1950, and speakers are placed throughout the acres of lawn for picnickers. Improvements continue in the park throughout the 1990s.

Jacobs has always lived on Chicago's south side. Until the completion of Chicago's expressway system in 1961, the drive to Ravinia from the south side of Chicago was on local roads. Often, this would take more than two hours. With the completion of the expressways, travel time was less and the nature of the audience changed from those who arrived by train to those who arrived by automobile. Even with the expressways, he had another obstacle each summer—road construction. Following retirement, he said that he never missed the drive to Ravinia.

The Ravinia Festival always hired conductors independently from the orchestra's winter season. The last conductor of the CSO's winter season to conduct during the Ravinia season was Desire Defauw in 1943. Four of the nine conductors in the history of the CSO [Rodzinski, Reiner, Martinon, and Solti] first appeared with the orchestra at Ravinia. In 1954, within a few weeks of each other, the orchestra was lead by Fritz Reiner—his last Ravinia appearance and Georg Solti—his first CSO appearance.

Principal conductors at Ravinia have been Seiji Ozawa (1968-69), Istvan Kertesz (1970-72), James Levine (1973-93) and Christoph Eschenbach (1995-). Regular guest conductors at Ravinia have included Leonard Bernstein, Antal Dorati, Otto Klemperer, Josef Krips, Erich Leinsdorf, Pierre Monteux, Eugene Ormandy, William Steinberg, Igor Stravinsky, and George Szell.[76]

Tours

The Chicago Symphony has established itself as the premier orchestra in the world by traveling often. It is impossible to list all tours by the CSO during Jacobs' tenure, as even the CSO Archives has only partial records. Included were many trips to points within the State of Illinois, and there was a concert series in Milwaukee for many years. Yearly trips were made for concerts in New York's Carnegie Hall and in Washington, DC's Constitution Hall, and, more recently, the Kennedy Center.

This is a partial list of the major tours on which Jacobs appeared:[77]

Jan. 20 to Feb. 5, 1946 - Midwest [Iowa, Minn., Ind., Mo., Ky., Ohio,

CSO in Carnegie Hall (1983)
From CSO Archives

Mich.];Mar. 10 to 22, 1947 - Midwest [Ill., Mo., Tenn., Ky., Mich., Ohio, N.Y.]; Jan. 26 to Feb. 8, 1948 - Southwest [Iowa, Kan., Okla., Texas, La., Ark.]; Oct. 6 to 20, 1958 - East [Mich., Ohio, N.Y., Vt., Maine, Pa., D.C.]; May 3 to 27, 1964 - West [Utah, Cal., Ore., Wash., Alaska, British Columbia, and Manitoba]; Feb. 22 to Mar. 14, 1966 - South / East [Fla., Ga., S.C., N.C., D.C., N.Y., Conn.]; Nov. 7 to 16, 1966 - East [N.Y., Conn., Pa., Maine]; Nov. 6 to 19, 1967 - East

[Ohio, Mich., N.Y., N.J., Conn., Pa.]; Aug. 26 to Oct. 6, 1971 - Europe; Apr. 30 to May 15, 1973 - U.S. [coast to coast]; Sep. 6 to 28, 1974 - Europe; June 3 to 29, 1977 - Japan ; Aug. 26 to Sep. 23, 1978 - Europe; Aug. 25 to Sep. 20, 1981 - Europe; Jan. 16 to 29, 1984 - Southeastern U.S.; Jan. 15 to Feb. 2, 1985 - Europe; Mar. 23 to Apr. 13, 1986 - Japan and Hong Kong; Jan. 26 to Feb. 16, 1987 - West Coast.

During the Reiner era, the State Department had proposed a tour of the Soviet Union as part of a cultural exchange. Reiner turned it down, stating, among other reasons, "It always rains in Moscow that time of year." Instead, the New York Philharmonic accepted the tour.

When Jacobs first joined the CSO, they primarily traveled by train. As air travel developed, the orchestra would fly, although at first they required multiple aircraft. In modern times the orchestra and their instruments can fit into one aircraft

Ticket for CSO Performance in Tokyo
From CSO Archives

with room to spare. He commented, "It has become a lot easier traveling with an orchestra throughout the years!"

The Music

Playing in orchestras for fifty-seven years, Jacobs has performed virtually all the standard repertoire. The tuba was not developed until the mid 1800s, so works written prior to about 1840 have no tuba part. Jacobs would always say that he was "on vacation" during a week that his colleagues would play works by Bach, Beethoven, Haydn, Handel, Mozart and others.

Not all repertory was written for the modern tuba. Berlioz and others composed for the ophicleide and Verdi wrote for the cimbasso. Today, with some exceptions, both are played on the modern-day tuba. While not a complete guide of orchestral tuba repertoire, the discography {see: Appendix A: Arnold Jacobs Discography} gives an idea of the orchestral tuba repertoire.

Jacobs is essentially a music lover, and has no "favorite" composition. Some of his most enjoyable works are the Mahler and Bruckner symphonies, Wagner's operas, music from the Russian School and jazz. One work he especially enjoyed playing was Mahler's *Symphony No. 6.* "It demands such an incredible range and is so challenging. I really enjoy myself."

On the other end of the spectrum, his least favorite work is the Dvorak *Symphony No. 9, from The New World.* The tuba part consists of fourteen notes, seven at the beginning of the slow movement, seven at the very end. "It's embarrassing to just sit there not playing for forty minutes."[78]

Recordings

The CSO is one of the most recorded orchestras in the world winning, by 1995, fifty-three Grammies awarded by the National Academy of Recording Arts and Sciences for CSO recordings. Included were seventeen awards for "Best Classical Performance by an Orchestra."

For many years the orchestra's concerts were taped for radio broadcast. Recording was suspended for a time but resumed again in 1976. Nationally syndicated, the programs are produced and distributed by Chicago radio station WFMT-FM.[79]

The Discography {see: Appendix A: Arnold Jacobs Discography} is a listing of all recordings that Jacobs has made. However, broadcast recordings are not included.

Until 1966, all recordings were done in Orchestra Hall, once one of the finest recording

During the taping of "Symphony Scene" (1950s)
Photo from the collection of Arnold Jacobs

environments in the United States. After the 1966 renovation, it was felt that a more reverberant environment was needed than the newly remodeled Orchestra Hall could provide {see: Chicago Symphony Orchestra: Orchestra Hall}.[80]

Sessions were, therefore, moved to Medinah Temple, a hall of more resonance located on Chicago's near-north side. In 1971 and 1972 the orchestra traveled to record in the Krannert Arts Center at the University of Illinois in Champaign-Urbana, Illinois. On the European tours of 1971 and 1974, recordings were made in Vienna's Sofiensaal, the frequent recording venue of the Vienna Philharmonic. From 1973 to the spring of 1981, work returned to Medinah.

After additional modifications of Orchestra Hall's acoustics in the summer of 1981, the hall, when empty, became a near-perfect recording environment. Since the 1981-82 season most recording work with the CSO has returned to Orchestra Hall.[81]

When Jacobs first recorded with an orchestra, state-of-the-art recording was on 78 rpm recordings. Technology has improved throughout the years with monophonic sound advancing to stereo, single-channel master tapes becoming multichannel, single miking to multiple, analog to digital, vinyl disc to compact disc, and many other improvements and refinements.

There are many recordings that stand out. Jacobs has mentioned a few:

Pictures at an Exhibition [Kubelik], recorded in 1951 - This was the recording that launched the CSO's reputation of producing great recordings. It was the first time that principal trumpet Adolph Herseth was recorded.

Ron Bishop, tubist of the Cleveland Orchestra writes, "On very short notice (two or three days) Kubelik told Jacobs that he better get the *Bydlo* ready on tuba because the tenor tuba player, who usually played it, was having some difficulty. Jacobs got a beat-up wreck of a double tuba (BB♭ and F Penzel) from T.M. (Ted) Koeder who got it to work, and he began trying to find a way to 'cover the part' if need be. He did have to do it at the session and to his surprise the high g♯ was more reliable on the BB♭—outrageous!!!"[82]

The *Bydlo* is traditionally played on a tenor tuba (euphonium). Jacobs played the same pitches on a BB♭ tuba, an instrument pitched a full octave lower than the tenor tuba!

Ein Heldenleben [Reiner], recorded March 6, 1954 - This was Fritz Reiner's first recording with the Chicago Symphony and he demanded perfection. Starting at 9 a.m., this was one of the most famous sessions in the history of the CSO.

On this recording, the euphonium player could not play softly enough for Reiner, so Edward Kleinhammer, at Reiner's command, played the soft tenor tuba

Excerpt of the Tenor and Bass Tuba parts from Strauss' Ein Heldenleben

parts on bass trombone. Jacobs remembers, "Reiner went over parts of it so many times that Ed Kleinhammer and I had to play the pianissimo passage about a dozen times."

Towards the end is a horn solo that can be difficult under normal circumstances. Jacobs recalls that around 11 p.m. Phil Farkas asked Reiner if they could continue with the recording the next day. Reiner declined and the session continued. At last, the final portion was recorded and Farkas' solo was brilliant.

Afterwards the orchestra began to leave, but Reiner ordered everyone back to their seats to record Strauss' *Dance of the Seven Veils*. The session ended after midnight—over fifteen hours!

Concerning Reiner's sessions, Jacobs said, "The recording sessions would go fairly well, though I must say fatigue on the part of the player never seemed to bother him. We could be taping long sessions and the fact that our lips got tired never bothered him in any way. He would just continue recording and ask for excellence. There was very little concession he would make to fatigue. Other than that the recording sessions were fine. Reiner's tension used to rise on Wagner and Strauss. Other than Wagner and Strauss, things used to go very smoothly."[83]

Alexander Nevsky [Reiner], recorded on March 9, 1959 was Jacobs' personal favorite recording with Reiner. He said, "This was the one chance I had to get close to a microphone."

"Quite often in a recording, you would have to force, you could not play comfortably. When they would want the tuba to be picked up, Reiner would say, 'play louder.' Many times this was not practical. I was already playing quite loud, and either it wouldn't be picked up, or I would have to change position and somehow try to get the bell pointing toward a microphone. In this one instance, they had a chorus mike maybe ten feet from the bell of the instrument, and it was picking up the tuba. I realized it, and could play fairly comfortably. It was one of the few recording sessions where I was quite comfortable as far as the tone production and balance were concerned."[84]

Symphonie Fantastique [Solti], recorded in 1972. The score calls for two tubas. Playing with Jacobs was Roger Rocco who remembers, "When we began to record the fourth and fifth movements, we noticed that there were no microphones for the low brass. Mr. Jacobs leaned over to me and said, 'We might as well cool it, since there are no microphones for us anyway.' We played at about half of our normal volume for the first take. Solti went to listen to the playback and returned to the stage with the directions for us to play at our normal concert volume.

Senza accel.

*Excerpt of the First Tuba part in the fifth movement of
Berlioz's* Symphonie Fantastique

"An engineer brought out a microphone and placed it directly in front of us (for this session, the tubas were located in front of the brass section). Solti said, 'Gentlemen, please play like you do at the concerts!' He then asked us to play some of the *Dies Irae* at the usual loud dynamic.

"Solti's face gleamed a smile and shouted to the offstage recording engineers, 'It sounds beautiful out here. How does it sound back there?'

"The engineer replied, 'Maestro, we can't hear the bassoons!'

"Solti answered, 'I don't care about hearing the bassoons!'

"I can honestly say that I was never even aware that the bassoons were playing along with us because we were so loud."

As a Soloist

The tuba has never been considered a solo instrument such as the violin, piano and, in the brass family, the trumpet or horn. But with a great artist such as Jacobs, the Chicago Symphony has featured him as a soloist.

Within his first three seasons (1944-47), he recalls performing Arcady Dubensky's *Fantasy on a Popular Folk Song for Tuba and Symphony Orchestra.* He had previously performed this work in 1938 with the Indianapolis Symphony {see: Professional Experience: Indianapolis Symphony Orchestra}. It was performed as part of a Saturday night popular series with Desire Defauw conducting. Preparing this solo involved playing this with piano accompaniment for DeFauw. The pianist for this occasion was Christine Querfeld who, in 2001 endowed the Chicago Symphony's tuba chair {see: Awards, Passing the Torch}.

He also recalls performing Florian Mueller's *Concert Music for Bass Tuba and Orchestra* [completed October 12, 1946] and at Ravinia, he performed the *Elephant and the Fly* with Pierre Monteux conducting.[85]

39

Arnold Jacobs: *Song and Wind*

Jacobs performed the first major concerto for the tuba, Ralph Vaughan Williams' *Concerto for Bass Tuba and Orchestra,* on the following occasions:[86]

Pops concert, Morton Gould, Conductor, January 27, 1968
Chicago Heights, Illinois, Morton Gould, Conductor, January 29, 1968
Quincy, Illinois, Henry Mazer, Conductor, May 7, 1972
University Night concert, Henry Mazer, Conductor, October 25, 1978
Subscription concert, Henry Mazer, Conductor, October 26-28, 1978
Evanston [Illinois] Symphony, conducted by CSO principal
cellist Frank Miller, December 11, 1978

The program notes from these concerts describe the work.[87]

"Ralph Vaughan Williams composed the *Concerto for Bass Tuba and Orchestra* in 1954, and dedicated the score to the London Symphony Orchestra on the occasion of its Golden Jubilee. The work was written for the tuba player of the London Symphony, [the late] Philip Catelinet, who was the soloist in the first performance of the work on June 13, 1954, at Royal Festival Hall. Sir John Barbirolli was the conductor.

"The Concerto takes full advantage of the musical and technical possibilities of the solo instrument. The first movement, *allegro moderato,* with its modal qualities, and the last movement *rondo alla tedesca* (the Italian name for the allemande—the German dance), exploit the range, the versatility and the agility of the tuba. The central movement, the *Romanza,* demonstrates the lyrical quality of tone and line in one of the most effective melodies Vaughan Williams composed."

On March 27, 1977, Jacobs recorded the concerto with Daniel Barenboim conducting the CSO. The previous season, a scheduled performance was canceled as Barenboim was needed at the bedside of his terminally ill wife, cellist Jacqueline DuPre.

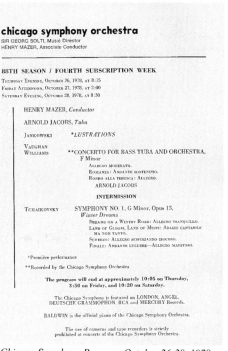

Chicago Symphony Program October 26-28, 1978

40

Prior to the recording, Jacobs was given a few weeks notice; there were no performances and little rehearsal time was provided.

At the recording session before actually recording, Jacobs played through the cadenzas unaware that Deutsche Grammophon's engineers were recording. When he asked to record the cadenzas, they told him that they had already recorded them. Jacobs was generally disappointed with the recording. Later, the Chicago Symphony released a significantly better recording from the live performances of October 1978 with Henry Mazer conducting.

For the recording and the 1978 concerts, Jacobs used an F tuba made by Boosey and Hawkes [Besson]. It is the instrument for which Vaughan Williams composed the concerto. On the other occasions, he used his York CC tuba.

Chicago Symphony Brass Quintet

In 1951, the Chicago Symphony Brass Quintet was formed—the forerunner of a multitude of quintets now in existence. The original personnel were Adolph Herseth and Renold Schilke, trumpets; Hugh Cowden, horn; Frank Crisafulli, trombone; and Jacobs.

The group was formed for a week-long tour of Wisconsin. Representatives from the Frank Holton Company heard a concert and were impressed, thus beginning a three-year relationship. Holton's affiliation with the group gave them another name, the Holton Brass Quintet.

Chicago Symphony Brass Quintet
Adolph Herseth, Frank Crisafulli, Wayne Barrington,
Arnold Jacobs, Renold Schilke

Holton arranged tours for the quintet during the breaks between the winter and summer seasons. Part of the affiliation required all members to play Holton instruments. At that time they made no CC tuba so Arnold Westphal of Holton measured Jacobs' York tuba and made a copy {see: York Tuba: Copies}. Sales of Holton's brass instruments skyrocketed. Later, as the symphony season lengthened, touring with the quintet became more difficult.[88] In 1954, the quintet made a recording for Audiophile Records [AP-21] in Milwaukee {see: Appendix A: Arnold Jacobs Discography}.[89]

Although the Holton relationship no longer existed, the quintet continued performing, primarily in the Chicago area. The February 1958 edition of the *International Musician* featured a cover photo of the quintet and stated, "The Chicago Symphony Brass Quintet gives regular clinical demonstrations in the schools of that city, in collaboration with the various music departments—informal sessions during which the student brings his instrument for consultation, instruction and personal advice from the members. The programs are aimed especially at elementary school children in the fourth to seventh grades."[90]

Over the years, the personnel of the group changed for various reasons. Other members of the group were trumpets: Vincent Cichowicz and William Scarlett; horns: Wayne Barrington and Richard Oldberg.

In the 1970s, chamber music concerts were presented in Orchestra Hall featuring the Chicago Symphony Brass Ensemble. The highlights of these concerts were large scale works performed by the full brass section.

"With a Little Help from My Friends"

Jacobs was, primarily, a one man section. If there were works that required a second tuba or when Jacobs was ill, a substitute player would perform. Generally, he called upon the tubist of the Civic Orchestra [the CSO's training orchestra] although a few times there were members of the bass section that doubled tuba—Fred Boos and Karl Walker. Some performed more than others, but they deserve recognition as a group. Here is a list of friends who helped Jacobs:

Clyde Bashand, James Blanden, Fred Boos, Forrest Byram, Daniel Corrigan, David Fedderly, Michael Grose, Charles Guse, Donald Hagner, Donald Heeren, Charles Hunter, James Johnson, Clarence Karella, Donald Little, Rex Martin, Michael Perrone, Robert Rada, Roger Rocco, Richard Schneider, Charles Schuchat, John Taylor, Bob Tucci, Karl Walker, Paul Walton, Russell Ward, and Peter Warhaftig.[91]

Colleagues

During Jacobs' tenure in the CSO, the brass section came to be considered the finest in the world. References were made worldwide about the great "Chicago Brass Sound."

Jacobs feels the principals in the brass section set the style. "We have a magnificent head in Adolph Herseth, who plays with very high standards and great authority all the time and right on down the line everybody follows along."[92]

Many members of the CSO brass section have commented, "We are supposed to fit between Herseth and Jacobs." They were the bookends of perhaps the greatest brass section of any symphony orchestra.

Chicago Symphony Orchestra, Sir Georg Solti, conductor (1980s)
From CSO Archives

Edward Kleinhammer states, "Don't build a foundation on sand, instead build it on rock. Arnold Jacobs was the rock that the brass section was built on."

Sectional rehearsals were infrequent. According to Jacobs, "If something came up that we need to work on, we always had time before concerts or rehearsals. We may try a few parts over together, but we had been playing together so long—we see more of each other on stage, probably, than we do of our families—that we know how each one thinks."[93]

Photo from the collection of Arnold Jacobs

Trombone Section

When Jacobs arrived in Chicago, parts of the CSO trombone section were already in place. When he was with the Pittsburgh Symphony, they hosted the CSO while they were on tour and [the CSO] played the overture to *Tannhauser*. Afterwards, Reiner gave Pittsburgh's trombone section a lecture on sound, using the trombones of the Chicago Symphony as an example.

From CSO Archives

In retrospect, Jacobs commented about the Chicago Symphony trombone section. "The section was excellent. I think everyone in the section was very interested in music and not just there to make money, but to enjoy the music. That is why we were such a good section. The whole bunch were an asset to the orchestra."

In comparison to other sections of the CSO, there were few personnel changes with the trombones. Frank Crisafulli and Edward Kleinhammer were already in the section before Jacobs arrived although both briefly left the orchestra during World War II for military service.

Frank Crisafulli

Frank Crisafulli had been in the trombone section for five seasons before Jacobs arrived and continued two more seasons after Jacobs retired. He had an amazing tenure of fifty-one seasons (1938-1989)! During this period, he has performed under the direction of every Music Director of the CSO except founder Theodore Thomas.

Crisafulli came from a musical family. A native Chicagoan, his father was a trombonist with the Chicago Civic Opera and the staff orchestra at WGN. His sister is a very fine pianist. Crisafulli entered Northwestern University as a liberal arts major although he played in the band, directed by Glenn Cliffe Bainum. He was then chosen as a member of the Civic Orchestra (1934-1937).

Frank and Dorothy Crisafulli with Arnold and Gizella Jacobs (1995)
Photo by John Taylor

In 1938, he auditioned for the assistant principal position in the Chicago Symphony, his first professional audition. According to Crisafulli, "I came in as an assistant to a man named Edward Geffert, a very wonderful gentleman. Shortly thereafter the bass trombonist became very ill and I was moved to second chair and the second trombonist, David Anderson, moved to bass trombone. This was the section for the remainder of the year. The following year Geffert, who was ailing, did not want the responsibility of being first chair and actually asked that I play first and he would become the assistant."

Crisafulli was the CSO's principal trombone for sixteen years and then second trombone from 1955 until his retirement in 1989. He was the only trombonist in the Chicago Symphony Brass Quintet.

Those who Crisafulli credits as his teachers included his father, Frank F. Crisafulli, Sr., Einor Passoja, Frank Rizzo, Donald Reinhart, and Arnold Jacobs. He taught at the Chicago State College and Northwestern University.[94]

Jacobs said, "Frank Crisafulli was a fine player no matter what part he played in the orchestra or quintet. He was an asset to the orchestra before I arrived until after I left. Frank is a fine gentleman and musician. I consider him a friend."

Frank Crisafulli passed away on November 5, 1998.

Edward Kleinhammer

Bass trombonist Edward Kleinhammer was born in Chicago in 1919, and at first played the violin. At age fourteen, in high school, he switched to the trombone. His teachers were CSO trombonists Edward Geffert and David Anderson. He was a member of the Civic Orchestra for two years starting in 1938, and played extra with the CSO. In 1940, he was a member of Stokowski's All-American Youth Symphony during their tour of South America. That same year he auditioned for the Chicago Symphony and a short time later signed a contract. He remained with the CSO until June 1985, and has played for all CSO conductors except Theodore Thomas.[95] He is the author of *The Art of Trombone Playing.*

Before Jacobs' arrival in the CSO, Kleinhammer had heard about him by his reputation. When Jacobs joined the CSO, Kleinhammer was in the Army (1942-45) and Elmer Janes had moved from assistant principal to bass trombone. It was after Kleinhammer's return to the orchestra that he met Jacobs for the first time.

Until Kleinhammer's retirement in 1985, he and Jacobs sat next to each other. Only on rare occurrences did the two of them work out parts. Kleinhammer once told Gizella Jacobs that the relationship between himself and Jacobs was, "Almost like being married." Jacobs stated, "They say that gradually a husband and wife learn how each other thinks and you practically become one. It's the same thing in the orchestral group. Without ever saying anything, we breathe together, and play the same length of phrase. We've played together so much, the communication does not need words. We hear each other all the time."[96]

According to Jacobs, "I had an ideal mate with Ed Kleinhammer. We never had a crossed word in all those years we played together. We didn't even have to talk about a part. It was as if each one of us knew what the other would do without saying a word. I could not ask for a nicer partner for all those years, believe me.

"The only time he ever took time off was when his [first] wife, Dorothy, passed away. He took one tour off and sent a substitute. Otherwise, he was there, always early, practiced and prepared his parts, and enjoyed himself. He has been a friend all these years."

Kleinhammer writes about Jacobs, "Arnold Jacobs, my friend and colleague for more than forty years, has ennobled and raised the spirit of all with whom he comes into contact. A world-class artist and tuba player, a kind and sympathetic person, it was my inherent great fortune to be his partner in the Chicago Symphony Orchestra.

Ed Kleinhammer with Arnold and Gizella Jacobs (1995)
Photo by Author

"Arnold would awe and humble one with his musicianship and 'Big Daddy' sound, be it a solo or an integral passage; he could make a 'concerto' out of a few notes. Between us a few words of suggestion were always welcome, and many are the helpful techniques I have learned from him. We had obscure signals between us that helped to keep us musically secure, and enjoyed a fine relationship. Likewise with many of his students—all carbon copies of Arnold's teachings. As a teacher he is world-acclaimed, and as a colleague and musician, I am thankful to God for Arnold Jacobs."

Edward Kleinhammer currently lives in Barrington, Illinois. An avid golfer, his home is located on a golf course.

Robert Lambert
Robert Lambert was born in Fruita, Colorado on April 15, 1920. He attended the Curtis Institute (1938-41) and was a euphonium soloist from 1941-46 with the United States Marine Band in Washington, D.C. Afterwards, he was associate principal trombone of the Philadelphia Orchestra (1948-55) and the Robin Hood Dell Orchestra (1946-55). He toured England and Scotland with Jacobs and the Philadelphia Orchestra in 1949. In 1955, he joined the Chicago Symphony as principal trombone, retiring in 1964.

Jacobs says, "Bob Lambert's leaving the orchestra had to do with the physical problems he was undergoing. Every now and then a brass player will develop physical problems that interfere with their careers, and we may lose a good player that way. Bob was not with us very long but we sure enjoyed him while he was here."

Lambert is currently living near Gunnison, Colorado.[97]

Jay Friedman

Jay Friedman is a native Chicagoan who, at first, played the euphonium which he continued playing into high school. At the same time, he developed an ambition to become a player in a symphony orchestra, never quite realizing that, "You can't make a living playing the baritone. Nobody uses the baritone." He was studying with Vincent Cichowicz, then second trumpet in the Chicago Symphony, and it was Cichowicz who suggested that Friedman switch to the trombone.[98]

Shortly thereafter, he joined the Civic Orchestra for four years and studied at the Chicago Musical College of Roosevelt University. He then spent two years as principal trombone with the Florida Symphony. One summer he studied as a scholarship student at the Yale Summer School of Musical Art, where he explored composition and conducting. His teachers include Robert Lambert, John Swallow, and Vincent Cichowicz, all members of the CSO.

In 1962, there was an opening for assistant principal in the CSO. Just three days before the season was to begin, Friedman got a call and was told to report for work as assistant principal trombone.

"The first year I was the typical assistant—I never got to play anything at all—you show up for concerts and rehearsals and you don't play." During Friedman's second season, Robert Lambert, the CSO's principal trombone, took a leave of absence. Friedman covered the first trombone part for the full season. The beginning of the next season, Lambert retired.

Friedman went to the personnel manager, John Weicher, asking if he could audition for the principal position. The response was, "What do you mean by audition? From what [Jean] Martinon [the CSO's conductor at the time] tells me, you've got the job."[99]

Beginning in April 1965, at the age of twenty-five, Friedman was appointed principal trombone—the youngest in any major orchestra and was the first trombone soloist to perform on a subscription concert in the history of the Orchestra.[100]

According to Jacobs, "Jay Friedman joined us while Lambert was still here—he was Lambert's student. When Lambert left us, we took a vote and recommended that the orchestra hire Friedman as principal, which they did. He is a fine player and has been a great asset to the orchestra."

James Gilbertsen

A native of Janesville, Wisconsin, James Gilbertsen began playing the trombone in the fifth grade. Later, he enrolled at the University of Wisconsin to study electrical engineering. He stayed only a year before transferring to Northwestern University where he could study trombone with Frank Crisafulli. Later, while he was working toward degrees in music education, he played first trombone in the Florida Symphony. After his audition, he joined the Chicago Symphony as assistant principal trombone in 1968 and since 1982, has held the title of associate principal.[101]

Jacobs states, "Jim Gilbertsen was a student of Crisafulli's. He is a fine player and an expert person in electronics, not only in using but in designing electronic equipment."

Charles Vernon

Following the retirement of Edward Kleinhammer, Charles Vernon emerged from the audition and joined the CSO in 1986.

A native of Asheville, North Carolina, Vernon attended Brevard College and Georgia State University. He has held the bass trombone positions in the Baltimore Symphony (1971-80), San Francisco Symphony (1980-81), and the Philadelphia Orchestra (1981-86). He has been on the faculties of The Catholic University of America (1972-80), Brevard Music Center (1972-81), and has taught at the Philadelphia College of the Performing Arts and the Curtis Institute of Music.

Among his teachers are Edward Kleinhammer and Arnold Jacobs.[102]

About Jacobs, Charles Vernon writes:

"As a student in the late sixties, I had listened to the Chicago Symphony for years, and like many people, considered the brass section to be the finest in the world. When I first heard the orchestra live, I was amazed by the sound of the brass, powerful and present at all dynamic levels. Of course, a large part of that sound was the legendary Arnold Jacobs. I began study with Mr. Jacobs in June 1969, and was in awe of his knowledge. In the beginning it was sometimes difficult for me to understand his concepts and scientific way of expressing himself, but he was patient and never let me go home until I was clear as to what he was trying to tell me. The main thing that I remember about my early study with Mr. Jacobs was his attention to tone quality and 'telling a story' when playing.

"From 1969-85, I was able to see Mr. Jacobs at least a couple of times a year, and with many telephone conversations, I was able to remain inspired and develop a friendship with him. In 1985, I was able to realize a lifelong dream and join the Chicago Symphony. Sitting on a daily basis beside the greatest tuba player and teacher in the world was one of the most memorable experiences of my life. My relationship with him changed from long time student to one of colleague and close friend. Occasionally during rehearsal, Mr. Jacobs would lean over make a playing suggestion, then sit back and listen to me try it. These 'mini-lessons' were wonderful for me. I always tried to help him out when I could, whether it was to carry his tuba up on stage, or, as his eyesight began to fail, have his music enlarged so that he could read it more easily. Before rehearsals and concerts, I would listen to him warm up. It was fantastic to watch him take a breath. So fast, easy and quiet, it was a picture of perfect execution.

"It was very sad for me to see Mr. Jacobs retire from the orchestra. We see each other occasionally after Thursday evening concerts, many of which he attends with his lovely wife Gizella. I am thankful that I was able to perform with a living legend, even for a short period of time."

Jacobs says, "Charlie is doing a fine job. The replacements [Charles Vernon and Michael Mulcahy, who replaced Frank Crisafulli] are excellent."

Glenn Dodson. Frank Crisafulli,
Edward Kleinhammer and Arnold Jacobs
From CSO Archives

Others

David Anderson was born in Chicago, May 14, 1894. He was second trombone (1929-1938), bass trombone (1938-40), and again second trombone (1940-55) before retiring from the Chicago Symphony. He played in the Civic Orchestra and had served in the military during World War II. Anderson died in Chicago on June 12, 1970.

Other players that have been members of the CSO trombone section from 1944-88 were Joseph Bejcek, Glenn Dodson, Elmer Janes, Byron Peebles, Robert Rada, Richard Schmitt, and John Swallow {see: Appendix B: Brass Personnel}.

Trumpet Section

Recalling the trumpet section, Jacobs said, "When I joined that orchestra, the trumpets were a normal section, but after Adolph Herseth came in the trumpet section became one of the leading sections of the orchestra. There was a wonderful spirit in that trumpet section. They are all fine gentlemen."

Renold Schilke

Renold Otto Schilke was a man of many talents. Besides being a great trumpet player, he was a repairman, designer, manufacturer of instruments, and a marksman.

Born in Green Bay, Wisconsin on June 30, 1910, he started playing the trumpet at age seven. At the age of nine he studied with Del Wright [United States Marine Band] and Jay Williams. He came to Chicago in 1929, and studied with the CSO's principal trumpet, Edward B. Llewellyn. Other teachers included Georges Mager, Boston Symphony; Max Schlossberg, New York Philharmonic; and Herbert L. Clarke, the famous cornet soloist of the Sousa Band.

Schilke's orchestral experience included the Civic Orchestra (1931-1936), Chicago Symphony (1936-1941,1942-1951), Grant Park Symphony (1944-1955), Tri-City Symphony (1945-1946), and the Chicago Lyric Opera (1954-1962). He was an original member of the Chicago Symphony Brass Quintet.

He taught at Northwestern University (1938-1954), DePaul University (1938-1958), and the Chicago Musical College (later merged as a part of Roosevelt University, 1939-1965). Many summers were spent teaching at Elon College, North Carolina, where he was awarded an Honorary Doctorate in 1976.

Schilke passed away in Sun City, Arizona on September 5, 1982.[103]

For years, Jacobs would bring repairs to Schilke. In the 1970s Schilke's company overhauled Jacobs' York tuba.

Jacobs remembers, "Schilke was a fine trumpet player. He was my friend and former roommate on tour. He became a very busy man during his career and his hobby was in the manufacturing of instruments, making mouthpieces and trumpets. He went from being a player to manufacturer. To this day, the Schilke trumpet is one of the major quality custom trumpets on the market. Of course Ren has since gone, but that trumpet is still manufactured by his family and is doing well."

Adolph Herseth

Jacobs has the highest praise for Adolph "Bud" Herseth. "I said it years ago and I'll say it again that Bud Herseth is the finest brass player I have ever worked with. He is a marvelous man. I am proud to have known him and proud to have worked with him. I consider him a friend."

Jacobs considers himself a student of Herseth's since he bases his conception of how a trumpet should sound by Herseth's playing. He is constantly telling trumpet players to, "Play it like Bud would."

When Jacobs joined the CSO, the trumpets were a normal section. According to Jacobs, "In the brass, it really started to improve dramatically with the hiring of Herseth, and of course, our trumpets really moved into a top flight relationship."[104]

"Herseth joined us at Ravinia, and the first work he played [under Reiner] was *Ein Heldenleben*. Reiner had been my conductor at the Curtis Institute of Music for seven years and five years in the Pittsburgh Symphony, so when he came here, I knew him quite well. He came up after the rehearsal and said to me, 'Where did you find that jewel?'"

At one time, Jacobs kept track of errors that Herseth made. "He made a mistake about once every three years—perfection all the time."

Adolph Sylvester Herseth was born in Lake Park, Minnesota on July 25, 1921. His father, who was a school superintendent in Bertha, Minnesota [population 510], introduced him to the trumpet. Jacobs, who lived in Willow Brook, California [population 400] has commented, "I'm the only person who came from a smaller town than Herseth."

Herseth got a trumpet when he was in second grade but essentially ignored it. Then his school got a new band director, his father got him a new instruction book, and he developed a new interest. "I found that the more I practiced, the better I played, and the better I played, the more I enjoyed it."[105]

It was in fourth grade that Herseth met his future wife, Avis who also played the trumpet. During the summer of 1937, Herseth went to the first state high

Adolph Herseth
From CSO Archives

school band camp that was held at the University of Minnesota. Here he studied with James Greco of the Minneapolis [now Minnesota] Symphony Orchestra.

After high school he enrolled at his father's alma mater, Luther College in Decorah, Iowa. He was not a music major but instead, studied mathematics. During World War II he served as a Navy bandsman at the Iowa pre-flight school and then attended the U.S. Navy School of Music. He ended his naval service with the Band of the Philippine Sea Frontier in the South Pacific.

After the war, he wanted to attend music school using the GI Bill. He wrote letters of application to four schools, the New England Conservatory, Curtis Institute, Eastman School of Music, and the Juilliard School of Music.

51

"I really did not have any intention of being a professional trumpet player. I wanted to get a master's degree for teaching purposes. I wanted to study with a high-class symphonic trumpet player because I found I enjoyed that kind of music and I enjoyed hearing those guys play."[106]

The New England Conservatory admitted him January 1946. He studied with members of the Boston Symphony, first with Marcel Lafosse, Boston's second trumpet. His final year was with Boston's principal trumpet, Georges Mager.[108] In 1948 h e g raduated from t he Ne w E ngland C onservatory. H e t hen r eceived a telegram from CSO conductor Arthur Rodzinski.

Herseth knew that Rodzinski was Music Director of the Chicago Symphony, but he never gave much thought to playing in a symphony. He just figured that Rodzinski was between appearances in Chicago and was looking around for some reserves, perhaps someone to play down at the end of the section. "I did not know how he got my name or anything else."

He went to New York and auditioned in Rodzinski's apartment for an hour and a half. When it was over, Rodzinski congratulated Herseth, "You are the new first trumpet player for the Chicago Symphony." Herseth was astounded. "I about went through the floor," he says. But he was not inclined to turn the job down.

Subsequently he discovered that the job had been offered to the first trumpet player of the Boston Symphony. He had turned it down but, having heard Herseth play, he recommended him for the job. The irony was that Rodzinski left the Chicago Symphony soon after that and Herseth never played under him. "I often joke that they fired him as soon as they learned that he hired me"—a twenty-four-year-old who hadn't finished his musical studies, as the first trumpet in the Chicago Symphony.[108]

Herseth's years in the CSO have included many solo appearances with the Orchestra and with Chicago Symphony brass ensembles. He is an original member of the Chicago Symphony Brass Quintet and he has been active as a soloist with community and regional musical ensembles and orchestras throughout the country. He holds Doctor of Music [Honoris Causa] degrees from Luther College and the New England Conservatory of Music and has given master classes throughout the world.[109]

After fifty two seasons with the CSO, Herseth retired in August 2001.

Others

Vincent Cichowicz was born in Chicago in 1927, and during high school played with the Houston Symphony (1944-1945) before joining the Army. Later, he played in the Grant Park Symphony (1947-1960) and studied at Roosevelt University with Renold Schilke. While first trumpet with the Civic Orchestra (1949-1950) he studied with Adolph Herseth and Arnold Jacobs. He joined the Chicago Symphony in 1952 as fourth trumpet, and moved to second trumpet seven years later and retired in January 1975. He was a member of the Chicago Symphony

Brass Quintet. Since 1959, he has been teaching at Northwestern University, becoming full-time in September 1974.[110] He passed away December 11, 2006.

A native Chicagoan, William Scarlett studied at Northwestern University with Renold Schilke. He played with the Civic Orchestra, studying with Adolph Herseth and Arnold Jacobs. While in the Army, he played with the Seventh Army Symphony (1957-1958). Next, he played in the Grant Park Symphony (1956, 1962-1964), and for five years was first trumpet with the Chicago Lyric Opera. In 1964, he became a member of the Chicago Symphony Orchestra and was appointed assistant principal in 1966. He also played with the Chicago Symphony Brass Quintet.

Scarlett has worked in the Schilke factory, and has developed an interest in antique brass instruments. He has an impressive personal collection and has been a consultant to many museums.[111]

Many fine players have been members of the CSO trumpet section from 1944-88 {see: Appendix B: Brass Personnel}. Those players include William Babcock, Sydney Baker, Charles Geyer, Robert Grocock, Frank Holz, Gerald Huffman, Frank Kaderabek, Timothy Kent, Ed Masacek, Rudolph Nashan, Philip Smith, and George Vosburgh.

From CSO Archives. Photo by Jim Steere

Horn Section

In 1944, Helen Kotas was the CSO's principal horn. She had previously played with Jacobs in the All-American Youth Orchestra. On the other end of the section was longtime CSO member Max Pottag who was in his final season with the orchestra. Two members of the horn section, William Verschoor and Joseph Mourek, were in the military and returned a few seasons later. Charles Jackson and Harry Jacobs were in the orchestra during this time. Clyde Wedgewood started his long career in 1943, dying tragically in 1969.

Philip Farkas

The late Philip Farkas was born in Chicago on March 15, 1914. In school, he had a conflict with his gym teacher, and fulfilled a physical education requirement by playing an old BB♭ Pan American tuba in the school's marching band.

Both Farkas and Jacobs had problems carrying their tuba on a streetcar, but their solutions were different. Reiner's chauffeur transported Jacobs and his tuba to and from the Curtis Institute. When a streetcar conductor banished Farkas' tuba, he switched to the horn.

Later, Farkas, while working as an usher at Orchestra Hall in Chicago, studied with Louis Dufrasne. While in high school, he joined the Civic Orchestra. At the age of eighteen he quit school to play first horn in the Kansas City Philharmonic (1933-36). He played in the Chicago Symphony (1936-1941), Cleveland Orchestra (1941-1945), Boston Symphony (1945-1946), and Cleveland, again 1946-1947. Finally, returning to the Chicago Symphony (1947-1960) as principal horn.

He joined the faculty of Indiana University in 1960, and was named a Distinguished Professor in 1982. During those years he continued to perform, including seventeen years at the Aspen Music Festival.[112] He wrote several books including *The Art of Horn Playing* and *The Art of Brass Playing*. Mr.

Philip Farkas
From *Art of Brass Playing*

Farkas passed away in Bloomington, Indiana, on December 21, 1992.

Farkas was with the CSO twice, from 1936-41 and 1947-60. He explained it thus:

"In 1936 I began my career in the Chicago Symphony and continued on through the 1940-41 season. After that season I was invited to the Cleveland Orchestra with Arthur Rodzinski, who became acquainted with me and my horn playing while at Ravinia, where he was guest conductor of the Chicago Symphony Orchestra. He offered me the job as first horn of the Cleveland Orchestra.

"When Arthur Rodzinski became the Music Director of the Chicago Symphony Orchestra, he insisted that I come back with him. Chicago was still my home, and the Chicago Symphony—the greatest orchestra in the world—was still in my heart. So I came back and stayed with the Orchestra from that season up through the 1960 season, going through the seasons of Rodzinski, Kubelik, and Reiner until I left to take up residency at Indiana University as a full professor of music."[113]

Jacobs comments, "Phil Farkas was a great horn player. He did not stay with us as long as I would have liked to have had him. He was surely an asset to the orchestra. When I sat behind him and listened, he sounded like a great singer singing a great aria. He played beautifully."

Dale Clevenger

Dale Clevenger started playing the piano at the age of seven. Four years later, he played the trumpet in the school band. "My father would not buy me a horn because it cost too much at that time, a second choice was the trumpet. So I played the trumpet for two years." When he was thirteen, the school bought a French horn. "I put the trumpet aside and I began playing the horn."

At the age of sixteen, Clevenger was hired by the Chattanooga Symphony as fourth horn. "I spent my last two years in high school playing in the Chattanooga Symphony." He enrolled at the Carnegie Institute of Technology in Pittsburgh where he studied with Forrest Standley, former first horn of the Pittsburgh Symphony. Clevenger played in many school ensembles and the Wheeling [West Virginia] Symphony. He also played as an extra in the Pittsburgh Symphony.

In the summers after his junior and senior years, he went to New York to study with Jacobs' cousin, the late Joseph Singer, then principal horn in the New York Philharmonic [see: Early Years]. "With Singer, I added touches with a different point of view, but with the same basic style of playing," After graduating from Carnegie Tech, he moved to New York.

In New York, he was playing extra horn with the New York Philharmonic and was a member of the Symphony of the Air and the American Symphony Orchestra. He toured Europe with the Pittsburgh Symphony and played with the Kansas City Philharmonic.

Clevenger then auditioned for first horn with the Metropolitan Opera and won plaudits—"One of the horn players who heard me said it was the best audition he ever heard played"—but the job went, instead, to the first horn from the Chicago Symphony. Clevenger promptly sought an audition for the first horn opening with the Chicago Symphony and was one of the two finalists, "But they didn't take anybody at that time."

He received a phone call from conductor Alfred Wallenstein, under whom he had played from time to time. Wallenstein said, "I've spoken to the conductor in Chicago about you. You should go out and audition for them." I said, "I just did audition for them, back in April, and I didn't make it." He said, "You go out again. You play for them again. They want a first horn player."

So one Sunday night, after playing a concert with Leopold Stokowski in Manhattan, he flew to Chicago and at 9:30 the next morning played an audition. Chicago did not hesitate this time. He got the job.[114]

In February 1966, he joined the CSO as their principal horn. He has since been a frequent soloist with the CSO and orchestras around the world. Additionally, he has done much work in the recording studios playing commercials and jingles.

According to Jacobs, "Dale Clevenger is a splendid horn player who is doing a beautiful job. He is at the top of his profession."

Frank Brouk

Frank Brouk is a native Chicagoan born on July 27, 1913. At the age of eight he began playing the cornet. He switched to the horn in high school and studied with Frank Kryl Sr. and Louis Dufrasne. In November of 1936, Brouk commuted between Chicago, where he played in the Civic Orchestra, and the Indianapolis Symphony where he was first horn (1937-41). This was the first job in a professional orchestra for both Jacobs and Brouk. After four seasons he joined the Rochester Philharmonic (1941-42) as principal horn.

In June 1942, Brouk joined the Army for two years. Afterwards, he became first horn of the Cleveland Orchestra (1947-50). He returned to Chicago in 1950, and played various engagements including the Grant Park Symphony (1946-49), WGN (1950-56), and the Lyric Opera (1956-59). In 1961 he was appointed to the Chicago Symphony, retiring in 1979.

Norman Schweikert writes, "During his almost eighteen years with the Chicago Symphony, Frank has officially played every position in the horn section except third horn—a feat not equaled by any past member of the section. He began as assistant and utility horn, and then became associate principal for the 1961-62 season. Twice he was principal horn (June 1962 to August 1963 and October 1965 to February 1966), each time returning to the associate principal position. In 1969 he asked to step down to a lesser position and became assistant principal in June of that year. After the tragic death of Clyde Wedgewood on Christmas Day, 1969, Frank took over the duties of second horn and continued in that position until he moved to fourth horn in September 1975."[115]

Hugh Cowden

Hugh Cowden was born in London on February 9, 1915. He trained with the National Orchestral Association in New York. During the mid-1930s studied with Bruno Jaenicke, principal horn of the New York Philharmonic. His first professional experience was with the New York Philharmonic and the New York Opera.

He was with Jacobs in the Pittsburgh Symphony (1942-44) where he played fourth horn. From there he played second horn in the Metropolitan Opera (1944-45), fourth horn in the Boston Symphony (1945-48) and rejoined Jacobs in the Chicago Symphony where he was assistant principal (1951-54) and an original member of the Chicago Symphony Brass Quintet. After the CSO, he played the Broadway Show *My Fair Lady*, beginning with opening night concluding with the last performance.

According to Jacobs, "Cowden was a great low horn player. When they brought him to Chicago, they put him on high horn. He was assistant principal, just where he didn't belong. He could play high horn, but he was an absolutely outstanding low horn player."

Philip Farkas said about Cowden, "He was a virtuoso hornist who could evidently play any orchestra horn position, high or low, and do it superbly."

Cowden died April 6, 1988, in Moanalua, Oahu, Hawaii.[116]

Norman Schweikert

Norman Schweikert has been a member of the Chicago Symphony since June 1971. Previously, he was a member of the Rochester Philharmonic while a student at the Eastman School of Music. He has taught at the Interlochen Arts Academy and Northwestern University.

Schweikert has been working on his book, *A Bio-Bibliographical Index of Symphony and Opera Musicians in the Major U.S. Organizations, 1842-1992*[117] and has been a contributor to *Arnold Jacobs: Song and Wind*. He offers these thoughts about Jacobs.

"Ever since experiencing Arnold Jacobs' impressive playing on recordings of the Chicago Symphony Orchestra under Kubelik and Reiner (most notably the former's recording of *Pictures at an Exhibition* and the latter's various Strauss offerings) I have been an ardent admirer of his art. Milan Yancich, my colleague in the horn section of the Rochester Philharmonic, 1955-66, had studied with him, and his recollections of the man and his methods only increased my admiration. It was, therefore, with great joy that I found myself working with Arnold in the brass section of the Chicago Symphony.

"Although I never formally studied with Arnold, I feel as though every day in his presence was a lesson of some kind. One cannot be around him without learning something valuable concerning breathing or a positive mental approach to performing. If one of my horn students was experiencing a physical problem I could not solve, I would send the student to Arnold or seek his advice myself. Positive results were always the outcome.

"It is a privilege to have performed with Arnold during his last seventeen years in the CSO and to count him among my friends. I am most pleased to have been able to assist during the research phase for this biography of one of the most important brass performers and pedagogues of this century."

Others

After Hugh Cowden left the orchestra, the Chicago Symphony Brass Quintet replaced him with Wayne Barrington. Barrington studied horn at the New England Conservatory graduating with a Bachelor of Music. He was in the military serving from 1943 to 1946. His orchestral career began as third horn of the San Antonio Symphony Orchestra (1949-50). He was then second horn in Pittsburgh (1951-54), third horn in Chicago (1954-64), and associate principal in Los Angeles (1964-66). During his years in Chicago he taught horn at De Paul University (1957-61) and since 1966 he has been a professor of horn at the University of Texas in Austin.[118]

The next horn player in the Chicago Symphony Brass Quintet was Chicago native Richard Oldberg. Born into a musical family, he attended Harvard University and received a degree from Northwestern University. His teachers include former CSO principal, Christopher Leuba. He joined the CSO in 1962 retiring in 1994.[119]

Other members of the CSO horn section (from 1944-88) include David Babcock, Nancy Fako, Alan Fuchs, Daniel Gingrich, Arthur Goldstein, Thomas Howell, Charles Jackson, Harry Jacobs, Helen Kotas, Arthur Krehbiel, Christopher Leuba, Joseph Mourek, Max Pottag, Louis Stout, Clarendon Van Norman, William Verschoor, Clyde Wedgwood, Gail Weimer, Gail Williams, and Milan Yancich {see: Appendix B: Brass Personnel}.

CSO Brass (1975)
From CSO Archives

Other Performances

During the later parts of the summers from 1961 to 1963, Jacobs traveled to Gunnison, Colorado where Western State College had a summer music camp. Conductors of the camp's Director's Band included Dr. Robert Hawkins, Cmdr. Charles Brendler [U.S. Navy Band], Lt. Col. William Santelmann [U.S. Marine Band], Glenn C. Bainum, Vincent DiNino, Charles Minelli, Al G. Wright, William D. Revelli, and others.

As the programming became more difficult, the director of the camp, Dr. Robert Hawkins, supplemented the group with faculty members from various professional orchestras.

Jacobs comments, "I remember playing a band transcription of the *New World Symphony*, playing the bass parts. I never knew what I was missing—it was marvelous. The orchestral tuba part consists of fourteen notes but the band part is a different world."

Many members of the CSO including Edward Kleinhammer and oboist Ray Still were on the faculty of Gunnison. During those summers, Jacobs was joined in the tuba section by Bill Bell.

"Bill Bell was a most unusual man. He was generous to a fault as he would give you the shirt off his back if you needed it. He was a fine musician and it was a joy to sit on stage and to play with him. I am glad I had the opportunity to play with Bell."

Arnold Jacobs and Bill Bell
Photo from collection of Arnold Jacobs

During the summer of 1963 they were joined by Harvey Phillips. "Harvey Phillips, Bill Bell and I were very advanced players. I have some records from Gunnison and you will hear some fine tuba playing from the three of us. Working with three tubas was so much fun. I guess we were a band director's dream team."

Harvey Phillips recalls that summer. "Like many musician colleagues, I have spent most summer months away from home base by teaching at one or more summer festivals and/or music camps. These summer positions are very important. They allow us to have renewed contact with old friends and to experience other colleagues who teach at a variety of schools around the country. Sharing pedagogical concepts, discussing different teaching experiences, and hearing others perform, inspires our continued growing as teachers and performers. Without a doubt, the most fulfilling and enjoyable summer I have ever experienced was the summer of 1963 at the Gunnison Music Camp in Gunnison, Colorado. Dr. Robert Hawkins directed the camp and conducted the Director's Band made up of faculty members (the listing of which read like a who's who of musicians). The tuba faculty that summer was William Bell, Arnold Jacobs and myself. I shall never forget what it was like to play in that tuba section, nor will I ever forget the relaxing dinners and impromptu parties which followed rehearsals and performances. As the youngest member of the section, I observed and listened. Never have I witnessed greater mutual respect and genuine comradeship than that displayed by William Bell and Arnold Jacobs for each other. The Director's Band did a lot of recording that summer, including the last concert which featured our tuba section in a unison (except for the last chord!) performance of Paganini's *Perpetual Motion*."

About Harvey Phillips, Jacobs says, "I first met Harvey Phillips many years ago when he came backstage following a performance with Fritz Reiner conducting the Chicago Symphony at Carnegie Hall. This was the start of our long friendship.

"Once, Harvey told me that he had decided to pursue a career as a solo tubist—unheard of

Carol and Harvey Phillips with Gizella and Arnold Jacobs Bloomington, Indiana (1994)
Photo by Author

in those days, as the solo literature for the tuba was almost nonexistent. Due to Harvey's time and energy encouraging new works for the tuba, the students of today have a great deal of material to choose from. He has led the way in making the tuba accepted as a solo instrument by setting high standards for performance."

Many recordings were made of the Gunnison band but were not commercially available. Jacobs performed as a soloist on a recording of Richard Strauss' *First Horn Concerto*. Jacobs and Bell recorded several duets and Bell, Jacobs and Phillips recorded Paganini's *Perpetual Motion* played in unison by all three {see: Appendix A: Arnold Jacobs Discography}.

After the summer of 1963, the camp was moved to Morehead, Kentucky and Fred Marzan became its director. However, due to increased activity with the CSO, Jacobs was no longer able to attend.

In June 1962, Jacobs was the first tubist to play at the Casals Festival in Puerto Rico. This festival was organized by cellist, conductor and composer Pablo Casals (b. December 29, 1876, d. October 22, 1973).[120] Although he enjoyed performing with the festival orchestra under Casals and the fishing was great, his luck was not very good. "I lost money every night at the casino."

In 1968, Jacobs traveled to Philadelphia with fellow CSO members Adolph Herseth, Vincent Cichowicz, Dale Clevenger, Jay Friedman, and Frank Crisafulli to record, along with members of the Philadelphia and Cleveland Orchestras, selected antiphonal music of Giovanni Gabrieli.

The music chosen was multiple brass choir arrangements of antiphonal sonatas and canzonas requiring two or three brass choirs. It won a Grammy for the best chamber music recording, a Gran Prix du Disque in Europe and was nominated for classical album of the year (1969).

Photo from Sony Classical. Used with Permission

The tubists were Jacobs and two of his students, Abe Torchinsky of the Philadelphia Orchestra and Ron Bishop of the Cleveland Orchestra.

Abe Torchinsky remembers, "The camaraderie was incredible at those sessions. When we finished the album, which was done in three, three-hour sessions, a group of us went to a local pub for lunch near the Academy of Music in Philly and someone said, 'Hey, we never tuned.' At that point someone said, 'Can you imagine if it were three woodwind groups. The oboe players would still be fighting over who gives the A!'"

The University of Miami boasted one of the finest tuba ensembles in the country directed by Connie Weldon. In 1969 they sponsored the International Tuba Ensemble Composition Contest. The judges were Connie Weldon, Bill Bell and Jacobs.[121] Jacobs made several trips to the University of Miami as his son, Dallas, was a student there for a few years.

In July 1971, the CSO low brass section made a recording of various orchestral excerpts {see: Appendix A: Arnold Jacobs Discography}. The personnel were Jay Friedman, James Gilbertsen, Frank Crisafulli, Edward Kleinhammer and Jacobs. Joseph Kreines conducted.

The second side of the recording features Jacobs as a soloist in Tomasi's *To Be or Not to Be*, accompanied by three trombones. This recording displays his incredible dramatic and singing style of playing as few recordings have.

Over thirty years later, in 2002, Jay Friedman and Vern Kagarice (from the University of North Texas) re-released this as a compact disc. Generations of low brass players had used this as a benchmark for section playing and are passing this to their students.

Conductors

During a performance career of fifty-eight years, Jacobs has played for most of the major conductors in the world. There are exceptions though, such as Arturo Toscanini, under whom Jacobs never played.

Music Directors of the Chicago Symphony Orchestra
With the exception of founder Theodore Thomas and his successor, Frederick Stock who collectively conducted the CSO until 1942, Jacobs has performed with seven of its musical directors, who are:

Desire Defauw
Desire Defauw was the third conductor in the CSO's history, from 1943 to 1947. It was Defauw who hired Jacobs for the Chicago Symphony.

Desire Defauw
From CSO Archives.
Photo by Anne. P. Dewey

Born on September 5, 1885 in Ghent, Belgium, Defauw graduated from the Royal Conservatory in Brussels. He became Belgium's leading conductor directing such groups as the Brussels Royal Conservatory Orchestra, Orchestre National de Belgique, Concerts du Conservatoire, and Belgian National Radio. He also guest conducted many of Europe's major orchestras.

In 1939, he made his American debut conducting the NBC Symphony Orchestra. When Hitler invaded Belgium in May 1940, Defauw was in Italy. He made his way to London where he led a concert with the BBC Orchestra. Later, he came to North America and conducted the Montreal Symphony from 1941-53.

Jacobs remembers, "I have pleasant memories of Desire Defauw. He had definite concepts, such as he wanted a happy orchestra, and went out of his way to make sure that we were. He was the only conductor that ordered you to be happy when you came to rehearsal in the morning. He was a very kind gentleman and was very proficient in some aspects of conducting, with a little acting here and there."

Following Defauw's departure from the CSO, Jacobs frequently saw him on the train on Chicago's south side as Defauw would travel to Gary, Indiana where he conducted the Gary Symphony (1950-58). Defauw died in Gary, Indiana on July 25, 1960.[122]

Arthur Rodzinski

Following Defauw was Arthur Rodzinski, who was with the orchestra for only one season, 1947-48. Rodzinski was born in Spalato, Yugoslavia, on January 1, 1892. Beginning with the 1926 season, he was an assistant to Stokowski with the Philadelphia Orchestra for three years. Concurrently, he was the head of the orchestra and opera departments at the Curtis Institute. He then conducted the Los Angeles Philharmonic (1929-1933), Cleveland Orchestra (1933-1943), and the New York Philharmonic (1943-46).

It was in 1938 he made his debut with the Chicago Symphony at Ravinia. He introduced the custom of presenting operas in concert form, a controversial move at the time. During Rodzinski's season in Chicago, the CSO was enduring a conflict between Rodzinski, management and the music critics. As Philip Farkas wrote, "Towards the end of the season that he was to leave, fights broke out in the audience—someone in the balcony would shout 'Don't fire Rodzinski, fire the Management!'—and someone would retort 'Shut up and sit down!' Then fist fights broke out. Finally, we had to have police protection and at the end of the last few weeks policemen were stationed at each corridor, the ends of each aisle, and out in the hall during the concerts to prevent out-breaks of this sort. It was quite exciting and when Rodzinski left after his last concert, of course, the entire audience rose to its feet and cheered and yelled, and he took several bows. When he finally came out for his last bow he brought his little son with him and took his last bow with this small child in his arms—there was quite a bit of weeping. It was simply amazing—the sort of thing you might see at one of our present day rock concerts."[123]

Arthur Rodzinski
From CSO Archives

According to Jacobs, "Rodzinski was a fine musician, and we did give some fine concerts with him. He had an erratic personality, but nobody in the audience could care about that. Evidently, he had problems with the orchestra management and the board of trustees, and he created problems with the orchestra. If he had stayed in Chicago, it would have been a very different orchestra in that second year than it was in his first year, as many of the CSO members would have been replaced that second year, had he stayed. I don't think he was terribly missed when he left."

Arnold Jacobs: *Song and Wind*

Coming from the New York Philharmonic the previous season, Rodzinski wanted a smaller sound from the CSO's low brass section. He encouraged the trombones to use smaller instruments and wanted Jacobs to do the same. This was shortly after World War II and production of musical instruments, especially tubas, had not returned to normal, and consequently Jacobs could not find a suitable instrument. Finally Rodzinski told Jacobs, "I like the sound of the instrument you are using [the York]," and the matter ended there.

Although Rodzinski was only with the CSO for one season, he greatly influenced the future of the Chicago brass sound by hiring a young, inexperienced trumpet player, Adolph Herseth {see: Chicago Symphony Orchestra: Trumpet Section: Adolph Herseth}.

After the CSO, Rodzinski conducted primarily in Europe. In 1958, he conducted several performances with the Chicago Lyric Opera before health problems forced him to retire. He died November 27, 1958.

The CSO then appointed Wilhelm Furtwangler to replace Rodzinski for the 1949-50 season. However, Furtwangler resigned before he had conducted a single concert due to questions raised regarding his wartime activities in Hitler's Germany. The CSO then had no resident conductor, and, instead, relied upon a series of guest conductors for the 1949-50 season.[124]

Raphael Kubelik

With the musical leadership of the CSO in turmoil, the orchestra hired Raphael Kubelik, who was Music Director from 1950-1953, and appeared as a guest conductor for many years thereafter. It was during this time that many fine recordings were made as the quality and techniques of recorded music began to improve.

Kubelik was born in Bychory, Czechoslovakia on June 29, 1914. He was the Music Director of the Czech Philharmonic from 1942-1948. During World War II, he refused to collaborate with the Nazis, and following the Communist control of Czechoslovakia in 1948, he left his native country. He conducted in England and Western Europe before coming to the United States, debuting November 17, 1949, with the Chicago Symphony. This led to his appointment as the CSO's Music Director the following season.

After Chicago, he conducted at the Royal Opera House at Covent Garden (1955-58), the Bavarian Radio Orchestra (1961-79), and the Metropolitan Opera (1972-74). Kubelik retired in 1985.

Raphael Kubelik
From CSO Archives. Photo by Austin Field

65

Jacobs says, "Raphael Kubelik came in at the right time for Raphael Kubelik. He was fairly well liked. Both Desire Defauw and Kubelik had similar problems. Most of the orchestras in this country had permanent conductors rather than guest conductors during that period. That meant that one conductor, for example Leopold Stokowski [with the Philadelphia Orchestra], conducted the entire season. This meant having a very large repertoire to draw from.

"Neither Kubelik nor Defauw had a very large repertoire. By mid-season, they were beginning to run short of material. By the end of the season Kubelik would be looking mostly at the melodic lines, and that would limit the performance potential quite a bit. In later years he was welcomed back as a guest conductor—as one of our favorites—and concerts were first-rate with him. He eventually gained experience and repertoire. That cannot come overnight, but comes from studying and digesting scores over a period of many years."

As a composer, Kubelik has written several operas and a variety of instrumental works. In 1985, the CSO premiered His *Symphonic Peripeteia for Organ and Orchestra*.[125]

Fritz Reiner

Fritz Reiner was born in Budapest, Hungary, December 19, 1888, and studied at the Royal Conservatory in Budapest. His first conducting position was Budapest's Volksoper (1911-14) and the Court Opera in Dresden (1914-21). He came to the United States as Conductor of the Cincinnati Symphony in 1922, and from 1931 to 1941, was Conductor of the Curtis Institute Orchestra. He was Music Director of the Pittsburgh Symphony Orchestra from 1938-48, followed by the Metropolitan Opera (1948-53). His tenure with the Chicago Symphony was from 1953 to 1963. Reiner passed away on November 15, 1963.[126]

Jacobs' relationship with Reiner began at the Curtis Institute when Jacobs was fifteen {see: Curtis Institute: Fritz Reiner} and where for seven years, Reiner conducted and Jacobs performed in the Curtis Institute Orchestra. Next, Reiner brought Jacobs to the Pittsburgh Symphony for five years. "I grew up with Reiner as my conductor, so everything since then had to be easier. He was a wonderful conductor."[127]

During the 1952-53 season, the CSO again had a series of guest conductors, and morale among the musicians dropped. It was rumored that the orchestra was considering hiring Reiner as conductor as he was no stranger to the CSO, having previously guest conducted the orchestra at Ravinia (1937-48).

However, Reiner's dark side was also well known among the CSO's musicians. Knowing Reiner and Jacobs were together at both the Curtis Institute and Pittsburgh, the musicians asked Jacobs about Reiner. He told them that, "Reiner would be a fine choice as the new conductor, and that he was not nearly as difficult to work with as it might appear. Reiner was hired and reunited with Jacobs again.

"I think he just kept following me around. I saw more of him, while I was growing up, than I did of my own father."[128] Jacobs and Reiner had spent a total of twenty-two years performing together.

Fritz Reiner

"Reiner had a bad reputation among musicians; he was a very difficult conductor to play under. I pointed out that he would probably be more mellow as he was getting older. When he came in, he was not only not more mellow, but less mellow. In Pittsburgh, he had his ups and downs, but in Chicago, it was mostly down."

The famous relationship with Reiner and the Chicago Symphony lasted from 1953-63. Later, Paul Haugan asked Jacobs, "Do you think Reiner was more or less responsible for building the Chicago Symphony for what it's known to be today?"

Jacobs responded, "The Chicago Symphony, for as long as I can recall, was an excellent orchestra—this was a great German orchestra before I ever joined it. I came here in the early 1940s, but I used to listen to concerts when Stock was the conductor. Reiner put his imprint on the orchestra very definitely, but he did not take an inferior group and make it into a superior group. He took a very excellent orchestra and then put on his style of interpretation. In much of what we are doing today, there are still some of the elements of the rehearsal time that we spent with Reiner, and those of us who had been with him and knew him over the years still have much of his style characteristics. But the question was, 'Was he responsible for this being a great orchestra?' I would say that he was very helpful, but it was a fine orchestra when he took it over."[129]

"Reiner did not want any nervous players in his orchestra, fearing that they would jeopardize his concerts. Finding out who these players were was difficult. He felt that all players would become nervous during rehearsal if they were subjected to a certain amount of pressure, and they would begin to react. If they were not able to hold up and produce sounds properly during a rehearsal under pressure, then they would have the same potential to fall apart during a concert. He didn't want people like that in his orchestra. It was his philosophy to test people occasionally. If he could get them a little unglued and they would fall apart, they belonged in some other orchestra, not his. This was planned on his part. We called him 'the great leveler' because you all took turns no matter who you were or how well he liked you, you took your turn regardless.[130]

"I remember the first time he conducted Wagner's *Meistersinger Prelude* with us [in Chicago]. He kept going over the same short passage, just a few brass chords. Nobody missed a note. Finally, after half a dozen times, he laughed and went on."[131]

Perhaps the most famous incident with Reiner's testing occurred when the orchestra was rehearsing Strauss' *Also Sprach Zarathustra*. Reiner kept repeating the well-known trumpet passage until it was apparent that he was testing Adolph Herseth. Herseth hit the high C every time. This legend has grown throughout the years as to how often Reiner repeated the section and Herseth's response. It seems that the rumors are better than the real story. Apparently, Herseth simply looked at his watch and said, "I've got until 12:30."[132]

Excerpt from First Trumpet part of Richard Strauss' Also Sprach Zarathustra

Reiner tested Jacobs about every third year. "I soon became aware of his testing, and at intermissions, particularly in Pittsburgh and Chicago, I would play the parts alone because he was always around listening. I would take the difficult parts and play them where he could hear them, and at my own leisure and pace. It would sort of get him off my back. He liked the idea that you would have enough initiative to cover the material without jeopardizing performances."[133]

"He wouldn't just fire people off hand. If you made good—he always asked for good playing—and if you made a few mistakes, he might hop on you and chew you out a bit. But if the playing came around and was what he wanted, he would always acknowledge it. It was not just a one-way street—he wouldn't just find fault. He would very definitely acknowledge good work."[134]

Not all of Reiner's firings happened behind the scenes when a player was dismissed and was suddenly not present at the next rehearsal. There were firings during rehearsals.

"At the start of one of our seasons in Pittsburgh, he brought in a percussionist. We were playing a work that involved the bass drum and there had to be accuracy. I don't recall—it was not the *Rite of Spring*, but it was something with a counting problem and the bass drummer miscounted. Reiner asked to go over it again. I think that around the fourth repetition, he said, 'You're not going to make it. Good bye. Go home. Don't come back.' They paid the man for the season, because he was under contract, but he was out!"[135]

Reiner purposely conducted with a small beat to force your attention to it. One day a bass player came with a telescope and asked Reiner "Hey pops, where's the beat?" "Reiner laughed—he fired him, but he laughed," said Jacobs.

Through all of this, Jacobs has the greatest respect for Reiner.

"Fritz Reiner was one of the truly great conductors of our age. I do not think he received quite the recognition he deserved. He did not use words nearly as much as many conductors. He was able to communicate through body language and facial expression. The stick technique was always very good. Even as a young conductor his stick technique was impeccable. He was a little stingy with it, but his philosophy was that a small use of the stick would force your attention to it."[136]

There is one thing that Jacobs has always wondered about Reiner. "Does anyone have a picture of Reiner when he is smiling?" An interesting story about this occurred when Philip Farkas retired from the CSO. Apparently, he approached Reiner looking for an autographed picture. Reiner was happy to oblige and asked Farkas which picture he would like. Reiner said "I have one mit me smiling and one mit me not smiling." Farkas told Reiner to give him the one with him not smiling—no one would recognize him if he were smiling!

Jean Martinon

After Fritz Reiner had redefined the German tradition and sound of the Chicago Symphony, they hired a French conductor, Jean Martinon. His often-controversial tenure with the CSO was from 1963 to 1968.

Martinon was born January 10, 1910, at Lyon, France. After studying the violin at the Lyon Conservatory, he attended the National Conservatory in Paris studying composition and conducting. In 1940, while a member of the French Army, Martinon was captured, and spent two years in a German prison camp. After the war, he conducted the Bordeaux Symphony (1943-45) and was Assistant Conductor of the Paris Conservatory Orchestra (1944-46). From 1947-49 he was Associate Conductor of the London Philharmonic. He headed the Lamoureux Orchestra in Paris (1951-57) and then directed the Israel Philharmonic (1958-60). He then conducted the Dusseldorf Symphony from 1960-66.

Martinon made his American debut in 1957, with the Boston Symphony. His first appearance with the CSO was at Ravinia in 1960. As the CSO's Music Director, he programmed many avant-guarde works, which drew criticism that ultimately led to his resignation in 1968. Following his tenure in Chicago, Martinon returned to France and conducted the French Radio Orchestra (from 1968) and the Residente Orchestra in the Hague starting in 1974.

A prolific composer, the Chicago Symphony premiered his *Symphony Number Four, "Altitudes"* on December 30, 1965.[137]

Commenting about Martinon, Jacobs said, "I enjoyed working with him. I think he was an underrated conductor. He was quite good, particularly

Jean Martinon
From CSO Archives

at the modern works. He had a magnificent technique and concept of how to organize some of the more difficult modern orchestral music, and how to rehearse it. I thought much of his conducting of the modern music was just marvelous. One of the best performances of the *Rite of Spring* that we have ever played was with Martinon. He always put a modern work on every program. I was always used to having a number of weeks off when there was an all-Beethoven or all-Mozart program. He would always mix the program with a modern number that used my instrument, so I rarely got a week off."

Martinon passed away on March 1, 1976.

Georg Solti

In 1968, after a season of guest conductors, Georg Solti was appointed Music Director. The relationship between Solti and the CSO has been one of the most successful marriages of conductor and orchestra.

Arnold Jacobs: *Song and Wind*

Solti was born in Budapest, Hungary, on October 21, 1912. At the age of thirteen, he enrolled at the Franz Liszt Academy of Music where he studied piano, composition and conducting. Although he made his concert debut as a pianist, he soon was engaged as conductor by the Budapest Opera. He was an assistant at the Salzburg Festival to both Bruno Walter (1935) and Arturo Toscanini (1936-37).

With the rise of the Nazis in Germany and Austria, Solti emigrated to Switzerland as a refugee. There, as a pianist, he was awarded first prize at the Concours International in Geneva in 1942. Following the war, he was invited to conduct a performance of Beethoven's *Fidelio* in Munich. The success of this performance led to his appointment as Music Director of the Bavarian State Opera (1946-52). For one season, 1960-61, he was Music Director of the Dallas Symphony, and was Music Director of the Royal Opera at Covent Garden from 1961 to 1971. A British subject, Georg Solti was knighted by Queen Elizabeth in 1972.

In Chicago, Solti was Principal Conductor at the Lyric Opera of Chicago in 1956 and 1957. He first conducted the Chicago Symphony at the Ravinia Festival in 1954 returning until 1958. At Orchestra Hall, he made his debut conducting the Chicago Symphony as a guest on December 9-10, 1965.

Solti held additional posts during his tenure in Chicago. He was Music Director of the Paris Opera (1971-73), Orchestre de Paris (1972-75) and Artistic Director of the London Philharmonic (1979-83).

Sir Georg remained Music Director of the Chicago Symphony through the centennial season (1990-91), and has continued conducting the orchestra, being named Conductor Laureate upon his retirement.[138] He passed away on September 5, 1997.

Jacobs has great respect for Solti.

"The first time I played under Solti, was in 1954 at Ravinia. We did one of the Bruckner Symphonies at the time. I always remember a very emotional, and very excitable man who talked a great deal during rehearsals. His

Sir Georg Solti
From CSO Archives

71

voice would shout out instructions, even when the full brass section was playing. I don't think anyone knew what he was saying during those loud passages, but he was full voiced trying to get instructions across to us.

"He was somewhat of a humanitarian, which I liked in a conductor. He had competence in many things, and was a fine musician. He was very fascinating. I liked Sir Georg."

In 1988, before his retirement, Jacobs was asked to compare Solti and Reiner. He said, "Although Reiner was the greatest conductor I ever worked with, I enjoy working with Solti more. He is more humane, much more of a diplomat than most conductors. He tries to be fair. With this orchestra, he usually takes things pretty much for granted, because he usually gets what he wants musically. I respect him very, very much."[139]

In 1988, when Jacobs retired, Solti wrote, "His tenure of over forty years with the Chicago Symphony Orchestra represents, to my mind, one of the most important contributions made by any single brass player to the history and development of symphony orchestras in our time. He is that rarest of jewels, a great and devoted musician combined with a warm and generous personality. Through his unstinting support and encouragement of generations of brass players the world over, he has justifiably become a legend in his own lifetime.

"We are going to miss him terribly, but I wish him many years of happy retirement and I feel sure, if I know him at all well, that these years will continue to be most fruitful for him and for those lucky enough to be his colleagues and friends."[140]

Daniel Barenboim

Although Jacobs retired in 1988 during Solti's era, Daniel Barenboim conducted the CSO often. He first conducted the orchestra in 1970, and assumed the post following Solti's retirement in 1991and remained until 2006.

Born in Buenos Aires, Argentina, November 15, 1942, Barenboim first studied piano with his parents, and in 1952, the family moved to Israel. He enrolled at the Accademia di Santa Cecilia in Rome, receiving his diploma in 1956. He made his American debut as a pianist in New York in 1957 and made his conducting debut with the New Philharmonia Orchestra in 1967. In 1975, he became Music Director of the

Daniel Barenboim
From CSO Archives

Orchestre de Paris holding the post until 1987. He has been a guest conductor of the world's leading orchestras.

In 1967, he married cellist Jacqueline DuPre who appeared with him on stage for many years before tragically being stricken and ultimately dying of multiple sclerosis.

In 1988, Barenboim was named Artistic Director of the Bastille Opera in Paris, but in a dispute over artistic policy, he was dismissed in January 1989. That same month he was named Solti's successor as Music Director of the Chicago Symphony.

Barenboim has recorded with the CSO for many years including the Vaughan Williams *Concerto for Bass Tuba and Orchestra* with Jacobs as the soloist.[141]

Jacobs says, "I am sorry I didn't get a chance to stay and play with him as his tuba player, but about when he was ready to arrive, I was ready to go out, so I only worked with him when he was a guest conductor. Barenboim is quite competent and a fine conductor."

Music Directors of the Ravinia Festival
The Ravinia Festival [summer home of the CSO] has its own Music Directors separate from the concerts at Orchestra Hall. From 1930 until 1963, there was no Music Director, only a series of guest conductors.

Seiji Ozawa
The Ravinia Festival's first Music Director, from 1964 to 1968, was Seiji Ozawa. Ozawa was born on September 1, 1935, in Fenytien, China, to Japanese parents. As a child he moved to Japan and graduated in 1959 from Tokyo's Toho School. In 1960 he was awarded the Koussevitzky Memorial Scholarship at the Berkshire Music Center. The next year he was one of Leonard Bernstein's assistant conductors with the New York Philharmonic.

On July 16, 1963, he conducted the CSO on short notice leading to his appointment as Ravinia's Music Director the following season. In 1969, when he was offered a position with the Salzburg Festival, Ozawa asked to he released from his contract although he was the Principal Guest Conductor at Ravinia during that season. He was succeeded by Istvan Kertesz who was Music Director at Ravinia from 1970-72.

Subsequently, Ozawa has been Music Director of the Toronto Symphony (1965-69) and the San Francisco Symphony (1970-76). In 1972, he became Music Director of the Boston Symphony Orchestra.[142]

Jacobs said, "Ozawa was a lot of fun to work with. We enjoyed making music with him, and enjoyed him personally."

James Levine

Ravinia's third Music Director was James Levine who directed the CSO for twenty-one summer seasons. Levine was born in Cincinnati, Ohio, on June 23, 1943 and made his professional debut at the age of ten as piano soloist with the Cincinnati Symphony. He attended the Juilliard School of Music, leaving to join the conducting staff of the Cleveland Orchestra from 1964-70.

His conducting debut at the Metropolitan Opera in 1971 was followed within a year by his appointment as Principal Conductor, beginning in the 1973-74 season. He was named Music Director of the Metropolitan Opera in 1976 and Artistic Director in 1983.

Levine made his Ravinia debut in 1971 and was Music Director from 1973 to 1994. From 1974 to 1978, he also served as Music Director of the Cincinnati May Festival.[143]

Jacobs states, "James Levine is a jewel. We enjoyed working with him very much. He is a fine musician and a fine conductor. We always played good music with him. I loved the summer we did the Mahler cycle."

The Ravinia Festival named Christoph Eschenbach to succeed Levine as Music Director starting in the 1995 season.

Others

During his career, Jacobs has played under hundreds of guest conductors. While listing them all is impossible, the most prominent [in alphabetical order] are:

Claudio Abbado

Claudio Abbado was a frequent guest conductor of the CSO, and from 1982 to 1986, was Principal Guest Conductor. Born June 26, 1933, in Milan, Italy, Abbado studied at the Verdi Conservatory where he was a student of Carlo Maria Giulini. He continued his studies at the Vienna Academy, and in 1958, won the Koussevitzky prize at Tanglewood, and in 1963, the Mitropoulos prize. Later he was Assistant Conductor of the New York Philharmonic. In 1971 he became Conductor of the Vienna Philharmonic, where he was named Music Director in 1986. From 1969 to 1986 he was Conductor and then Music Director of La Scala in Milan. He has been Principal Conductor of the London Symphony since 1979, and in 1989 was named Artistic Director of the Berlin Philharmonic.[144]

Leonard Bernstein

The late conductor/composer Leonard Bernstein guest conducted the Chicago Symphony at both Orchestra Hall and Ravinia. Bernstein was born in Lawrence, Massachusetts on August 25, 1918. He studied composition at Harvard University graduating in 1939. Later in 1939, he entered the Curtis Institute of Music [three years after Jacobs' graduation]. In 1943 Bernstein was appointed

Assistant Conductor of the New York Philharmonic. He was named Music Director in 1958. He retired and was named Laureate Conductor in 1969.

As a composer, Bernstein is one of the few who successfully wrote both in the classical and popular idiom. Although his more serious compositions have become part of the modern orchestral and operatic repertory, his collaboration with the Broadway stage has produced his most famous works including *On the Town* and his best loved and most familiar work, *West Side Story*. In preparing for the opening of the John F. Kennedy Center for the Performing Arts in Washington, D.C., Bernstein was commissioned to write the inaugural work *Mass*, which was premiered at the Center's opening concert in September 1971.

Jacobs remembers, "Leonard Bernstein was a great conductor and a most fascinating personality. He came to Curtis after I left, but I knew him then, and I have met him a number of times since. I enjoyed him very much."

Bernstein was the conductor of the 1988 CSO recording of the Shostakovich *First and Seventh Symphonies*, Jacobs' final recordings with the Chicago Symphony.

Bernstein died October 14, 1990.[145]

Fritz Busch

While discussing conductors with Jacobs, he mentioned Fritz Busch among his favorites.

Fritz Busch was born in Westphalia, Germany on March 13, 1890 and studied at the Cologne Conservatory. He was nineteen when appointed Musical Director at the Stadtstheater, later serving at Gotha and Aachen. Later, he conducted the Berlin Philharmonic Orchestra (1918). After that, he conducted in Stuttgart and in 1922, was appointed Musical Director and Conductor of the Dresden State Opera.

In 1933 he was dismissed from his Dresden post by the Nazis and left Germany. He made many appearances as a conductor with the Danish Radio Symphony Orchestra and the Stockholm Philharmonic. From 1940 to 1945 he was active mainly in South America, the Teatro Colon in Buenos Aires, and subsequently appeared in Chile and Montevideo. In New York, he conducted the Metropolitan Opera from 1945-49. Busch conducted the CSO in 1947, 1949, and 1950. He died in London on September 14, 1951.[146]

Carlo Maria Giulini

On November 3-4, 1955, Carlo Maria Giulini made his American debut as a guest conductor of the Chicago Symphony. In 1969, the CSO named him Principal Guest Conductor, a post created especially for him, and a relationship began that lasted nine seasons.

Born May 9, 1914, in Barletta, Italy, Giulini graduated from the Conservatory of Music of Santa Cecilia in Rome in 1939. From 1946 until 1953, he was conductor of the orchestras of Radio Roma and Radio Milano. In 1951, he made his opera debut at La Scala, where from 1953 to 1956, he was Principal Conductor. In 1978, Giulini left the Chicago Symphony to assume the post of Conductor and Music Director of the Los Angeles Philharmonic.[147]

Giulini was one of Jacobs' favorite conductors. "He was a real humanitarian—as fine a musician and conductor as a gentleman. He made work a pleasure."

In comparison to Reiner, "His type of musical communication was totally different from Reiner's, because it dealt primarily with the emotions. He would generate excitement through his intensity, his facial expression and his anatomy."[148]

Erich Leinsdorf

Erich Leinsdorf first conducted the CSO at Ravinia in 1945, and subsequently made many appearances at both Orchestra Hall and Ravinia.

Leinsdorf was born in Vienna February 4, 1912. He was an assistant to Arturo Toscanini at the Salzburg Festival, served as Conductor of the Metropolitan Opera from 1938 to 1943, and the Cleveland Orchestra in 1943. After serving in the U.S. Army, he conducted the Rochester Philharmonic (1947-56), New York City Opera (1956-62), the Boston Symphony (1962 to 1969) and was a frequent guest conductor for orchestras throughout the world.[149]

According to Jacobs, "Erich Leinsdorf was an excellent conductor. I liked him very much, but a lot of people did not. I knew him for years and years and got along well with him."

Erich Leinsdorf died in September 1993.

Pierre Monteux

For two decades, the late Pierre Monteux was a Ravinia institution. During Ravinia's fiftieth anniversary, the Ravinia Festival wrote, "There was seemingly nothing he could not play well—and the Orchestra loved him as much as did the public."[150] Many consider his recording of Frank's *Symphony in d Minor* as one of the CSO's finest.

Monteux was born in Paris, April 4, 1875. He was Conductor of Diaghilev's Ballet Russe (1911-14 and 1917). Next he conducted the Metropolitan Opera from 1917 to 1919, and from 1919 to 1924 he led the Boston Symphony. He was Associate Conductor of the Amsterdam Concertgebouw from 1924 to 1934. In 1929 he founded the Orchestre Symphonique de Paris which he conducted until 1938. He directed the San Francisco Symphony from 1936 to 1952, and was Principal Conductor of the London Symphony from 1961 until his death on July 1, 1964.[151]

Jacobs recalls, "Pierre Monteux was a wonderful conductor and a fine gentleman. What stood out more than anything was his sense of humor and his accent. He was a very interesting man to listen to and to play for."

Eugene Ormandy

Eugene Ormandy offered Jacobs a position in the Philadelphia Orchestra several times. In 1949, Jacobs toured England and Scotland with the Philadelphia Orchestra and Ormandy conducting {see: Professional Experience: On Loan to the Philadelphia Orchestra}. With the Chicago Symphony, Ormandy first conducted during the 1948-49 season, subsequently conducting both downtown and at Ravinia.

Born Jeno Blau in Budapest, Hungary, November 18, 1899, Ormandy studied at the Royal Academy of Music in Budapest. He came to the United States in 1921, to perform a violin concert tour that failed to materialize. Remaining in the United States, Ormandy became concertmaster of the Capitol Theater Orchestra in New York City, later becoming Conductor from 1924 to 1925.

In 1931, he substituted for ailing Guest Conductor Arturo Toscanini with the Philadelphia Orchestra. His performance led to an invitation to become Conductor of the Minneapolis Symphony Orchestra [now Minnesota Orchestra] remaining there until 1936. Then he was appointed Associate Conductor of the Philadelphia Orchestra, under Leopold Stokowski, whom he succeeded as Music Director and Principal Conductor in 1938. Following his retirement in 1980, he was named Conductor Laureate of the Philadelphia Orchestra.

Jacobs recalls, "I knew Eugene Ormandy very well. He was a great master of balancing and obtaining the great string sound that he got from an orchestra. He was proud of his ability to produce the Ormandy sound, which was actually derived from the Stokowski sound."

Eugene Ormandy died on March 12, 1985.[152]

Hans Rosbaud

Another lesser-known European conductor who was one of Jacobs' favorites was Hans Rosbaud.

Born in Graz, Austria on July 22, 1895, Rosbaud received his musical training in Frankfurt. Prior to World War II, he was active as a conductor in Frankfurt, Muenster, and Strasbourg. After the war, he was a conductor of the Symphony Orchestra of the Southwest Radio in Baden-Baden (1948). Later he was Music Director of the Tonhalle Orchestra in Zurich (1957). He became known as a conductor of modern works conducting, for example, the first performance of Schoenberg's *Moses und Aron* in 1954.

Rosbaud guest conducted the CSO a short time, from 1958-62. Besides his skills as a conductor, Jacobs remembers him as the only conductor that would personally greet every member of the orchestra as they left the stage at the conclusion of a concert. Rosbaud's final appearance with the CSO was on November 9, 1962. He passed away a short time later, on December 29, 1962.[153]

Fabian Sevitsky

Jacobs' first professional orchestral position was with the Indianapolis Symphony Orchestra, and also the first year for its Conductor, Fabian Sevitsky, who hired him.

Sevitsky was born in Vishny Volochok, Russia, September 29, 1891. He began his concert career as a double bassist under his original name, Koussevitzky. His uncle, conductor Serge Koussevitzky, suggested that he adopt a truncated form of the last name, and he complied to avoid a family quarrel.

Leaving Moscow in 1922, Sevitsky spent a year as a double bassist in the Warsaw Philharmonic. Next, he went to Mexico from where, in 1923, he emigrated to the United States. His first job was as a double bassist in the Philadelphia Orchestra. As a guest conductor, he appeared with the Los Angeles Philharmonic, the Washington Summer Concerts Orchestra, and the Paris, Berlin, Vienna, and Warsaw Symphonies. He lead the People's Symphony Orchestra in Boston from 1934 to 1936 and the Indianapolis Symphony Orchestra from 1937 to 1955. Sevitsky was reportedly the inspiration for the 1950s motion picture *Once More With Feeling*.

Jacobs says, "Sevitsky was a very interesting conductor. He was a very large man with big hands. He looked tall on the podium in comparison to Reiner, whom I was used to. When those hands stretched, it looked like he could reach over and touch you. I did enjoy working with him. He was a good conductor, but needed to conduct a lot more."

Later, he was Music Director of the University of Miami [Florida] Symphony Orchestra from 1959 to 1965. He died during a guest appearance in Athens, Greece, on February 2, 1967.[154]

Leopold Stokowski

Jacobs first played with Leopold Stokowski with the *All-American Youth Orchestra* in 1941. Later, Stokowski was a frequent guest conductor of the Chicago Symphony.

Leopold Antoni Stanislaw Boleslawowicz Stokowski was born in London, England on April 18, 1882. He studied at Oxford University, the Royal College of Music and in Paris and Munich. In 1905, he moved to the United States as Organist and Choirmaster of Saint Bartholomew's Church in New York City. Next, from 1909 to 1912, he was Conductor of the Cincinnati Symphony Orchestra.

During the next twenty-three years (1912-1938), he was Music Director of the Philadelphia Orchestra, making it into one of the world's greatest ensembles. Afterwards, he organized the *All-American Youth Orchestra*, which performed for two summers, 1940 and 1941. Later he conducted the NBC Symphony (1941-44 with Toscanini), the New York Philharmonic (1946-50), and the Houston Symphony (1955-62). In 1962, he founded the American Symphony Orchestra.

Stokowski was famous as an arranger and reorchestrator of music, particularly the organ works of Bach. He is known to the public through his three motion pictures, including Walt Disney's *Fantasia* (1940) featuring the Philadelphia Orchestra.

He continued conducting well into his nineties. His final recording session was on June 4, 1977. Three months later, on September 13, 1977, Stokowski died in Nether Wallop, Hampshire, England.[155]

Jacobs said of Stokowski, "I had great respect for him. I did a summer in the *All-American Youth Orchestra* with him, and he guest conducted frequently in Chicago. To me, he was a genius. He had such an ear for sound and color, and did everything he could to produce it. He couldn't have cared less about 'authentic' interpretation, but in putting his own stamp on music he was unique."[156]

Georg Szell

Another guest conductor of the Chicago Symphony, Georg Szell appeared annually at Ravinia until 1952. Later, he made several appearances at Orchestra Hall.

Born in Budapest on June 7, 1897, Szell studied in Europe. He conducted the orchestras in Strasbourg (1917-18), Prague (1919-21), Darmstadt (1921-22), Dusseldorf (1922-24), the Berlin State Opera (1924-30), the German Opera in Prague (1930-37), and the Scottish Orchestra in Glasgow (1937-39).

He was a guest conductor with the Metropolitan Opera from 1942 to 1945, and from 1946 to 1970, was Music Director of the Cleveland Orchestra. It was here that he was most famous for developing that orchestra into a great musical organization.

According to Jacobs, "Szell offered me a position with the Cleveland Orchestra which I declined. I had many phone calls from him asking my advice about who to hire on some of the brass instrument openings."

Szell died in Cleveland on July 30, 1970.[157]

Bruno Walter

Born Bruno Walter Schlesinger in Berlin, September 15, 1876, his first music instruction was from his mother, and he made his debut as pianist at the age of ten. At age eighteen, he was Assistant Conductor of the Hamburg Opera, where he began his friendship with Gustav Mahler, later becoming Mahler's assistant at the Vienna Court Opera. Walter conducted the posthumous premieres of Mahler's *Das Lied von der Erde* (1911) and *Ninth Symphony* (1912).

He founded the Salzburg Festival and held posts in Munich, Berlin, Leipzig, and Vienna. After being removed from Vienna by the Nazis, he settled in the United States in 1938, appearing at the Metropolitan Opera and serving as advisor to the New York Philharmonic (1947-49).

Bruno Walter was a frequent guest conductor with the Chicago Symphony. Jacobs recalls, "Bruno Walter was a classic conductor—he was a Mahler specialist. I still remember the first time I played the Mahler *Second Symphony* was with him and his interpretations were beautiful. I can still remember the rehearsals of it. I enjoyed him and got along real well with him."

Bruno Walter died on February 17, 1962.[158]

Retirement

While Jacobs was given marvelous musical abilities, he has not been as lucky with his health, even as a child.

When he was about eight years old, he contracted chicken pox aboard a ship from Long Beach, California to New York. At first his family tried to keep him in their cabin, but eventually the ship's crew found out. There was no infirmary on the ship so they put him in the brig. At first it was kept unlocked, but he ran away and was found in his mother's cabin. They brought him back and this time they locked the brig. He passed through the Panama Canal looking out through the bars of the brig's porthole.

The two youngest children of the Jacobs family, Arnold and Charlotte, contracted Friedreich's Ataxia, a hereditary disease.[159] Jacobs has told many that he had polio, a disease with similar symptoms. His father had learned enough during medical school to nurse his youngest children through the disease. Because Friedreich's Ataxia affected his legs, hips and reflexes, Jacobs was declared 4-F, making him ineligible for military service during World War II. He has always carried a flashlight with him to help him see when he walks.

One day when Jacobs was older, he was playing "spin the bottle." "The first girl I kissed gave me a disease," he said. He contracted scarlet fever, an extremely severe disease in the 1920s. A kidney complication arose when he developed nephritis, and was hospitalized for months. It was here that he began playing the mouthpiece, a practice he has continued his entire life.

During his career, Jacobs was a prime example of performing with medical problems. Many times he has played brilliantly while suffering from a variety of physical ailments. He has said, "It doesn't have to feel good to sound good. You get it to sound good, and then it will start to feel good. You don't go for the feel, you go for the actual musical product. I just flooded my brain with concepts as though I were a well person."[160]

Roger Rocco writes, "I recall the time that I was playing the second tuba part to *Symphonie Fantastique* with Jacobs and the CSO. He was really sick that day with a severe cold and could barely talk. His bad knee was also bothering him so much that he could not carry his tuba onto the stage. I remember bringing it up for him and thinking that I might have to play the first part. Not a chance! When the fourth movement started, he was playing the part with more energy and enthusiasm than I had ever heard before! I could only chuckle to myself in amazement and disbelief over what he was accomplishing in spite of how awful he felt!"

Jacobs has fought a lifelong battle against chronic lung disorders. After joining the Chicago Symphony, he contacted bronchial asthma. For a player of an instrument that requires the amount of air the tuba does, this could be devastating. Contrary to false legends, Jacobs has *two lungs,* but his breath capacity has been diminished {see: Physical Elements: Vital Capacity}.

"It is particularly bad when the skies lower over Chicago and the pollutants from autos and steel mills and the wretchedness of urban living concentrate in the air. When you breathe massive volumes of unfiltered air in or out of our lungs, as we do in heavy playing, continuous blowing, I think they should pass a law prohibitive of playing, because you're breathing unfiltered air," Jacobs states.

Again, Roger Rocco comments, "Mr. Jacobs knew that he had to find ways to overcome his own physical limitations and disabilities in order to maintain his career. I recall a time in the late 1960s when his career as a player was in jeopardy because of continuing respiratory health problems. His doctors were telling him that he would have to retire from the orchestra. He even told me to be prepared to finish the season for him if he could not continue. Just in time, new medications came on the market that allowed him to continue playing."

During the 1980s Jacobs was operated on for cancer that required radiation therapy, and later suffered a heart attack while in his studio. Following the 1986 CSO tour of Japan and Hong Kong, he was again hospitalized for a gall bladder problem.

In 1984, Jacobs stated, "I'm getting old and my lip hasn't felt good in years. I'm on medication for severe lung problems, and the physical comfort I had in playing when I was younger is gone. I'm an old cripple, but I still love to play."[161]

With all of these problems, for more than his final twenty years with the CSO, many asked, "When is he going to retire?" In 1979, Jacobs was asked about retirement and he stated, "I must say, my pension would have come through four or five years ago if I wanted to retire, but I still love to play. I think I have one of the best seats in Orchestra Hall. I hear wonderful concerts, enjoy it, and they pay me—I don't pay them! So I'm still enjoying playing. The tuba has been a part of my life, teaching has been a part of my life, and listening to music has been a great part of my life, so I'm still with it."[162]

Starting in the early 1980s, he began having problems with his eyes. Tongue-in-cheek, he ponders, "Could the cause of this be following Reiner's small beat for so many years?" Although he had cataracts removed, it was discovered that he had developed low pressure glaucoma and his vision has continued to slowly deteriorate. In his final years with the CSO, Jacobs had enlarged copies made of the music so he could see it.

"The doctors finally recognized the problem with my vision, and I had to go to Sir Georg and tell him that as much as I hated to, I was going to have to pull out of the orchestra. He wanted me to stay until 1991 [the centennial season] when he would officially retire [as Music Director] from the Chicago Symphony, but I knew by then that it would be a little ridiculous to even try to play. Not only couldn't I see the music, but I couldn't see his beat."[163]

From the collection of Arnold Jacobs

On September 29, 1988, Jacobs performed one of his final concerts with the Chicago Symphony. On that night, he was awarded the Theodore Thomas Medallion along with fellow retirees Leon Brenner, Samuel Feinzimer, Isadore Zverow and Donald and Margaret Evans. Jacobs thanked the audience for the years of support they had given him. Solti walked off the stage with his arm around Jacobs telling him, "I hope that this gives you enough energy to complete the season," as a replacement had not yet been found. Jacobs, in fact, finished the subscription series, completing his career as a performer.

"Oh, I will miss my colleagues—my musical family. It's a privilege to play with this great orchestra and brass section, it really is. I feel very fortunate to have been a part of it."[164]

He has moved from "One of the best seats in Orchestra Hall," on the stage, to a seat in the audience. For years Mrs. Jacobs had a season ticket for Thursday night concerts. They bought the seat next to hers and they regularly attended Thursday night concerts.

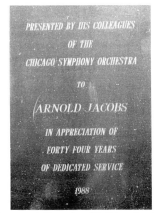

Plaque presented by members of the Chicago Symphony

"I look back on those years with really great pleasure. It was nice to have a job that when you wake up in the morning, you feel like going to work. You are anxious to sit down, get the horn out, join your colleagues making great music.

"Most of my life was based on professional playing, and enjoying it thoroughly. I miss it very much today. But we do have seats in the balcony of Orchestra Hall, and I see my colleagues performing. I feel a little strange about it sometimes because I feel I belong on the stage and not off. My horn is still there representing me. I sold it to the orchestra before I left, and Mr. Pokorny, the very fine tubist that they have today, enjoys it so much—he's playing it now. So I feel a little bit of me is still on the stage."[165]

Often as he picked up a horn, he cautioned the listener that he may embarrass himself, but few would refute that the rich vibrant sound was still there in all of its unique beauty. The eyes dimmed, the body had grown painful with arthritis, but the great musicianship and unique sound radiated in all their glory.

On June 7, 1998 Jacobs appeared on stage at Orchestra Hall for the last time as part of a Celebration of Adolph Herseth's fiftieth anniversary with the Chicago Symphony playing music of Gabrieli as part of a mass brass ensemble. He still presented masterclasses. and taught on Wednesdays and Saturdays.

On the morning of October 7, 1998 Mr. Jacobs woke up around 6:30 and briefly talked to his son, Dallas, before returning to bed. Shortly afterwards he quietly and unexpectedly passed away.

Arnold Jacobs did not leave us, he only changed his address. His legacy will live forever in every player of wind instruments, all concert halls and music studios throughout the world.

Awards

In the course of his career, Jacobs has received several honors and awards. His framed diploma from the Curtis Institute was always displayed in his studio on Normal Ave.

The Tubists Universal Brotherhood Association [TUBA] made him one of the first Honorary Life Members in 1984 [along with Bill Bell and Harvey Phillips] and presented him a Lifetime Achievement Award. TUBA's Chicago chapter, the Chicago Area Tuba Society [Metrocats] also presented him with a Lifetime Achievement Award in December 1983.

During the 1982 Fourth of July celebration in Evanston, Illinois, he was the Honorary Marshal. He took part in the town's parade and a concert was held that night conducted by Harvey Phillips.[166]

In June 1984, he was presented the highest award from the Second International Brass Congress. The plaque reads, "In appreciation and recognition of the unique and profound contribution of over fifty years through musical excellence, continuing inspiration to all brass players and a lifetime dedication to artistic tuba performance."

A year later (December 18, 1985) he was given the Medal of Honor from the Mid-West International Band and Orchestra Clinic. The late John P. Paynter presented the award which cited him as "God's gift to wind musicians everywhere."

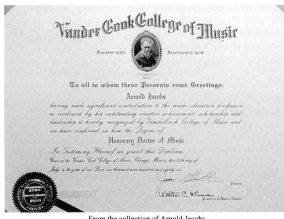

From the collection of Arnold Jacobs

On July 25, 1986, he again wore a cap and gown over fifty years after his graduation from the Curtis Institute. VanderCook College presented him with a degree of Honorary Doctor of Music [recommended by Roger Rocco]. This was in recognition for making significant contributions to the music education profession as evidenced by his outstanding creative achievement, scholarship and leadership.

Jacobs finally became a doctor. However, it was in music rather than medicine.

The Chicago Federation of Musicians named Jacobs "Musician of the Year" at the 30th annual Del Segno Brunch held on April 24, 1988.[167] He was further honored by the Chicago Federation of Musicians who presented him an award for Lifetime Achievement at the *First Living Art of Music Awards* on September 19, 1994.[168]

Chicago's DePaul University awarded Jacobs his second honorary doctorate on June 10, 1995, one day shy of his eightieth birthday. The citation, printed in the program was read by the Dean of DePaul's School of Music. Dr. Frederick Miller said, "The power and glory of your instrument delighted Chicago audiences and the citizens of the world for nearly half a century. Great orchestras are the cooperative effort of particularly gifted individuals, and as one of those so talented you helped create what many—critics and music lovers alike—regard as the world's greatest orchestra. We have had the privilege of sharing that marvelous group of musicians with you, but we share an equally meaningful bond with you. Your efforts as a teacher and a source of inspiration for generations of students, many of whom now reflect your talent and dedication worldwide, resonate our concern for those students who will delight and inspire legions of others in decades to come. Thus, it is our privilege to confer upon you the degree of Doctor of Humane Letters, Honoris Causa."

Arnold Jacobs following DePaul University ceremony, June 10, 1995
Photo by Author

As part of the International Tuba Euphonium Conference (ITEC) held at Northwestern University in June 1995, Jacobs was presented several honors.

Bernard Dobroski, the Dean of Northwestern's School of Music awarded Jacobs the first "Legends of Teaching" award. In addition, June 25, 1995 was proclaimed "Arnold Jacobs Day in the City of Chicago." The proclamation read by Edward Kleinhammer stated:

86

Arnold Jacobs: *Song and Wind*

"Whereas, on June 25, 1995, Arnold Jacobs will be honored at the International Tuba Euphonium Conference (ITEC) for his contributions to the music industry and musicians throughout his long career; and

"Whereas, Arnold Jacobs was the tuba player for the Chicago Symphony Orchestra (CSO) from 1944 until his retirement in 1988; and

"Whereas, during his legendary career with the CSO, his 'Rock of Gibraltar' sound allowed the rest of the ensemble to build the 'Chicago Brass' sound which no other orchestra's brass section could approach; and

"Whereas, his talent earned critical acclaim and greatly enhanced the prestige of the Chicago Symphony Orchestra and the entire City of Chicago; and

"Whereas, Arnold Jacobs is also known worldwide for his research and teaching, helping brass and wind players, as well as singers, in the areas or tone production, breathing and music-making; and

"Whereas, musicians of every instrument and vocal register have made special trips to Chicago to learn from this master teacher;

"Now, therefore, I, Richard M. Daley, Mayor of the City of Chicago, do hereby proclaim June 25, 1995, to be Arnold Jacobs Day in Chicago, and urge all citizens to recognize his many contributions to the Chicago Symphony Orchestra and musicians worldwide."

In May, 2001, the Chicago Symphony Orchestra announced that its principal tuba chair had been generously endowed by Christine Querfeld in honor of Arnold Jacobs. The tuba chair will be officially designated as The Arnold Jacobs Principal Tuba Chair, endowed by Christine Querfeld.. Long an enthusiastic patron of the Chicago Symphony Orchestra, Christine Querfeld enjoyed professional success in music performance, arts administration, and the law. Her gift honors Arnold Jacobs, whom she knew {see: Chicago Symphony: As a Soloist}, and bespeaks her life-long passion for the best in classical music.

On October 12, 2001 a reception was held in honor of Christine Querfeld. Gene Pokorny stated *Legacy is as permanent as time is fleeting. However we would all like to believe that orchestras are a permanent fixture. We orchestral musicians are "renters." For the most part, we attempt to at least fill the shoes of our predecessors, and then we too, move on. A great principle-centered institution will be willing to preserve the past but not at the cost of threatening its own future. Jacobs knew that there were other noble aspirations in his life to fulfill, and when it was time for him to "graduate" from the orchestra (as he called it), he did so graciously. He vacated the chair that he "rented" for 44 years from the Orchestra so he could more fully devote his efforts to passing along the invaluable information he had acquired over the decades to students. His love of performing was never dulled by his love for teaching, though he worried at times that his contribution as a performer might be overshadowed by his legendary skills as a problem-fixing coach. It is hard to believe that that would be the case especially since his imprint as a performer has hardly dulled in the 12 years since he has left the chair. Perhaps that is the definition of legendary and maybe it is one that we could all learn from.*

The Teacher

While Jacobs has earned a reputation as a world-class performer, equally significant are his teachings. In more than sixty years of teaching, he has been called the "Brass teacher's brass teacher" and a modern Aeolus, the Greek God of Wind.[169]

Henry Fogel, the Executive Director of the Chicago Symphony Orchestra writes about Arnold Jacobs, "Your achievements are legendary—something that can be said about few orchestral musicians. As a tubist, as a teacher, as a major influence on generations of brass players, you stand as a model for all who choose to serve the art of music. The excellence of your decades of performing is rivaled by your contributions as an instructor, and the result is that your art will live on forever."

In his introduction to the United States Marine Band, Conductor Colonel John Bourgeois said about Jacobs, "It is rare to have the master performer as the master teacher. Arnold Jacobs is both."

The Canadian Brass' Charles Daellenbach says, "This man was a great natural teacher who could have probably taught anything, but who just happened to be a wind specialist. He's the kind of legendary teacher that Liszt was for pianists of the 19th century."[170]

Dale Clevenger, principal horn of the CSO, writes, "Nearly every brass player in America has studied with Arnold Jacobs, whether they know it or not."[171]

Another colleague, former CSO principal oboist Ray Still says, "He is, simply, God's gift to wind musicians everywhere and I hope he lives forever."[172]

Sir Georg Solti praises Jacobs, "Through his unstinting support and encouragement of generations of brass players the world over, he has justifiably become a legend in his own lifetime."[173]

In 1932, the first of the thousands of musicians passed through Jacobs' studio. Ed Whitfield was his first student and wrote, "I was Arnold's first student, and his students of today may be interested in the fact that the going rate of tuba lessons from Jacobs in those days was exactly $1, and some of those sessions lasted all day!"[174]

He shares the sentiment of Jacobs' later students. In 1995, Whitfield wrote, "My affection for him and respect for his professionalism and achievements are undiminished over the years."

Among Jacobs' early students was Abe Torchinsky who was a member of the Philadelphia Orchestra from 1949-72 {see: Professional Experience: On Loan to the Philadelphia Orchestra}.[176] He tells about the early days studying with Jacobs, "My late brother, who was a fine saxophonist, worked with Arnold on club dates many times. When he decided I had some talent, he felt it was time to get a teacher, so he asked Arnold. I guess Arnold was too busy or didn't want to mess with a kid (I'm five years younger than Arnold) so he recommended I study with a man who had studied with him, Bob McCandless, who actually was more a bass player doubling on tuba and also an interior decorator and painter. After a short time, he felt he couldn't do anything for me so Arnold took me on at $1 a lesson. I studied with Arnold off and on until he went to Indianapolis, and then when he would come back to Philly to be with his folks. I certainly was among the earliest students and very happily so. I really feel that I owe my career to him and [the late] Bill Bell. Both were great influences in my life and I consider them special friends."

While Jacobs was with the Indianapolis Symphony (1937-1939), he held his first university faculty position, teaching at Butler University in Indianapolis. After joining the Chicago Symphony, Jacobs taught at Northwestern University in Evanston, Illinois, and was promoted to full professor in 1972.[176] In 1995, Northwestern's Board of Trustees appointed him Professor of Performance Studies, Emeritus.

Since 1982, Northwestern's School of Music continues to sponsor week-long workshops by Jacobs during the summer session. In addition to his Northwestern workshops, he has traveled extensively teaching workshops and master classes. A partial list of Jacobs' classes include: American Symphony Orchestra League; Baylor University; Cedar Rapids, Iowa; Celebration of the Tuba at Indiana University (1994); First International Women's Brass Conference - St.

From the collection of Arnold Jacobs

Louis (1993); Florida State University (1994); Gunnison, Colorado (1961-63); Illinois State University (1991); International Brassfest (1995); International Tuba Euphonium Conference (1995); Japan [for Yamaha during CSO tours in 1977 and 1985]; Minnesota Orchestra; Morehead, Kentucky; Music Educators National Conference; New College, Sarasota, Florida; Northern Illinois University (1994); Northwestern University (since 1982); Playing less Hurt—Minnesota; Playing Less Hurt—University of South Florida (1992); Roosevelt University (1977); Second International Brass Congress, Indiana University (1984); Trenton State University (1989 and 1990); Tuba Symposium, Indiana University (1973); United States Marine Band, Washington, D.C. (1991);

University of Arizona (1993 - Teleconference); University of Cincinnati - College Conservatory of Music (1994); University of Florida (1994); University of Michigan; University of Northern Iowa (1992); University of Ohio; University of Oregon (1991); and the University of Wisconsin.

Master class with the
United States Marine Band (1991)
Photo by Author

In 1978, Jacobs lectured at Chicago's Michael Reese Hospital before approximately 200 physicians on the use of playing wind instruments in the therapeutic treatment of asthma in children.[177]

Roger Rocco was one of the few musicians attending and commented, "Since Jacobs had been fighting his own asthma for years, he could speak from experience. He noted that he frequently 'felt lousy' before concerts, but always felt better afterwards. Using an inspirometer, he demonstrated how his ability to move air in and out of the lungs would increase as he played. He encouraged the doctors to use wind instruments as therapy for their patients."

In most master classes, the master teacher points out problems with a student's phrasing, musical style and other related items. Beyond these, Jacobs works with the student's musicianship, psychology and physiology. Those who play for him during these classes share one thing in common—they all sound better after fifteen minutes with him, one of the unique aspects of Jacobs' workshops.

Jacobs Students

Jacobs' phone is constantly ringing from students requesting a lesson with him. According to Roger Rocco, "Jacobs' first test of his students is the test of their will to overcome his rejection. He puts them off at first to determine if they really want to study with him or if they are just curious. Many times he asks new students to make several calls over an extended period before they get their first lesson appointment. I called at the exact minute that he requested. After several months of reintroducing myself over the phone, he realized that I was going to keep calling until I got my appointment. I finally passed my first test."

Many fine students are turned away due to his lack of time. The lucky ones travel from almost every part of the world to meet with him. Traveling from Europe or the Far East to have a few precious lessons with Jacobs is common.

When asked about his students, he responds, "My enrollment is in the hundreds, but they are of all instruments. I am not working with them as

90

developmental instrumentalists but working on normalizing their respiratory functions, making sure that their syndromes in terms of muscles are not involved in the wrong aspects of pressures or immobilization."[178]

Listing all of the musicians that Jacobs has taught is impossible—there are far too many and are not confined to just tuba players. Other brass instruments, all woodwind instruments and even singers and string players come for lessons. One student was not even a musician! Jacobs' students generally fall into one of the following groups:

Long term students
One or two timers
Referrals from others
Aging problems
Therapeutic

Ray Still said, "I send most of my students to him for at least a few lessons. His world-class reputation among musicians is based on what he knows about breathing, as well as about the psychology of making music. He's on my official resume as my most influential teacher, and no two instruments, in terms of the amount of air needed to make them sound, are farther apart than the tuba and oboe.

"He has helped countless older players who have come to him with reduced lung capacities, nervousness, or any number of problems they might be having from feeling their conductors don't like them, someone is after their job, or whatever."[179]

When asked about his specialty, Jacobs responded, "It's just a form of therapy, as though I were a physical therapist, in the sense of normalizing respiratory muscles, establishing the psychological, general attitudes in the brain as far as what thoughts to think in the art form. I do the physiotherapy, normally away from the instrument, normalize respiratory function away from music, establish patterns of normalcy, and then transfer them back to the instrument, so the brain is free to concentrate on the musical message."[180]

An important fact is that Jacobs knows that his role is only as a therapist. He holds no medical degree and does not treat anyone or prescribe medications. If he discovers a medical problem, he will immediately advise a student to consult a physician. In turn, several physicians have referred their patients to him, but only as a therapist. Jacobs will not give medical advice except to see a physician.

Philosophy of Teaching

The student absorbs information. The teacher imparts information and guides the student through his development. According to Jacobs, "The ability to learn is greater than the ability to teach.

"If one is going to be a teacher, one needs to have the ability to impart knowledge. A professional teacher must have a good sense of message, and the ability to deliver and influence a young person's mind. A teacher should be able to communicate as well with an instrument, because we are dealing with sound in this art form."[181]

Jacobs focuses on the fact that his students are musicians. "If you want to enter this profession, you have to do it as a musician. I don't like the word 'trombone player,' 'trumpet player,' or 'tuba player.' I know we play these instruments, but we are artists, we are musicians. We choose these particular instruments as a medium in which to express ourselves."[182]

An important consideration in Jacobs' philosophy of teaching is that all students are different, as every person has his own way of thinking. One person may be highly developed in visual stimuli, such as shades of color that are valuable in art. Another person may have developed in the sense of hearing and pitch recall that is beneficial in music. There are those who think with logical thought and others who think emotionally—it all depends on the individual. Students also have different physical needs, strengths, weaknesses, experiences, desires, and other variables.

Because there are as many teaching problems as there are students, Jacobs treats each student individually. He is concerned only with the student sitting in the chair beside him. Often, he will tell one student one thing and change emphasis with the next student—what he is looking for are results.

This is a common trait among great players. Adolph Herseth states, "A lot of potentially good horn players have been screwed up by teachers, who insist that the only way to play is the way they play. That's a crock. Each person has to do it his or her way. There is no secret about how you learn to make a good sound. You work your butt off."[183]

According to Jacobs, "You have to talk to the student and get an insight into his motivations. If you have a student who tends to think very mechanically, and he becomes very involved in playing an instrument like the tuba, very frequently his thoughts will be on his instrument—on the fingering patterns, the parts of his tissues, embouchure, respiratory system, tongue—very frequently the music is a minor part. You would give it a rating of maybe 15 percent of his intellectual capacity and attitudes, then 85 percent would be on the technique. I always like to reverse it, so that 85 percent has to be based on the phenomenon of sound that is inspirational thinking, on intuitive aspects of the brain, and 15 percent is awareness of structures and functions of all types including the instrument."[184]

There are those who have studied with Jacobs who have interpreted the way that he taught them as *The Arnold Jacobs Method*, and attempt to imitate Jacobs' style with their own students. Jacobs taught them as individuals and the methodology would therefore change with the next student. There is no set Arnold Jacobs method of teaching *all* students. Jacobs individualizes the methodology to the *individual* student. He is the master with his vast knowledge and decades of experience.

Jacobs separates performing from his teaching. He states that he wears several hats. While performing, he wears a performer's hat. When teaching, he wears a teacher's hat. When investigating respiration, he wears an investigator's hat. He knows when to put a hat on, and more importantly, when to take a hat off. When he performs he only wears the hat of the performer. It is not the time to investigate or analyze. Those hats are removed to avoid making simple procedures complex.

"All good teaching is a simplifying process, a weeding out of what is unnecessary or distracting."[185] Jacobs is always looking for simple methods to solve a problem although the process may be complex. Often a student will be thinking with too much complexity that can cause what he calls "Paralysis by Analysis." {see: Mental Elements: Analysis}

Jacobs sees a tendency among students to focus concentration on the clinical aspect of playing. "The act of going to school, of acquiring knowledge as a youngster, is receiving, not sending. It has to be turned around so that performance is always being able to tell a story in music, even at the most elementary stage. The attitude must always be that of somebody imparting knowledge to somebody else, even while he is learning."[186]

"Students seem to want to know 'how to' do something. Many teachers respond that way, but there are several things that do not need to be taught."

Unlike many teachers, Jacobs works with the student's strengths—what he is doing correctly being dominant over what he is doing wrong. For example, many students come to him with an unorthodox, but functional embouchure. While many teachers would work with a student to change it to perfection, Jacobs may leave it alone, as it is perfectly functional, and concentrate on other problems.

Jacobs relies on a multi-sensory approach to teaching. Students learn through their senses and Jacobs uses tactual, visual and aural clues. He rapidly imparts the strongest message for the particular student using the various senses.

With the aid of external devices {see: The Jacobs Studio: Equipment} he motivates students with different senses. Away from the instrument, he may have a student blow a ball to the top of a tube. During this time he is making the student aware of the feeling of the physical activity. Finally he will have the student play on their instrument and tells them to forget the external device and return to the art form of music.

When asked what was his philosophy of teaching, Jacobs responded, "I try to help the student based on what I perceive to be the problem. We have to first make sure that he has good equipment, or at least satisfactory equipment. At that point, we delve into the problems of the player. I have to know where the problems are. I need to know what is motivating the student.

"Frequently, it's not just what he tells me is motivating him. I have to go through a series of physical tests to find out what he is motivating. I make a survey of what that student is like when he comes into the room, based on the way he approaches his instrument and musical characteristics, and based on physical characteristics as well.

"I try to be helpful to the student, primarily in his art form, so that music is dominant over potential problem areas. The positive aspects of what must be right musically are what we enhance. There are vast differences in structural aspects between individuals.

"You can't teach one way in terms of physical application. You teach principles."[187]

To Jacobs, the art form must come first, last, and always. Making music should be approached as an artist rather than as a mechanic. The art form, creative thought, or *song* is 85 percent of music. The artist must prevail in musical thoughts.

Jacobs is not teaching a player of a particular instrument, but, rather, teaching an artist who plays a particular instrument. All students, from the beginner on up, are performers, although their levels vary from elementary to highly advanced. While technique is important, they should put the study of music first and the methodology [technique] second.

As an actor uses his body to express emotions, a musician uses the qualities of tone, rhythm, and other things creatively. A musician must be a storyteller of sound.

"Make it an art form that should be enjoyed by all the participants. I would keep a heavy dominance on this thought—no matter how elementary a person's command of an instrument, as soon as he picks that instrument up, he is a performer. Bad sounds can be made into good sounds—silence cannot."[188]

Jacobs usually reserves a student's first lesson to evaluate the student's strengths and weaknesses. This allows him to set a course of study for the student. The largest number of problems with students are with improper respiration [not using enough air] and the tongue.

Beginning Students

Although most students who pass through Jacobs' studio are advanced students or professionals, during master classes he is commonly asked about teaching beginners. Once, a friend of Mrs. Jacobs' had a son who was a beginning student and Jacobs was asked to teach him.

He started with this student by demonstrating sound. He played the student's instrument to demonstrate that the only variable was the player and not the instrument. Jacobs told him, "'Listen to this carefully. This is what a good note sounds like on your trumpet.' I then have them think about it for a moment to establish recall in silence. Then I ask them to try to sound the way I did. Imitation is like putting a player piano roll on so that the keyboard knows what to do—the act of trying to sound like a very good player."[189]

The student would buzz on the mouthpiece and play familiar songs, first on the mouthpiece and later [after learning some fingerings] on the instrument. Jacobs wanted the emphasis to be on the study of the *sound* of the instrument.

He sent the student home with instructions to play on his instrument and mouthpiece. The boy then played for his father and told him, "This is what Mr. Jacobs sounds like." The resulting sound from the boy was not very good and his father was probably wondering what was going on. Rapidly, patterns in the student's brain evolved to *sound* a certain way.

"We take a young mind, we take somebody who is just learning something new. We are showing him excellence, not musculatures in terms of activities, but results. Here's your trumpet, here's your mouthpiece, and it can sound beautiful. Imitate by trial and error. Be willing to make a mistake. It's no big deal if there is something wrong. But have a very definite concept of what you want the audience to hear. It's a very important type of thought to have."[190]

"Even in the most elementary stage, a very young player should not be focused on learning to play the instrument. Rather, he should learn how an instrument should sound. In the act of learning the sound, he is learning the instrument. The emphasis is then on the creative aspect of the sound phenomena, what he wants to do with it—his product is sound, and what he is going to do with it in terms of phrase, dynamics, emotion. He has to communicate.

"He has to become an artist. In the beginning, he is an elementary artist, but he is still an artist when he plays a scale, all the ingredients of the scale. He should also recognize that all these could be transferred into a solo. A scale could be in the style of Mozart or in the style of Brahms. A long tone should not just be a long tone as an exercise. It should be a tone that is used as part of a fine solo, or as part of an accompaniment. It should not just be a fog-horn sound. It should have quality and expansion. But always your plan is the art-form, rather than the meat, the muscles."[191]

A beginner is an elementary artist, "Extremely elementary, but he is still in an art form," as Jacobs states. After a few months with his beginning trumpet student, he received a call from the student's bandmaster. He told Jacobs that the student, "had the sound of a professional but could not read a note of music." Later, as the student progressed, he learned more of the technical aspects of playing, but his first exposure was concentrating on making music.

Jacobs also takes into consideration the student's physical limitations. "You have to recognize that young people usually have small lung capacities. The lung capacities become fairly sizeable with their growth in height and usually around the ages of eighteen to twenty-one it becomes maximal, but if you are dealing with twelve-year-olds, people at grade school level, they have not achieved their heights and lung capacities.

"There is a danger with a young student playing long phrases. Since they are not yet fully developed physically, they should be allowed to break up these phrases to a point of which they are physically capable."

Greatest Teaching Problem

During more than sixty years of teaching, Jacobs has seen many problems with students. Once during the evaluation process, he encountered a student that seemed to be tone deaf. This turned out to be the greatest teaching problem he has ever encountered.

When Jacobs sang a note and asked the student to sing the same note, he could not. Next he had the student sing a child's song. When he sang it in tune with all the intervals, Jacobs believed that this student had the ability to recall pitch.

To help this student, Jacobs used a keyboard, tape recorder and a twelve-window electronic tuner. He would play a single pitch on the keyboard, and after a long silence, another note. Surrounding the notes with silence allowed the student to recall the pitch in his mind.

To bring in the sense of sight, the twelve-window tuner was used. Watching the tuner, the student would sing a pitch and try to stop the window on the tuner. At this point, he would know whether he had properly recalled the pitch. The tape recorder was used so the student could recall the previous session. Rapidly, a pattern of recognition was established, and the student's pitch recognition developed normally. This student has since enjoyed a fine career with a professional orchestra.

Physical Elements

Many consider Jacobs to be the world's foremost expert on the study of respiration as applied to wind instruments. Before Jacobs, most of the principles in relation to wind instruments were essentially non-existent. In the nineteenth century there were studies conducted, but the subjects, for the most part were, large males, primarily vocalists, whose air requirements are different from those who play wind instruments. Many problems encountered by smaller males and women resulted from the misapplication of the techniques of larger males to all others. The school of thought with brass teachers for years was the "tight-gut method." Generations of players were taught this style of respiration for playing believing, among other things, that the diaphragm is located below the navel.

Jacobs is the pioneer of modern-day knowledge of respiration in relation to wind instruments. His research was conducted through thousands of hours of independent research studying the normals and abnormals of respiration. Several doctors, most notable Dr. Bruce Douglass and Dr. Benjamin Burrows, worked with Jacobs. Many have said that Jacobs knows more about the mechanics of respiration than many physicians, although he is primarily self-taught. There is truth in this because physicians are more concerned with diseases and not as concerned with the physiology of respiration as is Jacobs. Jacobs realizes his limitations, and if he senses a medical problem with a student, he always recommends that a physician be consulted immediately.

As a boy, Jacobs had some exposure to human physiology. His father, Albert, had attended medical school but never completed his studies. Arnold Jacobs was a very successful performer with knowledge of the physiology of the human body, although limited, quite impressive for a wind player. During his early years in the Chicago Symphony, Jacobs visited his doctor.

"The doctor that I used to visit in the early 1940s said, 'You're too much music, everything is always music. You need a hobby. You have to do other things.' I think he intended for me to go out to play golf, but I had a problem with my legs so rather than playing golf, I decided to study the structure and function of the human body as a hobby. I was interested even from childhood. I was so fascinated with the study that I stayed with it."[192] This has continued throughout his life.

He first he asked his wife, Gizella about physiology, as Jacobs told Dee Stewart, "My wife is excellent in physiology. In her high school days, they had a physiology class at Calumet High School in Chicago, and she really excelled. She became very competent at the medical drawings—anatomy drawings. While talking with her about breathing, I mentioned the diaphragm and pointed to my navel. She said, 'No, it's not there, it's up here!' and described the effect of the dome of the diaphragm and how it descends and so forth. This was from my wife. She knew more about it than I did, and she was a dancer! I decided I was going to look into the subject.

"My wife had a girlfriend who was a nurse and I called her. I said, 'What do you know about diaphragms?' She wouldn't speak to me! I finally got across to her that I was talking about respiratory functions. She then sent me a book of anatomy and physiology that nurses used in their training. I read through it and found it fascinating.

"At that time, we had a lovely lady who was our family physician, Dr. Margaret Buck. I talked to her about my desire to learn a bit of structure and function. She guided me through this period in terms of advising me on literature and where to start. She suggested that I study the skeletal structure first, then learn about anatomy, but do it on a sensible basis. 'Don't just start with the respiration. Learn what human beings are, how we are structured.'

"I had plenty of time and the interest was there, so I started a program that I thought would be of short duration. That was in 1944, and I'm still at it—I've never stopped."[193]

At first he kept his studies away from music, but eventually he saw differently as he stated in an interview with Jim Unrath on Chicago radio station WFMT-FM.

"I had no intention of using the biological studies that I was doing in the teaching pursuit at all. Once I began to learn how we function, then it was obvious. If I saw phenomena existing in an individual in the way he uses his musculature, and I know that he cannot move air at that point, I may work with him a little bit as a therapist just to establish the air flow, to get him back into the use of the bellows activity that we have in respiration."[194]

The subject fascinated Jacobs. He read medical books and audited classes at a medical school. "I took a considerable amount of time to study illness and health. What happens to our body when we are ill, what happens when we are healthy."

"This was just a never-ending study of enormous complexity. If I had known this at the time I started, I probably would have closed the book and said, 'No way!' I would want to go fishing and have some fun. But there was an ever increasing fascination."[195]

Many musicians thought that Jacobs was in deep left field working with the physiology of breathing to students. Then his students started capturing positions in many orchestras. As a teacher, he became more popular and others came to him for advice, including physicians.

At one point, Jacobs reached a crossroad in life. He considered resigning from the Chicago Symphony and enrolling in medical school. Then reality set in. He asked himself the age-old question, "Who pays the bills?" The idea was abandoned. Jacobs would have made a great doctor—a loss for the medical world but a gift for musicians.

Mechanics of Breathing

Jacobs has always stated, "Great music can be made without the specific knowledge of the body." Just as most motorists know little or nothing about the mechanics of their car, most musicians know little or nothing about the mechanics of breathing. For general driving of a car, a knowledge about what is happening under the hood is not required. However, in more serious driving, such as racing, a more detailed understanding of the car's mechanics would be helpful.

The same is true in understanding the mechanics of breathing. For everyday breathing, it is better just not to think about it. For more specialized breathing, such as playing a wind instrument, a more detailed understanding of the physiology of breathing could be beneficial.

This very complex subject is something that Jacobs has spent more than fifty years studying. "The mechanics of the body are marvelous, but as a musician, I teach music. The normals and abnormals of the mechanics are too complex."

The key here is when to analyze and when not to. When a race driver is in the pits, it is time to analyze the mechanics of the car. When out on the race track, it is time to only drive. During a concert it is not the time for the musician to analyze the mechanics of breathing, it is time to perform.

Jacobs states, "When I am investigating respiration, I wear an investigator's hat. When I am teaching, I wear a teacher's hat. When I put on the performer's hat, I am not concerned with the mechanics of breathing."

Uses of the Respiratory System

The most common use of the respiratory system's musculature is to exchange gasses, a requirement to sustain life. This is only one of three phenomena of life supported by the musculature of the respiratory system.

The second use is for the contraction of the muscles in isometric opposition where muscles become rigid. This is useful for sports or combat, but not in playing a wind instrument.

About the final use of the respiratory system, Jacobs says, "I learned more about the lungs not by studying wind for playing my instrument, the tuba, singing, or trumpet playing, but by studying defecation and childbirth—the study of what happens with breath pressure."[196]

The pelvic pressure syndrome uses the respiratory musculature for both childbirth and defecation. Abdominal muscles bear down, increasing internal air pressure. The throat closes to contain the pressure [the Valsalva maneuver]. Inside the body, air is under considerable pressure, far more than required to play a wind instrument.

Often during master classes, Jacobs has a man blow into a modified blood pressure gauge with as much air pressure as possible. Usually he can only blow three pounds of static breath pressure as sensors in the lungs protect the tissue and prevent larger pressures.

Pat Sheridan with Jacobs and gauge
Photo by Author

Next, he has this man lie flat on his back on the floor and tense up the muscles of his abdomen by isometric opposition. A small woman [usually Mrs. Jacobs!] then stands on his chest and abdomen.

"On the trumpet, which is the highest pressure instrument in the brass family, I have measured many people and they hardly go up to three pounds of pressure. The average will be between one-half and one and one-half pounds. When they are working really hard, they may get up to two to three pounds."

Gizella Jacobs standing on Pat Sheridan
Photo by Author

This demonstration shows that the muscles of the abdomen can only sustain a pressure around three pounds, but can also support 100 pounds or more. "Physically, we have reflexes in each lung that will not permit us to use any of this kind of strength. Anytime you exert a great power in these powerful muscles, this has to do with reduction. There would be an enervation of the muscles that make you large. That would cancel it out and this goes on all the time. It's foolish to use enormous strength when you are dealing with one to two pounds."[197]

Excess contraction of the abdomen's musculature is unnecessary, as it limits the potential of the respiratory system. It is contrary to the old "tight-gut" method that decades of wind players have been taught.

For respiration, humans breathe by first taking air into the lungs [inspiration] and then expelling it [expiration]. These two acts make up a complete breath. The average adult normally takes about sixteen breaths per minute when awake and about six to eight per minute when asleep. Under stress that rate may increase to one hundred per minute.

Control of Breathing

The human body has developed a complex series of feedback loops that stimulate or inhibit breathing. Some are simple biochemical sensors, in the neck or primitive brain [the medulla oblongata]. Some are tied directly to our emotions and cannot be anatomically located. In response to a low level of oxygen and build up of the acidity of the blood caused by carbon dioxide, a signal is sent through the nerves to the respiratory muscles for more rapid and deeper breathing. In certain circumstances, one or the other may dominate, but in healthy musicians, both oxygen and acidity are equally important in stimulating the sensation that it is time to breathe. Overcharging the oxygen level of the blood is possible by hyperventilation {see: Physical Elements: Hyperventilation}.

At times the need to breathe is increased. For example, if one were to breathe as at rest, but walk at two-and-one-half miles per hour at sea level on a level pavement, the oxygen content of the blood would quickly drop to a level equal to what would be found in a person at the top of Mount Everest. This is a blood/oxygen level that is not compatible with life.

Even mild exercise clearly requires increased breathing. The normal reflex is to shorten exhalation, while not changing the time of inhalation. Increased oxygen consumption will first increase the frequency of breathing rather than volume of each breath.

Breathing to play an instrument is clearly different from breathing to live. Mechanical wind is needed to produce sound rather than a chemical exchange needed to produce homeostasis [a stable physiologic environment].

Upper Respiratory

We inhale and exhale air through the mouth and nose. For wind musicians, the goal is to inhale with what Jacobs calls "minimal friction." Yawning is one of the best examples of a good inhalation. During exhalation, Jacobs says, "The psychology of wind is where it lands, not the feel in the oral cavity."

Jacobs does not recommend breathing only through the nose [the sniff breath]. "I cannot see anything wrong with nasal breathing except that it is slower." He feels that a larger breath can be taken through the larger opening of the mouth in the same amount of time. If only small amounts of air are taken through the mouth, it could be significant to take air in through the mouth and nose simultaneously. "The two together can complement each other. If you can take air in through the nose and mouth together it can be a plus."

Closure of the throat [pharynx] can constrict the air flow. Jacobs often feels under a player's chin to check for closure of the throat. "I do not want more space in the mouth than the space of the pharynx. I need the resistance to air at the lips, not at the throat. If we take air comfortably through the lips, there will still be a moderate friction in the pharyngeal region. If too much air is taken in, there will be a massive resistance in the throat, which is very hard to cope with."

The most common cause of a constricted air flow is pressurization of the air in the body. To block the pressurized air from the embouchure, either the throat is closed or the tongue is used. The blockage can cause pressure to build up in the

STRUCTURES
OF THE THROAT

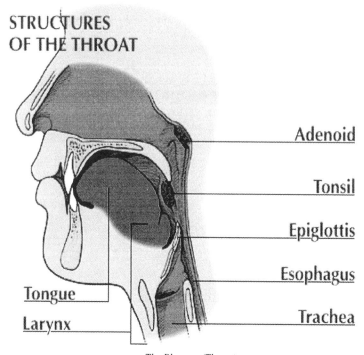

Adenoid

Tonsil

Epiglottis

Esophagus

Tongue

Larynx

Trachea

The Pharynx (Throat)

lower respiratory system as in relation to Bernoulli's law {see: Physical Elements: Tongue}. This can cause pelvic pressure syndrome. The throat must remain open. "An open throat is a relaxed throat."

The larynx contains the voice box and the associated musculature. It is used to close the air passageway when swallowing and when downward pressure is required as in the Valsalva maneuver used for childbirth and defecation, not for normal breathing or playing an instrument.

At the International Brassfest [Bloomington, Indiana] in 1995, Jacobs demonstrated this with a student.

AJ - "I want you just to blow out as wind, I'll demonstrate [he blows out then makes a choking sound followed with a choke].

"Can you describe that feeling?

Student - "It feels like I'm going to die."

AJ - "Well don't die—it's too hard to get volunteers. There should be a choking sensation, a sensation in the throat. Try this in the audience."

"Do you all feel the pressure in the neck?

"You should feel pressure in the neck. When that happens there are changes not just in the neck, but there are changes throughout the entire respiratory system. This is used in nature as part of the Valsalva Maneuver to increase pelvic pressures. Those women who have had babies had to bear down [he makes a pushing sound] in order to get the infant out.

"I've had players galore that use a form of this while they are playing the instrument. They can get the air out under high pressure, but they cannot use very much air. There is not much room for the reduction phenomenon that takes place with emptying or taking the air out of the lungs."[198]

Air can be felt above the larynx, but not below. Jacobs does not advise the use of laryngeal muscles for beginning and ending notes.

The windpipe [trachea] is the start of the bronchial tree. About halfway down the chest, it divides into a right and left bronchus, or branch, each entering a lung. "If there is insufficient air volume moving up the trachea, the glottis will close and the tongue will have too much pressure behind it and there will be starvation of air to the embouchure."

Lungs

The lungs are designed to exchange gasses between the inspired air and the blood. They are like a series of separate bellows, so parts of the lungs will be usable in any position the body puts them. Although their outer surface area is relatively small, they provide a very large inner surface to exchange gasses. Both lungs are not identical, the right lung has three lobes, the left two.

The bronchial tree in the lungs resembles an upside-down tree with the trachea as the trunk. The trachea divides into the five lobes of the lungs and into smaller and smaller branches called bronchioles. Each bronchiole ends in a cluster of tiny air sacs called alveoli. The lungs have about 300 million of these clusters. Wrapped around each alveolus are pulmonary capillaries, the smallest blood vessels in the lungs. The capillaries are so narrow that red blood cells must pass through in a single line. This is where gas exchange takes place. Each red blood cell leaks carbon dioxide and absorbs oxygen through the thin walls of the capillaries and alveoli.

From the trachea to the last bronchial branch there are twenty-three divisions of the bronchial tree, increasing the cumulative diameter of the bronchioles to more than 2000 times that of the trachea. This division increases the surface area of the alveoli from less than one-half a square meter [the outer surface area of the lung] to more than seventy square meters [approximately the size of a tennis court].

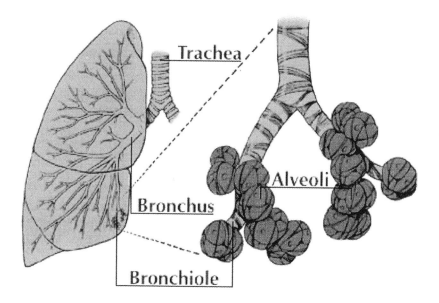

From the time we are born and take our first breath, the lungs have air in them. Residual air always stays in the lungs. Without the residual air to keep the lungs inflated, they would collapse. This is what happens when a lung is punctured. Simply breathing in will not reinflate it. The residual air is mechanically not usable for respiration.

The lungs lie within a muscular and bony framework that expands, when inhaling, creating a negative pressure within the chest compared with the outside air. Boyle's Law dictates that pressures must be equalized between two gaseous compartments [outside the body and the lungs inside the body] by the movement of air from the higher pressure compartment to the lower, if the two compartments are freely connected. During normal inhalation, the pressure within the trachea is about 2.5 millimeters of mercury below the pressure outside. Air then moves into the lung and the lung expands.

The surface area of the lungs is expanded by the lowering of the diaphragm {see: Physical Elements: Diaphragm} while the rib cage moves up. The ribs move upwards as they are attached to the vertebrae in the rear. The eighth, ninth, and tenth ribs rotate and there is a lateral motion as they ascend while taking a breath.

Many musicians only breathe from the abdomen [diaphragmatic breathing], abandoning upper chest breathing. A full breath cannot be taken without expanding the lungs in the upper chest. Jacobs will commonly tell a student, "Think of Dolly Parton and allow the upper chest to expand."

The body can lie. Jacobs tells students, "Breathe to expand, don't expand to breathe." Many players show all of the outward and visible signs of taking a breath but are taking in very little air. They are enlarging their bodies to take air in, but little air comes in.

"Many people that come to my studio do not let blowing air be psychological but based upon anatomy. They move their bodies in order to blow. They are doing physical maneuvers, but they are lying to their own tissues. If they would simply move air out by blowing, they would understand the concept right away and blow.

"Like a bellows, when you blow it gets smaller and when you breathe in, it gets larger, but your body can lie like crazy. If you go by the changes in the body, you may or may not be getting the results. You think you should because you might say, 'Well, the body is supposed to get smaller when you blow.' It does not have to, some other part can get smaller and make up for it. Your body can fool you, but if you tell the truth to your body that you want to blow wind, you have to sense air as it leaves the body."[199]

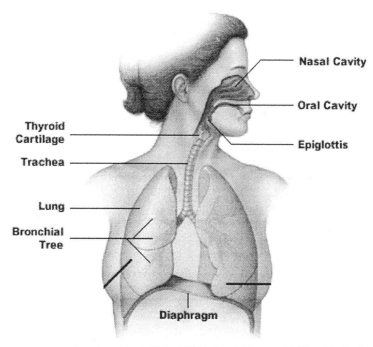

Nasal Cavity

Oral Cavity

Thyroid Cartilage

Epiglottis

Trachea

Lung

Bronchial Tree

Diaphragm

Jacobs demonstrates this concept by having the student put his hands on his [Jacobs'] chest and feel the expansion as he breathes. Next he puts his hand over his mouth and nose and expands his chest without taking in any air. The motion is the same in both instances.

Although the upper parts of the lungs extend to the base of the neck and shoulder muscles, many musicians dramatically raise their shoulders as part of body expansion [clavicular breathing]. Jacobs discourages students from this maneuver. "In a complete capacity breath there is some shoulder raising. This occurs because of the lungs being full of air to capacity. However, the deliberate raising of the shoulders should be avoided."[200]

Dr. Richard Nelson comments, "The energy expended raising the shoulders probably exceeds the respiratory gain by approximately 3 percent."

Diaphragm

The diaphragm is a muscular partition between the thoracic and the abdominal cavities. Its location, in the front, is at the base of the sternum [breastbone] and in the back on the spine and at the base of the rib cage.

During contraction, the diaphragm descends, the chest cavity is enlarged and air pressure is lowered. This is responsible for 75 percent of the normal volume increase of the lungs. It is a physical impossibility to use the diaphragm to *raise* intrathoracic pressure.

For deeper breathing the ribs are elevated and expanded outwards, further expanding the chest by the external intercostal muscles. Small increments in volume can be obtained by further elevation of the ribs by muscles of the neck and back.

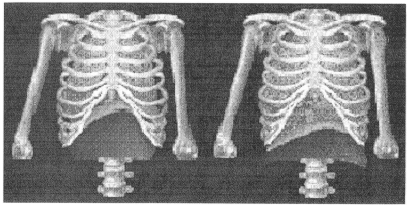

Diaphragm at upward position during exhalation (left) and downward position during inhalation (right) Notice the expansion within the rib cage

From Bodyworks CD-ROM © 1994 Softkey Multimedia, Inc., a subsidiary of Softkey, International, Inc. Used with permission.

Because the diaphragm can only move up and down, Jacobs commonly makes the analogy of the diaphragm to an old-fashioned insect sprayer. "With the bug sprayer, if you pull the handle out, the pressure decreases. If you push it in, the pressure increases—the diaphragm is like a piston."

There are no nerves in the diaphragm to tell the brain what position it is in. The diaphragm has only pain sensing nerves.

Many teachers use the phrase, "blow from the diaphragm," and use the term "diaphragmatic support." "The term 'support' raises questions in itself. Many people make the mistake of assuming that muscle contraction is what provides support. The blowing of the breath should be the support, not tension in the muscles of the body, but the movement of air that is required by the embouchure or reed.

"Support is always a reduction phenomenon. Wherever the player is going to build pressure, according to Boyle's Law, he is going to have a reduced chamber. The chamber can be reduced anywhere it is previously enlarged. It gets bigger when you take air in. It gets smaller when you move air out. When you blow, the brain will deactivate the diaphragm, normally. If you are using air to create pelvic pressures, the diaphragm will not deactivate—it will remain stimulated. Abdominal muscles that would normally be expiratory will start contracting, and there will be a closure at the throat or the tongue or the lips, which causes the air pressure to bear down on a downward-contracting diaphragm to increase the pelvic pressure for expulsion of fecal matter. Of course, to bypass this we have to have a blowing phenomenon that is different," Jacobs says.

The ability of the diaphragm to move is directly related to the position of the body {see: Physical Elements: Posture}. The respiratory system should not be thought of as a single bellows, but as a series of segmented bellows. "If I lean to the right, the use of the right lung is diminished. By leaning to the left, the use of the left lung is diminished. By leaning backwards, the upper lung motion is diminished. By leaning forwards, the diaphragmatic activity is diminished [as less air can be taken in]."

Exhalation

Exhalation begins with the relaxation of the inspiratory muscles. During normal breathing, exhalation is passive. In forced exhalation, such as playing a wind instrument, the relaxed diaphragm is lifted by contraction of the abdominal muscles [neural inhibition] and the chest is drawn downwards and in by the internal intercostal muscles.

Breathing out can be inhibited by either contraction of the diaphragm [the paradox or perversity of "diaphragmatic support"], or by obstruction of an outflow at the larynx. Both these "brakes" are used during normal respiration and especially during straining maneuvers.

Emptying the lungs in a normal person may take only four seconds. Eighty percent of the air should be dischargeable within one second and the remainder in the next two or three seconds. By pulling in the lower abdomen, the diaphragm is forced up and a bit is forced out—something Jacobs does not recommend.

The best advice is to take in a full breath. Jacobs says, "There is no reason not to take a full breath—it's free, it costs nothing."

Brain

The human body is one of the most complex organisms on earth. The central nervous system, including the brain, controls all organs of the body and intelligence. Jacobs makes the distinction between anatomy and function through what he calls the "computer activity of the brain," which is separate from the "thinking part of the brain." Human intelligence, or as Jacobs calls it the "thinking part of the brain," should be used for coping with life around us, not for the self-analysis of life within us {see: Mental Elements: Thinking Part of the Brain}.

Jacobs compares the control of the human body with that of an automobile. Under the hood of the car are many complex systems such as the engine, cooling system, brakes and other similar devices. The car is designed with a simple set of controls to operate the complex mechanical portions of the car.

During an interview with Jim Unrath on Chicago radio station WFMT-FM, Jacobs explained, "Whenever you build a machine, you must put in a set of controls. From the moment you have the controls in, you do not work the machine by its individual component parts, but what you want the machine to accomplish. To do this, you communicate through the control system. Our controls are in the brain. We never play by segmented tissue, such as diaphragms and lips and various segmented parts of our tissues. We play by *song*. We use our motor activities based on the flow of *wind*, which is our fuel supply.

"We have a level of the brain that I call the computer level—a region above the brain stem that we know today has a great deal to do with the coordinate phenomena of function—and we allow this computer level to coordinate our physical movements. We have to order the products, what we want. It's very much like in this speech. I'm using very complex tissues, but I don't know a thing about them. The controls are in the brain and based on conditioning and habits that are already formed. I'm ordering products constantly. But you really cannot segment into the individual components of the body."[201]

Often, Jacobs will use the analogy of reaching for a glass of water. "Here, you are not concerned with the musculature of the biceps and triceps in the arm. You are not concerned with compensating for the gravitational pull of the earth while lifting the glass. These are complexities that the brain manages. A simple command is sent to the brain to get a drink of water and the brain controls the complexities of an action. It would be a waste of time to analyze the complexities that the brain automatically performs in the subconscious."

Muscles

Body motions require the use of muscles. According to Jacobs, "You have 659 muscles in the human body, 654 paired as antagonists to each other. There is some variation on these thoughts depending upon the researchers, but this is the basic information. These 654 muscles maneuver the skeletal structures, permit you to perform everyday functions such as drinking a glass of water, and other things we do not think about."

With muscles paired as antagonists, the body's musculature is capable of great stiffness. Just as contracting both the biceps and triceps simultaneously can result in no arm motion because of opposing forces, other muscles can counteract each other, creating problems for musicians. If one part of the body has tension, other parts are affected. Although Jacobs encourages relaxation while playing an instrument, he prefers using another term.

"I usually take the word 'relaxation' out and use the term 'minimal motors.' The muscles always have some type of activity going on, so we have to return to a minimal state of activity.

"If you have a sudden dramatic change of blowing (when you breathe in), you suck so that the stimulus for inhalation is the pulling of air into the space between the lips. It has to go somewhere—so it goes straight into the lungs, which is where it is suppose to go. When that happens, the brain will automatically deactivate the muscles that are moving the air out. They completely deactivate the muscles to the point of even taking muscle tone out at the same time they activate the muscles that have to make you large [neural inhibition], which will lower the air pressure and take the air in. It is done without any effort on your part.

"You simply have to give the order of what you want to do with the air on the lips. You are blowing out and it is done so fast that you do not have to relax. If you stop and relax it is going to take you a few moments and you would not be able to do this. When you are not doing anything, you should be relaxed. There should not be any tension except the norms."[202]

Often Jacobs feels a student's body as he plays his instrument. He is feeling muscular contractions to determine if muscle groups are fighting each other. "Your muscles have the potential for great stiffness. You must find weakness through minimal effort. Strength is your enemy—weakness is your friend."

Hyperventilation/Hypoventilation

The concentration of oxygen and carbon dioxide in the blood stream constantly varies. During the respiratory cycle, the blood carries oxygen to the tissues that require it, and carbon dioxide is the waste product.

Unlike others, who refer to hyperventilation as the increase of the blood's oxygen level, Jacobs would rather refer to hyperventilation as the lowering of carbon dioxide. The symptoms of hyperventilation are not due to an accumulation of oxygen but a lowering of carbon dioxide levels in the blood stream, with resulting alkaline shifts in the blood's pH. The brain gets its signals in this situation, from the amount of carbon dioxide, not the amount of oxygen in the blood—it is a negative-feedback system.

Hyperventilation can cause problems especially with high flow rate instruments such as the flute or tuba. "The problem with playing the tuba is that there is a very moderate amount of hyperventilation associated with the instrument.

"When you hyperventilate a bit, you actually alter the pH of the body. The alkaline/acid relationships are affected, and a person is apt to feel a little bit peculiar with very moderate hyperventilation. Usually it will start out as dizziness. How will I say it—a little leaving of the ground—you begin to float a little bit.

"The symptoms of hyperventilation are due to a lack of carbon dioxide and its effect on the brain. The carbon dioxide is washed out of the blood by the heavy breathing [increased ventilation] of the respiratory system. Keeping the air flow into the tuba at the maximum, makes the person feel dizzy." he says.

Jacobs performed studies with research scientists at the Pulmonary Functions lab at the University of Chicago, and every indication was that he should have been suffering from severe hyperventilation, but he was not.

As he told William Barry Furlong, "According to their tables, with the volume of air that I was moving in and out of the lungs, I should have been in massive hyperventilation. The question was, 'Why not? Why don't tuba players, as a rule, suffer from massive hyperventilation, particularly after arduous numbers?' They perceived, of course, that the breath expelled into the instrument contained carbon dioxide—the carbon dioxide that he was exhaling. When he took a breath to replenish his lung supply, he would get fresh air in through the corners of his mouth—that is how tuba players learn to breathe—but he is also inhaling some of the air he had expelled into the instrument. That air contained an excess of carbon dioxide and, when he brought it back into his mouth, it created enough of an excess of carbon dioxide in the breath going into his lungs—and then to his brain—to cancel the pure-oxygen [loss of acidity] effect on the brain.

"When I get into these huge, massive blowing episodes, like *The Great Gate of Kiev* at the end of *Pictures at an Exhibition*, I will deliberately take the air back through the instrument to forestall hyperventilation."[203]

In addition to the air requirements for a particular musical passage, the physical energy required to play an instrument at a loud dynamic level will cause the body to demand more oxygen in the blood stream. Obviously, this will have an effect on the oxygen/carbon dioxide level in the blood.

While teaching, Jacobs generally has a student perform only three or four full inhalations in a row with test equipment. After that he has them rest for almost a minute in order for the carbon dioxide level to increase in the body. After that period, he will continue with more respiratory cycles.

Hypoventilation is the opposite of hyperventilation. Jacobs refers to hypoventilation as the accumulation of the carbon dioxide level. This is particularly a problem with low flow rate instruments such as the oboe.

Many oboists have come to Jacobs with problems playing long solo passages, such as Tchaikovsky's *Symphony No. 4,* where there is a solo phrase that lasts up to one minute. The problem is while having enough air for the passage, the body is demanding a breath.

Because of the accumulation of carbon dioxide in the blood stream [hypoventilation] and the demand of oxygen, the body is ordering a breath although the lungs are still full of air. To treat this, Jacobs has a student do three or four deep inhalation/exhalation cycles before a long phrase [in an unobtrusive manner], just as a swimmer might do prior to prolonged activity underwater. This will decrease the carbon dioxide level temporarily delaying the body's need for the next breath. Then they take a full breath to play the phrase.

Vital Capacity

Once we reach maturity, we achieve a certain amount of lung tissue with the physical capability of holding a certain volume of air. Total lung capacity cannot be increased beyond what nature grants to a particular body. Only the elasticity of the lung tissue or chest wall can be increased. Jacobs compares lung capacity with the length of a stringed instrument's bow. A small capacity requires

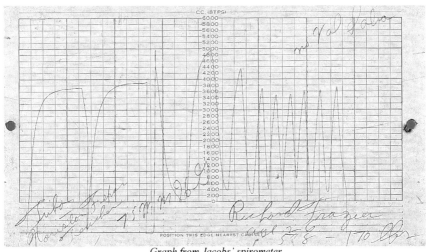

Graph from Jacobs' spirometer
Courtesy of Richard Frazier

breathing more often, like using an undersized bow on a violin requiring more up and down strokes.

To determine a person's vital capacity, a test is given on a respirometer or spirometer {see: The Jacobs Studio: Spirometer}. Other devices such as a Voldyne® {see: The Jacobs Studio: Voldyne®} and a measured air bag {see: The Jacobs Studio: Air Bag} can also be used with less accuracy. These tests determine how much air [in liters] can be moved in or out of the lungs in a single breath.

The following formulas can determine an estimate of a person's vital capacity [in liters] based on height, age and gender. They are from the American Thoracic Society.[204]

These are only estimates. Age is entered in years and height in meters. To convert inches to meters, divide height in inches by 39.37. For example a height of 6 feet [72 inches] equals 1.83 meters [72 / 39.37].

Male: Height^2 X $(((1.541 - (4.06$ X Age$) / 1000)) - ((6.14$ X Age$^2)/100000))$
Female: Height^2 X $(((1.332 - (4.06$ X Age$) / 1000)) - ((6.14$ X Age$^2)/100000))$

For example, using these formulas, a forty-year-old male with a height of six feet would have an estimated vital capacity of 4.28 liters. A female thirty-years-old and five feet tall would have an estimated capacity of 2.68 liters. The charts on the following pages can be used for ages twenty to eighty in increments of five years.

In hospitals, after determining both the estimated vital capacity [from the formulas] and the actual vital capacity [from pulmonary function testing], the ratio is reported. It is determined by dividing the actual capacity by the estimated capacity. If, for example, a person has an actual capacity of five liters and an estimated capacity of four liters, this person would have a capacity of 125 percent of normal. Wind musicians seem to have a higher than normal vital capacity.

Body typing [or somatotyping] is used to estimate a person's vital capacity. The relative role of several factors involved in the estimate are sex (30%), age (8%), height (20%), weight (2%), ethnic differences (10%), technical (3%), unexplained (smoking, active or passive, occupational exposures, pollution, socioeconomic status, genetic, allergies, or past or present respiratory health status) (27%). [205]

When a student comes to Jacobs, he always asks them their age, height and weight. Through experience, he can estimate their capacity. Occasionally he is fooled. Before entering the trumpet section of the Chicago Symphony, William Scarlett was a student of Jacobs. While measuring his vital capacity, Scarlett blew the top off Jacobs' spirometer. Although Scarlett is only five feet ten inches tall, he has a vital capacity of six-and-one-half liters. According to Jacobs, "It's a matter of the torso's shape." In Scarlett's case, he has a long torso and short legs.[206]

Children usually have smaller lung capacities in comparison to adults. "The lung capacities become fairly sizeable with growth in height and usually around the ages of eighteen to twenty-one, vital capacity becomes maximal. People at grade school level, twelve-year-olds for example, have not achieved their heights and full capacity." Those who teach younger players must realize this and not push them into playing longer phrases with their reduced capacity.

	Estimated Vital Capacities of Male and Female 5'6" Tall, Ages 20-80		
Age	Male	Female	% Less
20	4.0	3.4	14.5%
25	3.9	3.3	14.9%
30	3.8	3.2	15.3%
35	3.7	3.1	15.7%
40	3.6	3.0	16.3%
45	3.4	2.8	16.9%
50	3.3	2.7	17.6%
55	3.1	2.5	18.4%
60	3.0	2.4	19.4%
65	2.8	2.2	20.5%
70	2.6	2.1	21.8%
75	2.5	1.9	23.4%
80	2.3	1.7	25.3%

Women have a lung capacity below that of a man of the same size. The average women's vital capacity is between three and four liters. By using the formula for vital capacity from the American Thoracic Society [207] for both males and females, a man and woman, both five feet six inches tall would have a difference in estimated vital capacities ranging from 14.5 percent at age twenty to 25.3 percent at age eighty {see: Physical Elements: Aging Process}.

Women do not have the capacity for inhaling, storing, and using air that men do. "Their potential for moving air out rapidly from their lungs should be quite high, but they do not have the quantity—it's quality without quantity. Most of the time you will find that women will have quite a percentage less lung capacity due to the contouring of the ribs and the general smallness of their structure, compared to the males.

With smaller vital capacities, women cannot waste air, they must take in a comfortably large breath and use it efficiently. "A large male can afford to limit his breathing. A small female cannot."

	20	25	30	35	40	45	50	55	60	65	70	75	80
4'	2.1	2.1	2.0	2.0	1.9	1.8	1.8	1.7	1.6	1.5	1.4	1.3	1.2
4' 1"	2.2	2.2	2.1	2.1	2.0	1.9	1.8	1.8	1.7	1.6	1.5	1.4	1.3
4' 2"	2.3	2.3	2.2	2.1	2.1	2.0	1.9	1.8	1.7	1.6	1.5	1.4	1.3
4' 3"	2.4	2.4	2.3	2.2	2.1	2.1	2.0	1.9	1.8	1.7	1.6	1.5	1.4
4' 4"	2.5	2.4	2.4	2.3	2.2	2.2	2.1	2.0	1.9	1.8	1.7	1.6	1.4
4' 5"	2.6	2.5	2.5	2.4	2.3	2.2	2.1	2.1	2.0	1.8	1.7	1.6	1.5
4' 6"	2.7	2.6	2.6	2.5	2.4	2.3	2.2	2.1	2.0	1.9	1.8	1.7	1.5
4' 7"	2.8	2.7	2.7	2.6	2.5	2.4	2.3	2.2	2.1	2.0	1.9	1.7	1.6
4' 8"	2.9	2.8	2.8	2.7	2.6	2.5	2.4	2.3	2.2	2.1	1.9	1.8	1.7
4' 9"	3.0	2.9	2.9	2.8	2.7	2.6	2.5	2.4	2.3	2.1	2.0	1.9	1.7
4' 10"	3.1	3.0	3.0	2.9	2.8	2.7	2.6	2.5	2.3	2.2	2.1	1.9	1.8
4' 11"	3.2	3.1	3.1	3.0	2.9	2.8	2.7	2.5	2.4	2.3	2.1	2.0	1.8
5'	3.3	3.3	3.2	3.1	3.0	2.9	2.8	2.6	2.5	2.4	2.2	2.1	1.9
5' 1"	3.4	3.4	3.3	3.2	3.1	3.0	2.8	2.7	2.6	2.4	2.3	2.1	2.0
5' 2"	3.6	3.5	3.4	3.3	3.2	3.1	2.9	2.8	2.7	2.5	2.4	2.2	2.0
5' 3"	3.7	3.6	3.5	3.4	3.3	3.2	3.0	2.9	2.8	2.6	2.4	2.3	2.1
5' 4"	3.8	3.7	3.6	3.5	3.4	3.3	3.1	3.0	2.8	2.7	2.5	2.4	2.2
5' 5"	3.9	3.8	3.7	3.6	3.5	3.4	3.2	3.1	2.9	2.8	2.6	2.4	2.2
5' 6"	4.0	3.9	3.8	3.7	3.6	3.5	3.3	3.2	3.0	2.9	2.7	2.5	2.3
5' 7"	4.2	4.1	4.0	3.8	3.7	3.6	3.4	3.3	3.1	2.9	2.8	2.6	2.4
5' 8"	4.3	4.2	4.1	3.9	3.8	3.7	3.5	3.4	3.2	3.0	2.9	2.7	2.5
5' 9"	4.4	4.3	4.2	4.1	3.9	3.8	3.6	3.5	3.3	3.1	2.9	2.7	2.5
5' 10"	4.5	4.4	4.3	4.2	4.0	3.9	3.7	3.6	3.4	3.2	3.0	2.8	2.6
5' 11"	4.7	4.6	4.4	4.3	4.2	4.0	3.9	3.7	3.5	3.3	3.1	2.9	2.7
6'	4.8	4.7	4.6	4.4	4.3	4.1	4.0	3.8	3.6	3.4	3.2	3.0	2.8
6' 1"	4.9	4.8	4.7	4.6	4.4	4.2	4.1	3.9	3.7	3.5	3.3	3.1	2.8
6' 2"	5.1	5.0	4.8	4.7	4.5	4.4	4.2	4.0	3.8	3.6	3.4	3.1	2.9
6' 3"	5.2	5.1	4.9	4.8	4.6	4.5	4.3	4.1	3.9	3.7	3.5	3.2	3.0
6' 4"	5.3	5.2	5.1	4.9	4.8	4.6	4.4	4.2	4.0	3.8	3.6	3.3	3.1
6' 5"	5.5	5.4	5.2	5.1	4.9	4.7	4.5	4.3	4.1	3.9	3.7	3.4	3.1
6' 6"	5.6	5.5	5.4	5.2	5.0	4.8	4.6	4.4	4.2	4.0	3.8	3.5	3.2
6' 7"	5.8	5.6	5.5	5.3	5.2	5.0	4.8	4.6	4.3	4.1	3.8	3.6	3.3
6' 8"	5.9	5.8	5.6	5.5	5.3	5.1	4.9	4.7	4.4	4.2	3.9	3.7	3.4
6' 9"	6.1	5.9	5.8	5.6	5.4	5.2	5.0	4.8	4.6	4.3	4.0	3.8	3.5
6' 10"	6.2	6.1	5.9	5.7	5.6	5.4	5.1	4.9	4.7	4.4	4.1	3.9	3.6
6' 11"	6.4	6.2	6.1	5.9	5.7	5.5	5.3	5.0	4.8	4.5	4.2	4.0	3.7
7'	6.5	6.4	6.2	6.0	5.8	5.6	5.4	5.2	4.9	4.6	4.4	4.1	3.7
7' 1"	6.7	6.5	6.4	6.2	6.0	5.8	5.5	5.3	5.0	4.7	4.5	4.2	3.8
7' 2"	6.8	6.7	6.5	6.3	6.1	5.9	5.7	5.4	5.1	4.9	4.6	4.3	3.9
7' 3"	7.0	6.8	6.7	6.5	6.3	6.0	5.8	5.5	5.3	5.0	4.7	4.4	4.0
7' 4"	7.2	7.0	6.8	6.6	6.4	6.2	5.9	5.7	5.4	5.1	4.8	4.5	4.1
7' 5"	7.3	7.2	7.0	6.8	6.5	6.3	6.1	5.8	5.5	5.2	4.9	4.6	4.2
7' 6"	7.5	7.3	7.1	6.9	6.7	6.4	6.2	5.9	5.6	5.3	5.0	4.7	4.3

*Estimated vital capacities for **males** in liters. Follow height (in left column) and age (at top, in five year increments). Based on a formula from the American Thoracic Society[205]*

	20	25	30	35	40	45	50	55	60	65	70	75	80
4'	1.8	1.8	1.7	1.7	1.6	1.5	1.5	1.4	1.3	1.2	1.1	1.0	0.9
4' 1"	1.9	1.8	1.8	1.7	1.7	1.6	1.5	1.4	1.3	1.3	1.2	1.1	1.0
4' 2"	2.0	1.9	1.9	1.8	1.7	1.7	1.6	1.5	1.4	1.3	1.2	1.1	1.0
4' 3"	2.1	2.0	1.9	1.9	1.8	1.7	1.6	1.5	1.5	1.4	1.3	1.1	1.0
4' 4"	2.1	2.1	2.0	1.9	1.9	1.8	1.7	1.6	1.5	1.4	1.3	1.2	1.1
4' 5"	2.2	2.2	2.1	2.0	1.9	1.9	1.8	1.7	1.6	1.5	1.4	1.2	1.1
4' 6"	2.3	2.2	2.2	2.1	2.0	1.9	1.8	1.7	1.6	1.5	1.4	1.3	1.2
4' 7"	2.4	2.3	2.3	2.2	2.1	2.0	1.9	1.8	1.7	1.6	1.5	1.3	1.2
4' 8"	2.5	2.4	2.3	2.3	2.2	2.1	2.0	1.9	1.8	1.6	1.5	1.4	1.2
4' 9"	2.6	2.5	2.4	2.3	2.2	2.1	2.0	1.9	1.8	1.7	1.6	1.4	1.3
4' 10"	2.7	2.6	2.5	2.4	2.3	2.2	2.1	2.0	1.9	1.8	1.6	1.5	1.3
4' 11"	2.8	2.7	2.6	2.5	2.4	2.3	2.2	2.1	1.9	1.8	1.7	1.5	1.4
5'	2.8	2.8	2.7	2.6	2.5	2.4	2.3	2.1	2.0	1.9	1.7	1.6	1.4
5' 1"	2.9	2.9	2.8	2.7	2.6	2.5	2.3	2.2	2.1	1.9	1.8	1.6	1.5
5' 2"	3.0	3.0	2.9	2.8	2.7	2.5	2.4	2.3	2.2	2.0	1.9	1.7	1.5
5' 3"	3.1	3.1	3.0	2.9	2.7	2.6	2.5	2.4	2.2	2.1	1.9	1.7	1.6
5' 4"	3.2	3.2	3.1	2.9	2.8	2.7	2.6	2.4	2.3	2.1	2.0	1.8	1.6
5' 5"	3.3	3.2	3.1	3.0	2.9	2.8	2.7	2.5	2.4	2.2	2.0	1.9	1.7
5' 6"	3.4	3.4	3.2	3.1	3.0	2.9	2.7	2.6	2.4	2.3	2.1	1.9	1.7
5' 7"	3.6	3.5	3.3	3.2	3.1	3.0	2.8	2.7	2.5	2.3	2.2	2.0	1.8
5' 8"	3.7	3.6	3.4	3.3	3.2	3.1	2.9	2.8	2.6	2.4	2.2	2.0	1.8
5' 9"	3.8	3.7	3.5	3.4	3.3	3.1	3.0	2.8	2.7	2.5	2.3	2.1	1.9
5' 10"	3.9	3.8	3.7	3.5	3.4	3.2	3.1	2.9	2.7	2.6	2.4	2.2	1.9
5' 11"	4.0	3.9	3.8	3.6	3.5	3.3	3.2	3.0	2.8	2.6	2.4	2.2	2.0
6'	4.1	4.0	3.9	3.7	3.6	3.4	3.3	3.1	2.9	2.7	2.5	2.3	2.1
6' 1"	4.2	4.1	4.0	3.8	3.7	3.5	3.4	3.2	3.0	2.8	2.6	2.3	2.1
6' 2"	4.3	4.2	4.1	3.9	3.8	3.6	3.4	3.3	3.1	2.9	2.6	2.4	2.2
6' 3"	4.5	4.3	4.2	4.0	3.9	3.7	3.5	3.3	3.1	2.9	2.7	2.5	2.2
6' 4"	4.6	4.4	4.3	4.2	4.0	3.8	3.6	3.4	3.2	3.0	2.8	2.5	2.3
6' 5"	4.7	4.6	4.4	4.3	4.1	3.9	3.7	3.5	3.3	3.1	2.9	2.6	2.3
6' 6"	4.8	4.7	4.5	4.4	4.2	4.0	3.8	3.6	3.4	3.2	2.9	2.7	2.4
6' 7"	4.9	4.8	4.7	4.5	4.3	4.1	3.9	3.7	3.5	3.3	3.0	2.7	2.5
6' 8"	5.1	4.9	4.8	4.6	4.4	4.2	4.0	3.8	3.6	3.3	3.1	2.8	2.5
6' 9"	5.2	5.0	4.9	4.7	4.5	4.3	4.1	3.9	3.7	3.4	3.2	2.9	2.6
6' 10"	5.3	5.2	5.0	4.8	4.6	4.4	4.2	4.0	3.8	3.5	3.2	3.0	2.7
6' 11"	5.5	5.3	5.1	5.0	4.8	4.6	4.3	4.1	3.9	3.6	3.3	3.0	2.7
7'	5.6	5.4	5.3	5.1	4.9	4.7	4.4	4.2	3.9	3.7	3.4	3.1	2.8
7' 1"	5.7	5.6	5.4	5.2	5.0	4.8	4.5	4.3	4.0	3.8	3.5	3.2	2.9
7' 2"	5.9	5.7	5.5	5.3	5.1	4.9	4.7	4.4	4.1	3.9	3.6	3.3	2.9
7' 3"	6.0	5.8	5.6	5.4	5.2	5.0	4.8	4.5	4.2	3.9	3.6	3.3	3.0
7' 4"	6.1	6.0	5.8	5.6	5.4	5.1	4.9	4.6	4.3	4.0	3.7	3.4	3.1
7' 5"	6.3	6.1	5.9	5.7	5.5	5.2	5.0	4.7	4.4	4.1	3.8	3.5	3.1
7' 6"	6.4	6.2	6.0	5.8	5.6	5.4	5.1	4.8	4.5	4.2	3.9	3.6	3.2

*Estimated vital capacities for **females** in liters. Follow height (in left column) and age (at top, in five year increments). Based on a formula from the American Thoracic Society[205]*

The largest lung capacity Jacobs has measured is that of Michael Johnson, a British tubist who attended a master class. He had an amazing capacity of 7.94 liters! On the other end of the spectrum, Jacobs' wife, Gizella, has capacity of approximately two liters. A former dancer, she plays no musical instruments.

Jacobs has never had a large lung capacity. Contrary to legend, he has *two lungs* but with diminished capacity. Early in his career he had a capacity of nearly five liters but after cancer surgery in the 1980s, his capacity

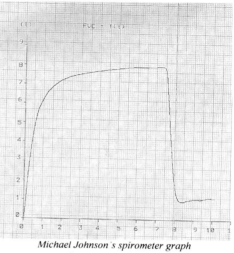

Michael Johnson's spirometer graph
Courtesy of Michael Johnson

diminished to approximately 2.75 liters. With time he was able to get it back to 3.8 to 4.4 liters—his normal capacity during the latter part of his career.

For wind players with small lung capacities, Jacobs is an inspiration. During his tenure with the Chicago Symphony, his capacity at its best was only four to five liters and he played the tuba—an instrument that requires large volumes of air to play!

The most obvious question is, "How does Jacobs do it?" A valid question but impossible to completely answer. "If I play soft, I can hold a phrase longer. I can sometimes hold as long as seventeen to twenty seconds or longer. I have students who have double my lung capacity that can obviously go twice as long. If a very large person with a seven-liter lung capacity plays softly using a fifteen-liter-per-minute flow rate, he has considerable phrase length. The potential for longer phrases is there."[208]

However, most wind players use less than one-half of their vital capacity when playing their instrument. "One of the difficulties, with men as well as women, is that the player rarely, if ever, uses all the usable air in their lungs. They may have a vital capacity of four-and-a-half liters, but that is not what they use. They use only a fraction of that capacity. A trained person might use 75 or 80 percent of their vital capacity, others will use half or less.

Jacobs uses his small lung capacity to its full potential. "It is better to use 80 percent of a four-liter vital capacity than 50 percent of a six-liter vital capacity, but it is better to have a large vital capacity to begin with."[209]

While most believe that Jacobs advocates a full breath, that is not precisely the case. For overall playing, he suggests a breath of 75 to 80 percent of capacity.

116

Of course, this will vary depending on the requirements of the music being played. During a loud passage on a high flow rate instrument, a full capacity inhalation will be required.

For those with small capacities, Jacobs recommends that they concentrate on their musical attributes. They should realize the size of their capacity and not be frustrated by attempting to achieve that which they cannot physically achieve.

Relaxation Pressure Curve

Part of the respiratory process is the movement of air into the lungs by the lowering of air pressure within the chest. As the diaphragm lowers, air pressure is reduced within the chest below the pressure of ambient air and air flows into the lungs from the outside.

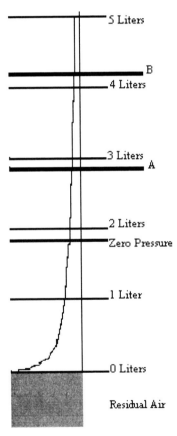

<<Time<

Relaxation Pressure Curve

Jacobs uses a graph generated while exhaling with the time factor running right to left. It is the sort generated by a drum spirometer {see: The Jacobs Studio: Spirometer} as shown with the *Relaxation Pressure Curve* graph. The top of the graph is total lung capacity and increments are in liters. The bottom is the residual air that will remain in the lungs and is unusable for musicians.

In the positive pressure zone, when breathing out normally, large quantities of air naturally and easily flow from the body to the lower pressure outside the body. To play an instrument, this is the ideal range in which to work.

The zero pressure line on this graph is the point where passive exhalation ends [not playing an instrument]. Pressure inside and outside the body are equal. Above this point, air will flow out with no musculature assistance.

Below the point of zero pressure is what he calls the "negative pressure zone." Here it feels as if the pressure in the body wants to be lower than pressure outside the body. Though air naturally wants to come into the body at this point, great muscular effort is needed to maintain air flow out of the body, actually to the point of "squeezing" it out. [notice the irregularity of the line towards the bottom of the graph].

For playing wind instruments, this creates the problem of diminished quantity. The body naturally wants to inhale, but muscular contraction is exhaling air to play the instrument. The air quantity is diminished and air is being forced out—an uncomfortable situation.

Unfortunately, most wind players are shallow breathers, taking in far less than a full breath [starting with a breath at point "**A**" on the graph]. Their starting point with a breath is too low on the positive end of the curve. Greater muscular effort is required than is desirable, especially below the point of zero pressure.

For a short phrase, there is no problem. For a long phrase, when entering the negative portion of the curve, air volumes are diminished and there is great discomfort. Jacobs encourages his students to breathe deeply and frequently and avoid dipping below the point of zero pressure where they would have to work too hard and use more effort to move the air.[210]

The solution is simple. Instead of taking in a shallow breath [for example 50 percent of the total capacity], a larger capacity breath [80 percent or more] should be taken [starting with a breath at point "**B**" on the graph]. This results in a higher volume of air flow with less discomfort. If possible, avoid going into the negative pressure area. Most important, second and third breaths must have as much quantity of air as the first breath.

This is a very complicated subject that many students have had problems comprehending. To help simplify this concept, during an interview with Jim Unrath, Jacobs stated:

"If we just relate this to fuel, on my car I have a twenty-gallon gas tank. If I were to fill it halfway and run to empty, I would be simulating what some of my students will do with their lung capacity. They may take a breath only to half-full and play towards empty. There are complications in this. The last quarter of the fuel tank becomes very hard to empty. It gets very difficult to get the air out of the lungs and increasingly so, the closer you get toward empty. But, if we were to have three-quarters of a tank of fuel and play down to one quarter, we would still use a half-tank, but locate it a little more towards full, we avoid the complications near the end of the breath. And it's much freer to replace the air, much more comfortable to use in blowing an instrument without the signs of strain and without some of the physical evidence of pulmonary malfunction, which comes from emptying the lungs too much."[211]

Air Flow/Air Pressure

Wind can only be experienced as it enters and leaves the body through the lips. Within the body, it can only be detected as air pressure. To move air outside the body, air pressure is required as moving air requires pressure. Jacobs calls this, "the phenomenon of wind."

The relationship between air flow and air pressure has been puzzling to wind instrument players. Air as pressure uses the same musculature as air as *wind*. However, the musculature is used in different ways. "With *wind* there is always air pressure. With air pressure, there is not always *wind*." He often tells students to play with *Song and Wind*, not song and air pressure.

In 1995 at the International Brassfest in Bloomington, Indiana, Jacobs commented: "You learn to differentiate between air pressure and *wind*. With *wind*, there is always air pressure. If you think about it, there can never be *wind* unless there is air pressure. If you have a piece of tubing and put your hand near one end, you feel a little air coming out—the air pressure can be measured. Where it enters the tubing you will find it higher than where it comes out. When you use an anemometer, you can measure the differences in the air pressure, and you will always find that where there is wind, there are differences in pressures. When you order wind, a gentle wind [he blows softly], or a powerful wind [he blows hard], there is a great difference in pressure in those two that you actually measure flow and pressure.

"The psychology of *wind* is very different than the psychology of pressure. If you go by the psychology of pressure, you can have pressure with practically empty lungs."[212]

To show air pressure, Jacobs has students place a finger over their lips and then blow. When they release the finger, there is a pop. This is air under pressure. At first, there is a large volume of air, but this is not sustained for more than a few moments, unless they continually blow.

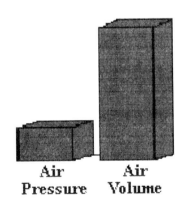

Air Pressure   Air Volume

For air flow, Jacobs differentiates this as thin air and thick air. To show thin air, he has a student hold his hand in front of his mouth and say "sssssss." The air is under high pressure, but there is little quantity. Blow "whoooooo" (as in who) for thick air. The feeling is a considerable volume of air under low pressure.

Jacobs draws two lines to demonstrate the air pressure in the oral cavity and air volume (flow) in the instrument. There is nearly four times the air volume.

All wind instruments have their flow rate—the quantity of air required to play a note on an instrument for one minute. Variables include the instrument, range and dynamic. Just as there are variables for air flow, air pressure has the same variables.

In the brass family, the trumpet uses the least amount of air flow but under the greatest amount of pressure, around one-half to one pound of pressure [of mercury]. In extreme circumstances, the pressure can be as high as three pounds. The tuba uses the greatest air flow, but under the least pressure—one to ten ounces.

In the 1950s, Dr. Bruce Douglass, a tubist and physician from the Mayo Clinic, traveled to Chicago for lessons with Jacobs. Douglass put him in contact with Dr. Benjamin Burrows then at the University of Chicago's Billings Hospital. It was here that Jacobs did research with full laboratory equipment.

In 1959 or 1960, four members of the Chicago Symphony, with instruments, traveled to the University of Chicago for tests. They were Adolph Herseth, trumpet; Philip Farkas, horn; Robert Lambert, trombone; and Jacobs, tuba.

Jacobs spoke to Bill Russo on Chicago radio station WFMT-FM about these tests:

Russo, (BR) - What's the difference between [brass] instruments?

Jacobs, (AJ) - "The trumpet would use the least amount of breath, but under the greatest amount of pressure of any of the brass instruments. The tuba would be just the reverse. It would use the most in terms of volume of air and flow, but under the least pressure. We found that the flow rates in very high range playing would be very low—say maybe ten-liter-per-minute flow rate under a pressure of sometimes in excess of a pound-and-a-half to two pounds. In his lower range, he might be playing with a flow rate of maybe twenty-five to thirty-liters-per-minute under a pressure of maybe eight or ten ounces.

"On the tuba, my intra oral pressure—the pressure as measured in the mouth cavity while playing—we inserted a little tube into the mouth while playing, and the pressure was read—goes as low as two ounces in general playing, but at the same time, my flow rates may go anywhere from seven-liters-per-minute playing as softly as I can, to well in excess of 120 liters-per-minute playing in full volume.

"Dr. Benjamin Burrows who helped me with these experiments was rather intrigued with the fact that you could draw one curve for the entire brass family in terms of how much air is used, and how much pressure is used in producing this flow rate on the instruments.

"Wherever we played notes that were enharmonic, even though they were on different instruments—our work efforts and flow rates were practically identical. As an example, when I played a high C at a given dynamic that we were working to, I was using about six ounces of intra oral pressure and about ten liters flow rate per minute, and in graphing this we found that Mr. Herseth, on exactly the same note, was using practically identical pressure and flow.

"On a different note, with Mr. Farkas, again we found that my pressure and his were about the same. Flow was about the same—even though we were using different instruments. Our embouchures in coming to a given size and shape had a certain requirement for the breath in terms of pressure and movement."

BR - "The flow rate increases for lower notes on a given instrument?"

AJ - "In the brass family, yes. At a given dynamic level, the flow rate is almost invariably greater in the low range compared to the high range."

BR - "And the pressure decreases for the lower notes?"

AJ - "Exactly."

BR - "But now, when you say that different instruments have the same flow rate and same pressure for a given same note . . ."

AJ - "Enharmonic, yes."

BR - "Say for middle C, does that mean then that as the tuba increases its flow rate to ten, the trumpet decreases its flow rate down to ten?"

AJ - "Exactly. As the trumpet goes into his low range, the pressure eases off and his flow increases—as I go into my high range on the tuba, my pressure increases and the flow decreases."

BR - "Terrific. What are the implications of this? There must be millions."

AJ - "Well, there are many implications, as you say, one is psychological to those of us who play the tuba. We must realize that we do not have to work very hard when we play in the high range. I have many students who will go into severe isometric contraction simulating the work effort of the trumpet when he is working in his high range, when actually it is not needed."[213]

"Tuba players use their breath up about three times as fast as the horns and trumpets do, and as a result, should be permitted to breathe more frequently. [This comment is based on playing at the same proportionate volume levels as the higher pitched instruments]."[214]

The embouchure for the tuba requires low pressure air but in large quantities. For soft playing, the flow rate can be as low as seven liters per minute. In a work involving low, loud playing, for example the Wagner *Ring* operas, the flow rate can be as high as 140 liters a minute. At the other end of the scale, an oboe may require seven liters at a loud dynamic. Because of the high flow rate required by the tuba, its players commonly suffer from hyperventilation {see: Physical Elements Hyperventilation/Hypoventilation}.

Going up an octave almost doubles the amount of intra thoracic pressure. Jacobs states, "On the trumpet, if you use ten ounces of pressure while you are playing, for the next octave you may go to approximately twenty ounces of pressure. That again is simply tied into the mass of air so that you blow with greater volumes of air—thick air. It will be that thick volume of air based on the resistance of your embouchure in that particular register. You cannot use this as a blanket rule for the entire spectrum of notes on your instrument. It will be different in the bottom as well as the top register."[215] The trumpet, conversely, is a low flow rate instrument compared to trombone and tuba, and therefore uses less air but under higher pressure.

The oboe requires the least amount of air of all wind instruments. In pianissimo playing, the flow rate is about two and one-half liters per minute and in fortissimo, would go up to about five liters per minute.[216]

Jacobs elaborates on this. "The oboe is almost like a static breath pressure. Ray Still [former CSO principal oboe] has the lung capacity of slightly more than five liters. He has a flow rate of about five liters per minute (in loud playing). So, if he were to take a full breath at that particular flow rate, he could obviously hold a note for a full minute. Now, if he is playing softly, he will have a flow rate of maybe three liters per minute. So he can go considerably more than a minute."[217]

The musculature of the body is capable of extremes with the use of air pressure. For example, to equate pressure to speed, a cough can generate a release of air up to one hundred miles an hour.

Lips [Embouchure]

Although many students come to Jacobs complaining about embouchure problems, he rarely finds problems with the embouchure.

"The most common problems I have seen over the last sixty-odd years I have been teaching are with respiration and the tongue. Surprisingly enough, I rarely find problems with the embouchure. That might sound strange because people come to see me because of problems with their embouchure, but frequently it is the embouchure reacting to a bad set of circumstances and failing—it is simply cause and effect. If we change the cause of the factor, it is easy to clear up the embouchure. The embouchure is not breaking down, it is trying to work under impossible conditions. When you are starving the embouchure for air volume, giving it all sorts of air pressure but not quantity, it cannot work. Very quickly you will be struggling to produce your tone. Just increase your volume of air not by blowing hard, but by blowing a much thicker quality of air. Very frequently the air column is just too thin."[218]

The three basic requirements for sound are pitch vibration, motor function and resonance {see: Instruments}. For brass instruments, pitch vibration is done through the embouchure based on length, thickness and tension. Motor function is the breath that fuels the vibration of the lips and the motion of the fingers to press a valve or key. The amount of air needed to play an instrument depends on the needs of the embouchure.

The source of stimulus for the embouchure is a signal from the brain passed through the seventh cranial [facial] nerve to the lips. Neurons in the brain transmit the same signal to each muscle fiber in the embouchure. The fifth cranial nerve [trigeminal] is the sensor sending signals from the lips back to the brain but it receives little information from the embouchure {see Mental Elements: Nerves}.

The signal coming through the seventh cranial nerve from the brain to the lips has to motivate a message. "When we use wind, we have the motor activity of the lips. But the lips do not have to respond to wind. They can resist wind and not respond at all. They must have a message and wind. On the scale of importance, I would put 85 percent into psychological attitudes of *song* so that the lips will have a message, and 15 percent into *wind* as a matter of movement."

Jacobs compares singers with brass players. "Instead of vocal chords in the larynx, we have vocal chords in the larynx of the tuba, which is the embouchure."[219]

The lips vibrate from the center of the lips outward towards the mouthpiece rim. In the development of tissue, there is hypertrophy of fibers (an increase in size rather than the number of constituent cells). The musculature of the embouchure is not only the orbicularis oris. It is not made up of a simple muscular group but a "basket-weave" of muscle tissue to protract, retract, elevate or depress the lips. In elementary players, the tissue has not yet developed and their range and endurance are affected. As students continue to play their instruments, their muscle fibers are developed and skills will develop. This is true of all muscle groups whether from lifting weights or playing a brass instrument.

To help build the embouchure's muscles, Jacobs suggests, "Continuous sound in itself is embouchure building and when it is carried throughout the range of the horn, [and we must include dynamic range as well as pitch range], we will certainly bring about embouchure strength. If we include fast changes of pitch in interval form as well as scale form, then we will achieve our goal as velocity tends to refine the embouchure form and to reduce the amount of change in musculature involved."[220]

Unfortunately, younger brass players try to control the embouchure tissue to control sound. Jacobs simply tells them to do the opposite, "Control the sound to control the meat. Think less of the muscle fibers and think like a great artist."

Throughout the years, there has been much misinformation disseminated about the embouchure. For example, as a youngster, Jacobs read that an embouchure does not vibrate!

"The embouchure has to be a source of vibration. It cannot vibrate without air—without a moving column of *wind*. If we could substitute electrical current in the lips to create vibration, we would not need *wind*, but we would still need the vibration."[221]

Both brass and woodwind families of instruments share the need of air to fuel vibration. For woodwind instruments, with the exception of the flute family, vibration is from the instrument's reed. For brass instruments, the mouthpiece rim isolates the vibrating area of the lips. Unlike many teachers, he is not overly concerned with mouthpiece placement.

"There's too much attention paid to the appearance and feel of an embouchure. There should be more attention paid to how you sound and function.

If you set rules you will limit the ability to advance."[222]

An embouchure can be just as effective whether it has an upper / lower ratio of fifty / fifty or seventy / thirty. It does not necessarily have to be centered on the lips. Jacobs' own embouchure is not perfectly centered!

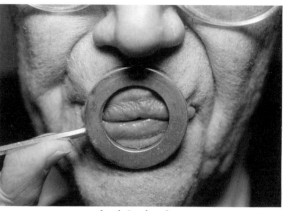

Jacobs' embouchure
Photo by John Taylor

"I'm not putting the embouchure down, but we cannot teach embouchure. We are all born with lips, and lips develop as we play music. They become what we call an embouchure, but embouchure comes into being through the music we play, not by mechanical procedures. They can appear unorthodox and still work. An embouchure that looks perfect might be silent because there is no signal along the nervous system ordering the sound. You have to order the note by the sound of it, not by shaping the lip and blowing against it as if it were a wooden reed."

Jacobs says this in a simpler way. "You don't need to control the embouchure to control the sound—you need to control the sound to control the embouchure."

During master classes, Jacobs demonstrates embouchure by playing something simple like *Pop Goes the Weasel* on a mouthpiece rim. First he will play it with his normal embouchure, then on the extreme right of his lips followed by the extreme left. Finally, he will cross his upper and lower lips and play it. It sounds better with some embouchures than others but the point he is making is that the signal being sent from the brain to every muscle fiber in the lips is the same. The fibers are not equally developed across the lips, but they are being sent the same message.

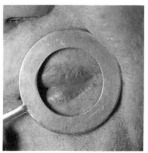

Photo by John Taylor

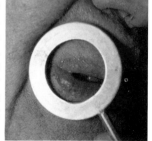

Photo by John Taylor

124

"Too much emphasis is placed on the appearance and feel of the embouchure rather than the resultant sound. If you set rules, there will be a diminishing advancement of the player."

"Many players will have considerable difficulty playing in the low range at first, but usually the embouchure learns to cope with the low vibratory rate on a trial and error basis. There is a general principle of embouchure involved in producing range on the tuba. In descending into the lower range of the tuba, we play with somewhat thicker surfaces as they will vibrate more slowly and still give a firm sound. The opposite is true in the extreme upper range. Rotate the lips inward upon themselves rather than assuming a broad smiling position. The resulting tighter lip surfaces will vibrate faster. We must be sure that the lips do not become stiff, or it will be difficult to obtain proper response."[223]

There has been much controversy about shifting the placement of the mouthpiece for various ranges. When Jacobs first entered the Curtis Institute, he had difficulty with the high range. "When I got to classes and to my private studio with Philip Donatelli, I could hardly play the high notes. One day I asked Donatelli to play a passage from Berlioz's *Overture to Benvenuto Cellini.* I was having problems getting the high G in that particular piece

Excerpt of the tuba part to Berlioz's Overture to Benvenuto Cellini

"Because he had a short upper lip, Donatelli had a mouthpiece with the top of the rim cut off making a flat section so it could fit under his nose. He simply shifted the mouthpiece placement up where he would play into the small section of the mouthpiece near the bottom when he would go up to high G.

"Here I was, a former trumpet player and thought, 'My God, he is changing his lip—his embouchure!' I had read articles that advised never to change the embouchure. I had accepted this advice and never changed. When I saw him change, I took the horn back and tried the same thing. I played the G above high C, and the G above the G above the high C. I practically had all the high notes on the tuba that I did on the trumpet by using a trumpet embouchure. I never had any trouble with high notes after that."

Some mouthpiece pressure against the lips is important to ensure a proper seal around the vibrating portion of the lips. However, unlike a wooden reed, the lips need proper blood circulation. If too much mouthpiece pressure is applied, tissue can be damaged. To help, Jacobs suggests, "In general, the lips have good circulation. Under extreme conditions they can be bruised. The usual result of this mistreatment is a circulation problem. When a player holds the mouthpiece on the lips too long, swelling develops. If swelling disrupts the embouchure, rest is the best cure. When that is not possible, use a slightly smaller dynamic range and avoid the very top notes of the instrument. The swelling from fluid accumulation will clear up with twenty-four to forty-eight hours of rest. The best procedure keeps the brain occupied with music, keeping it from self-analysis and possible downward spiral."

A common problem is that of a double buzz, or as Jacobs calls it, "segmentation." This happens when the embouchure is set for vibrations higher than what is actually desired. A major factor is insufficient air to fuel the vibration. It is, in fact, hardly ever an embouchure problem. The tongue's position is too high and forward in the mouth. To correct segmentation, adjust the embouchure to vibrate at the pitch that is desired—play with a thicker air stream and keep the embouchure open.

When asked "How can I get power in the trumpet's high register?" Jacobs responds, "The small embouchure surface needed for high pitch and the big push needed for amplitude makes a delicate situation. Danger lies in pushing against resistance. Instead of hard blowing, move toward a bigger sound based on the buzz of the embouchure. Zero-in on the buzz of the lips in a lower octave then keeping the same feeling for buzz, play in the upper octave."

Tongue [Articulation]
Next to problems with respiration, the most common problems with which students come to Jacobs are those concerning the tongue. The tongue is an unruly organ and has nothing to do with vibration, but can easily get into the air stream and negatively affect the tone's production.

Just as no two performers are alike, no two people's tongues are alike. Therefore, the correct tongue position depends on the person. Jacobs commonly checks the size of a student's tongue and the presence of tonsils.

"Some people's tongues take up most of the oral cavity. There are others with huge tonsils, some have moderate tonsils and a fairly big tongue. I frequently find crowded conditions to the point where even relaxed and properly used oral equipment does not work right simply because it is taking up too much space."[224]

The size of the tongue is important, and should be a consideration in the study of the passage of air through the oral cavity. Any attempt to control the tongue as a muscle will cause disappointment. Focus should not be at the tongue, but at the vibrating lips. The tongue should be given little importance in relation to the lips. Since the amount of air needed to play an instrument depends on the needs of the embouchure rather than the needs of the tongue, Jacobs commonly tells students, "Blow to the lips, not the tongue."

Dutch-born Swiss mathematician Daniel Bernoulli is most famous for his work in the field of hydrodynamics [fluid mechanics]. Bernoulli's law was published in 1738 and is used in many areas, such as aviation as the principle of air compression in jet engines.[225]

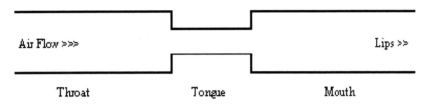

For brass players, the throat [pharynx], tongue and lips form a Bernoulli tube. As air flows from the throat [pharynx] to the smaller opening caused by the tongue, pressure increases in the throat. The least amount of pressure is in the third tube, the mouth. If the tongue is positioned too high, pressure can build in the throat as air compresses to pass through the smaller opening created by the misplaced tongue.

Training the tongue by musculature is difficult if not impossible. Jacobs prefers solving problems of the tongue through speech, with consonant and vowel relationships. For example, the syllables "ooh-thu" and "kee-hoe" are used for the back and forth motion. "Hah" vs. "sssssss" move the tongue from the lower to upper portions of the mouth. To experience a constricted air flow, say "tee, yee, tee, yee." To experience an open airway, say "ah, oh, ooh."

Jacobs spoke about an oboe player who was having problems with her respiration. Her biggest problem was that she had an oversized tongue—"Her tongue in repose was taking up too much room in her oral cavity."

His method of dealing with the problem was not to lecture her about her tongue—there was nothing that she could do about its size. Instead, he started by giving her speech exercises. "We had to do it by opening up the airway. You cannot communicate with a tongue. It will just stiffen up and be very uncooperative. But you can communicate beautifully with it through speech." He started by making the speech out of vowels. He also started by showing her how to compensate for an airway blocked by the tongue. "Take a drowning person, what do you do? He is choking on his tongue—you pull his chin forward and pull out his tongue. Just moving your chin forward will tend to open the pharynx. So she could see right away that she could compensate for her tongue by opening her airway more." He demonstrated how it is done reflexively in speech by the use of vowels. Then bit by bit he built on this insight so that she learned over many months to tie into a vowel concept in which her airway became subconsciously open.[226]

Rather than concentrating on the position of the tongue, Jacobs relies on a proper signal being sent from the brain with the musculature of the tongue responding naturally.

The sensory nerves of the tongue provide very little information to the brain. "I would suggest that the student be more aware of what good articulation should sound like, rather than what it should feel like. With success, in good articulation, will come sensations with which the player can familiarize himself."[227]

Attacks

Jacobs feels the word attack is used improperly. An "attack" is simply the start of vibration of the lips or a reed.

Wind players use only a few consonants to attack notes. The "D" consonant is commonly used for playing legato passages, "K" is used in double or triple tonguing. Jacobs occasionally uses the "H" consonant eliminating movement of the tongue.

The most common is the "T" consonant. In speech, "T" is unvoiced as it only builds up static pressure behind the tongue. In playing a wind instrument, the tongue should be used as a focusing tool, not as a valve to stop the air. If internal air is compressed before it is time for the note to begin, it must be prevented from reaching the embouchure by either blocking it with the tongue or closing the throat. Blocking with the tongue can cause rough or delayed attacks, harsh tone quality, and excessive effort when playing.[228] This can even trigger the Valsalva Maneuver whereby the throat closes to allow the air pressure of the lungs to push down the diaphragm.

Vowels

The tone of an instrument is the vowel, not the consonant of the attack. The "T" of the attack must be minimized. Jacobs emphasizes this by spelling an attack "tAH" or "tOO" rather than "Tah" or "Too." He recommends using the lower vowel forms, "ah," "o," "ooh," and "u." The color of the tone can be changed by using vowels. For a veiled pianissimo, the higher vowel forms, "e" and "i" are used.

With the placement of the tongue, the lower vowel forms create a more open airway than the higher vowel forms. The tongue is its shortest with the "Oh" vowel. "I recommend precise diction in tonguing with the use of the syllables 'tOO' or 'tAH'. Which is chosen does not matter. It is important that the tongue remain as relaxed as possible at all times, with frequent rests to remove any sense of muscle fatigue or strain."[229]

Double and Triple Tonguing

As with all tonguing, multiple tonguing should be approached by using speech patterns. After the "T" attack, using the "K" consonant on the next attack moves the tip of the tongue in an up/down motion. This is great for fast articulations. Unfortunately, while simple in theory, it takes practice to develop properly. Jacobs suggests, "Multiple tonguing should not be attempted until a free use of single tonguing has been achieved. When the student begins multiple tonguing, I usually prefer that he start first with triple tonguing as he does not face the maximal use of the 'K' consonant. The student first attempting to triple tongue should use only short groups of notes."

1 & a	2	3 & a	4
Tu Tu Ku	Tu	Tu Tu Ku	Tu

"I recommend the use of a metronome to encourage rhythmical precision. The tempo should be a comfortable one that the student can cope with while single tonguing. One should learn to pronounce 'Tu-Tu-Ku-Tu' rhythmically in speech and then without voice, but while blowing a column of air, somewhat simulating the conditions of playing. When this maneuver has been extensively practiced, then the application to the instrument begins. It must be stressed in the beginning phases to do the exercises in mid range, using only a monotone for some time. This avoids coordination problems inherent in the use of the valves, and pitch changes in the embouchure."[230]

Releases

Several forms of releases are used on a wind instrument. The most common is simply to stop the air that in turn stops the vibration as if saying "tAH" or "tOH." Many players use the tongue for the release as if saying "tAAt." In this release the tongue is used as a valve to start and stop the air flow to the embouchure. While not as common, many fine players use this type of release.

Staccato

Jacobs feels that a staccato is not a short note, but a short sound with a short vibration or buzz. He spells the staccato's articulation "tOOt." Often a player will emphasize the unvoiced "T" attack and release spelling a staccato note "TooT." The result is a note with too much consonant and not enough tone [the vowel]. Many play a short note based on the tongue. "A short staccato note should be based on vibration in the lip, not the tongue."

Arnold Jacobs: *Song and Wind*

When saying "hut" and holding the final "t," the tongue will hang up on the top of the mouth. By repeating "hut" several times, the tongue springs up and down. It is lowered by the vowel and springs up with the "t." The vowel moves the tongue out of the way of the air column but the "t" consonant blocks the air like a valve. The vowel must be dominant over the "t" consonant or the embouchure will be starved of air.

Jacobs compares a staccato note to a loaf of bread. Bread is cut in whatever thickness needed but the ingredients remain the same. Staccato notes must have the same tone quality as longer notes—the tone should not deteriorate because the note is short.

Although short notes are not always staccato, shorter notes should have more emphasis since the longer ones naturally have that emphasis. The short ones should be brought to that level.

Posture

A common problem with students is poor posture while playing their instrument.

"Posture is very important. We are structured so that the maximal use of air comes in the standing posture. Standing offers the greatest ability to move large volumes of air in and out of the lungs. The closer you get to the supine [laying flat on the back], the poorer it becomes.

"If you think of the respiratory system, it should be thought of not as one bellows, but as a series of segmented bellows, depending on your posture. When lying on your back on the floor, you will find there is little ability to use chest breathing, but you will have a marvelous use of diaphragmatic breathing, which is more than enough to sustain life. However, the diaphragm isolated from the rest of the rib cage provides a rather small breath. There is no such thing as a full breath without the use of the sternum [the breast bone and cartilage that supports the ribs]. If I lean back on the chair and reach over my head, the motion pulls the rib cage up, which is already in the expanded position. That means I cannot use it for breathing in or out. If I bend forward, pressure in the abdominal region under the diaphragm is such that I have great difficulty using diaphragmatic function."

Jacobs tells students to "stand while seated." He has them stand at their highest possible height. They are told to imagine "There is a string pulling you up—like a puppet on a string," There is a small inward curvature of the spine in

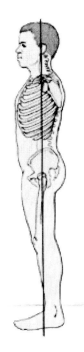

the lower lumbar region just above the belt. As the student sits, he wants them to retain that curvature of the spine. He wants the same upper body position in the sitting position as in the standing position—the idea of standing from the hips, keeping the spine long.

Many slump while playing, resulting in the torso being compressed and expansion of the respiratory system inhibited. A long, straight line, standing position moves air easily.

Aging Process

Professionals from orchestras throughout the world travel to Chicago to see Jacobs for one of his finest specialties, dealing with the body's natural aging process. Many come to him with their career in jeopardy.

"Usually the life of a brass player in a symphony orchestra is not as long as a string player. They used to have a pension arrangement in the Chicago Symphony where a brass player would be eligible for a pension at the age of fifty-five, because so many brass players break down by that age."[231]

Many say, "I would not be playing now if it were not for Arnold Jacobs."

Part of the reason that students come to Jacobs for advice on aging is that he practices what he preaches. Throughout his career he has suffered from a variety of illnesses {see: Retirement}.

Early in his career, Jacobs' peak lung capacity was around five liters {see: Physical Elements: Vital Capacity}. He could expel as much as 80 percent of his capacity in the first second. As he grew older, at times his capacity fell to slightly more than three liters but he was only able to expel 50 percent of his capacity in the first second.

In 1984, he said, "How your body feels when you are playing is not important. I'm getting old and my lip has not felt good in years. I'm on medication for severe lung problems, and the physical comfort I had in playing when I was young is gone. I'm an old cripple, but I still love to play. If you provide your seventh cranial nerve with an excellent musical message, your body and your instrument will respond."[232]

A person's pulmonary functions and lung capacity will peak at eighteen to twenty-one years of age. Afterwards there is a downward curve—a loss of lung capacity that continues for the rest of a person's life. The following graph shows the loss of capacity based on the formula by the American Thoracic Society {see: Physical Elements: Vital Capacity}.[233]

Lung capacity decreases due to the calcification of the costal cartilages and the loss of elasticity, which becomes noticeable in the middle forty age bracket. With illness, lung capacity can also be dramatically changed. Additionally, pressure in the throat and difficulty with the tongue increases with age. Due to the physiological changes, psychological changes follow.

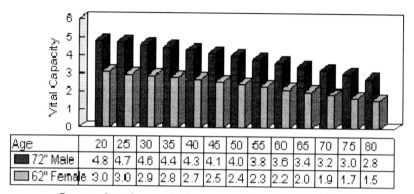

Projected vital capacity for men and women ages 20-80

Age	20	25	30	35	40	45	50	55	60	65	70	75	80
■ 72" Male	4.8	4.7	4.6	4.4	4.3	4.1	4.0	3.8	3.6	3.4	3.2	3.0	2.8
□ 62" Female	3.0	3.0	2.9	2.8	2.7	2.5	2.4	2.3	2.2	2.0	1.9	1.7	1.5

Jacobs advises, "When you get older, your body changes. The time comes when you must learn to use your body differently. It's like learning to play a new instrument. If you become frightened about loss of air, your muscles will tense and you will cut off even more air. For a singer or a wind player, you must have confidence in your capacity to properly use air or you are lost. It is a lot like driving a car. Some cars need to be filled up when they get down to one quarter of a tank. The human body is like that too. As you get older, you must change the way you breathe to correspond with your needs.

"One's vital capacity lowers without the individual realizing it. If he is using limited amounts of air—say he is used to taking half a breath, the air that he may draw from that fuel supply may be adequate to play his instrument at the age of twenty, but not at forty-five or fifty or fifty-five. When the fuel supply lowers, the half that he gets is a smaller quantity than it was at twenty, and one can run into very severe problems."[234]

Nature is unkind to us with deterioration of the body due to the aging process. For many, the biggest problem is to condition themselves for the natural changes within the body. Players must compensate when this happens but it is beneficial to form habits of using a full breath when young. "It is much better to have too much air than to have too little. As you grow older, this becomes more important."[235]

Breathing Exercises

During master classes, Jacobs has students do a variety of breathing exercises. These are physical skills that should be learned *away* from the instrument. As challenge precedes development, be patient with the development of these skills.

Remember when doing these exercises, take breaks when feeling dizzy to avoid hyperventilation. While pausing, reflect and evaluate how much air is in the lungs and how much of the unused air capacity is left in the lungs [such as a glass that is half filled with water]. For visual reinforcement, do these exercises in front of a mirror. As skills develop, sustained notes on the instrument can be played.

It is important to learn how to take the fast breath by analyzing the slow breath.

To open oral cavity:
>In a regular pulse, say "ah, oh, ooh, ah, oh, ooh" then inhale.
>>[Inhale in time.]
>Discover the sensation of inhalation through a large oral cavity.

To eliminate pressurization:
>Take a full breath with the gesture of surprise, keep the throat open
>With a resonant voice say "one," pause with the throat open,
>Say "two," pause with the throat open,
>Say "three,". . . continue.

Exercise of slow full breath:
>Slowly move an arm toward the body in a count of six while inhaling
>>until a full breath is taken.
>Next, in a count of six, move the arm away from body while exhaling.
>Use the arm as a measuring device, when half the breath is exhaled,
>>the arm should be half way.

Study of slow breath in thirds:
>Use arm motion, moving an arm at the elbow toward the mouth in thirds
>>to give visual aid of inhaling and exhaling air while imagining
>>the quantity of air moving in thirds. When ordering a breath, do
>>not focus on air velocity as the primary factor, focus on quantity
>>of air.
>Move air in one third of total capacity.
>Pause [two or three seconds] and reflect on how much air has been taken
>>in and how much room is left for additional air.
>>Take a period of silence to judge the quantity of air.
>Move air in a second third, Pause and reflect.
>Move air in the final third, Pause and reflect.
>Move air out one third, Pause and reflect.
>Move air out two thirds
>Move air in three thirds
>Move air out two thirds

133

Move air in one thirds
Repeat using various combinations, one third, two thirds, three thirds.

Study of fast breath:
    Establish a steady, rather slow beat, about 60 beats per minute.
    In 5/4 time: blow out for counts 1 through 4, breathe in on count 5
        (5) | 1 2 3 4 (5) | 1 2 3 4 (5) | 1 2 3 4 (5) | 1 etc.
        [Inhale on beat (5)]
    In 4/4 time: blow out for 3½ counts, breathe in for ½ count
        4+ | 1 2 3 4 + | 1 2 3 4 + | 1 2 3 4 + | 1 etc.
        [Inhale on the (+) of beat 4]
    In the various meters above, use different tempi.

Study of slow breath:
    Stand with arms at your sides, palms down.
    While inhaling raise arms to encourage the rib cage to elevate and
        snap fingers while counting to five.
    On beat 5 - your hands should be above your head and your lungs should
        be absolutely full. When you hold your breath, do not close
        your throat. Keep the airways open.
    Drop hands to sides while continuing to hold your breath.
        Notice just how full of air you are and how expanded you are
        from the bottom of your lungs to the base of your neck.
    Exhale over five counts.
    Repeat several times.

Although all these studies may be mastered in a week, a year of significant practice may be necessary for full integration into everyday playing.

Mental Elements

While Jacobs' reputation is for his studies related to the physical aspects of playing an instrument, his thoughts on the mental elements of music are equally important.

According to Roger Rocco, "Mr. Jacobs completely understands how the brain creates a physical accomplishment, which is what playing a brass instrument is. He had to overcome his own physical weakness with mental strength! He is a master of the psychology of playing!"

In the brain, Jacobs makes a distinction between anatomical function and intelligence. The physical action needed to accomplish a task is based on the "computer activity of the brain" {see: Physical Elements: The Brain}. The "thinking part of the brain" handles motor impulses carried by nerves throughout the body and human intelligence. "Intelligence copes with the study of the world around us, not the study of the world within us."

Nerves

The brain sends and receives information through the body's system of nerves. They are divided into these systems:

Autonomic - controlling body functions such as heartbeat and normal breathing

Sensory [receptors] - the input to the brain

Motor [effectors] - the output from the brain

These nerves transmit neural impulses to and from the brain traveling only in one direction, like a one-way street.

Among the sensory nerves [or receptors], are the five senses [sight, smell, touch, hearing, and taste] that send information to the brain. These nerves transmit to the brain signals about our relationship to the external world. Information is *gathered* through sensory nerves.

One example is learning in which information is *gathered* through the senses and sent to the brain for evaluation. "Much of a young person's life is spent in acquiring knowledge. In an art form, you are always imparting information—whether it comes from you or is transferred from somebody else through you, you are in a process of imparting knowledge to others.

"You use different nerves. It is the psycho-motor aspect of being a musician. Your thoughts have to come from the brain and are imparted to somebody else as a form of communication, whereas the act of going to school, of acquiring knowledge as a youngster, is receiving, not sending. It has to be turned around so that performance is always being able to tell a story in music, even from the most elementary stage. The attitude must always be that of somebody imparting knowledge to somebody else, even while he is learning."[236]

Information is sent or *departed* through motor nerves [effectors]. "As human beings we move about, we influence the external environment through motor activity—psycho motors, the thought processes that stimulate motor functions. They go down a very special type of nerve from the brain or the spinal cord, to what we call an effector. Maybe it is a finger. Maybe it is the embouchure, a buzz, or the violin bow being effected by what you do with the bow affecting the string on the violin. These messages are motor messages. They are not sensory."[237]

During master classes, Jacobs often says, "When I move this microphone, I'm doing it through motor systems. When I talk to you, I'm using motor systems. You're listening to me using sensors."

The external environment is observed through sensory nerves and affected through motor nerves. When playing an instrument, the brain sends commands to the motor nerves. For observation, sensory nerves send data to the brain for evaluation. Although complex relations between nerves and tissues exist, the body responds best to simple orders.

As with the physiology of muscles {see: Physical Elements: Muscles}, it is better to study the product rather than the methodology. Unfortunately, many musicians, especially students concentrate on the mechanical aspect of performing.

Charles Lipp tells about his experience. "To improve my sound, I played long tones. I sought a norm for tone color. I desired to control each sound to meet the demands of my inner ear. I sent orders to my mouth, lips, jaw, and oral cavity. Each pitch required a unique combination of orders to make an acceptable product. Matching orders with pitches became an end in itself. This strategy resulted in drastic interference with my body's abilities to perform.

"My blunder was to zero-in on individual body parts. I thought they were responsible for individual parts of music making. Instead of training my brain for musical thought, I practiced drills to gain strength and speed. Physical work mis-directed mental energy. Desire for physical control replaced musical thinking. I developed the habit of isometric tension (muscles contracting against muscles with no work being done).

"I lost my music-making ability."

Often a teacher will mistakenly work with a student to alter the methodology of an action rather than the resulting product. The teacher may give "machine like" methods that are not efficient to enable a person to learn. Most of the time, the answer is in the simplicity of psychology, not the complexity of anatomy.

Conceptual

Jacobs has always said that he plays two tubas simultaneously—one in the hand and the other in the mind. The tuba in his hand is the mirror image of his thought. It plays a pitch a split second after the proper signal is sent from the tuba in the mind—the brain. "It does not matter what octave you sing in the mind. What comes out of the instrument should be a mirror image of the conceptual thought of the brain. It is a conceived sound." Although conceptual thoughts such as these have been around for years, Jacobs has formalized them for musicians.

Although he uses the tuba as an example, this philosophy can be applied to all instruments, and to other disciplines. Among Jacobs' students is Bob Carpenter, who, in addition to being a tubist, is an engineer working for NASA.

When he designs a system to do its appointed task, he must conceptualize its use in the vacuum of space with zero gravity that cannot be tested on earth. Another consideration is what may happen in relation to other components of the spacecraft. Most important, he must think of the result of a malfunction as a problem that can have severe consequences and builds a backup system to compensate. He conceives what he would like as an end product and works backwards to achieve it.

On the opposite extreme, imagine a contractor constructing a building using no plans. Problems would occur such as retaining walls not bearing the weight of floors above and the result could be disastrous.

Unfortunately, many musicians play without a concept of the end result—the sound coming from the instrument. Their concept is like the builder with no plans. They play with the instrument in their hand but no instrument in their mind and many mistakes occur. Instead they should conceptualize on the end product—the sound coming from the instrument.

"A constant effort must be made by the student to think musically. He should develop the ability to hear the sound in his mind that he wants to hear from his instrument. This tremendously important concept should be encouraged by renewing it daily."[238]

"The important thing is not what you *sound* like. It's what you *want to sound like*. I have people who come to me and only listen to themselves—they are not conceiving."

Arnold Jacobs: *Song and Wind*

When asked "What do you think about when you play?" Jacobs response was, "I sing in my head what has to go out of the horn. It is like the relationship between a player-piano roll and the keyboard. I am always on the player-piano roll, and never at the keyboard. I don't care how the lip feels—I don't care how I feel. The psycho-motor aspect of playing is a message from one part of the brain that is fed to the lip through the seventh cranial nerve. It goes through a computer activity that you have in the brain, but you are always conceiving the message, just as though you had vocal chords, but had them in the lips. So my whole concentration is not on what I feel like or what I sound like, but what I want the audience to hear. It's like telling a story, but instead of words you tell it with concepts of sound."[239]

Frequently, he will have a student put words to a particular piece of music (usually something silly). This encourages the student to sing in their head.

Often, if a student has rhythmic problems, he will have them use numbers rather than words. A flute student had rhythm problems with Mendelssohn's *Midsummer Night's Dream*. The problem was a lack of *song* from the brain so

Excerpt from the first flute part to Mendelssohn's Midsummer Night's Dream

Jacobs had her sing in her mind to the pitches of the music: *One two-and three-and one two three, one two-and three-and one two three.* When the proper message was sent from the brain, the body responded and the problem was quickly solved.

Imagination is a tool that Jacobs uses frequently. He once told a trumpet player during a master class, "Imagine what the worst player in the world would sound like. Let's hear Ralph Rotten."

The resulting sound was horrible.

"Now, close your eyes and think about what it would sound like if a great artist like Adolph Herseth were playing it. Imitate for me what you just heard in your head—play it like Herseth would."

The young man closed his eyes, listened for a moment to something the rest could not hear, and played the passage again.

The difference in sound was amazing.

Song and Wind

One of Jacobs' most famous phrases is *Song and Wind*. During his lecture at the 1995 International Brassfest in Bloomington, Indiana, he explained:

138

"My approach to music is expressed as *Song and Wind.* This is very important to communicate a musical message to the audience.

"This approach is one of simplicity as the structure and function of the human being is very complex, but we function in a simple manner. When we bring it to the art form it becomes very simple.

"*Song*, to me, involves about 85 percent of the intellectual concentration of playing an instrument, based on what you want the audience to hear.

"You cannot get anywhere without *wind.* If you think of a car, the wheels will not turn without an energy source—the engine. Brass players must have a source of energy as there must be a vibrating column of air for the instrument to amplify and resonate. The musical engine is the vibration of the lips. However, the lips cannot vibrate without *wind.*

"When we combine *Song and Wind*, the musical message, *song*, is the principal element comprising 85 percent of the consciousness. The remaining 15 percent is the application of the breath, *wind*, to fuel the vibration of the lips."[240]

Adolph Herseth puts it another way, "You have to start with a very precise sense of how something should sound. Then, instinctively, you modify your lip and your breathing and the pressure of the horn to obtain that sound."[241]

Wind is the energy source used to fuel the conceptual message of the *song* from the brain. His emphasis of *Song and Wind* shows how much importance Jacobs gives to musical conception. "Study the product, not the method. Mentalize music by making statements, not by asking questions."

Storyteller

Many musicians play beautifully, but very mechanically. They do not convey a message. Jacobs wants a story told, even at the most elementary stages. "We have to be storytellers of sound. Unlike singers, who use words, we use phrase, emotion, and other such tools."

"It is very important that we study emotions in music, style characteristics in music, the art form of music. You can make people laugh, you can make people cry, you make people want to enlist in the Army, you can help them by the moods that the music can be associated with. You have all sorts of abilities to communicate and tell a story through sound."[242]

Acting

Jacobs encourages the study of acting to help musicians put emotion into their music. In musical studies, a student should devote equal time for absorbing and imparting information.

A good actor knows how to communicate to an audience. If he wants to convey rage, he draws upon his experiences that involve rage. If he shows hate, his facial musculature may contract and the audience will sense this without the actor saying a word. For a musician, emotions must be conveyed to the audience through his playing.

To Jacobs, an acting class is a way to study presentation and to play the role of the presenter. He would like to see this incorporated as a part of the curriculum of music schools.

Solfege

A subject that Jacobs strongly recommends is the study of solfege. During his studies at the Curtis Institute, he was enrolled in a solfege class the entire time {see: Curtis Institute: Renee Longy-Miquelle}.

"Solfege converts written notes to sound, a great mental and musical exercise. You should convert printed notes to sounds as quickly and surely as you convert printed words to ideas. The printed word *run* stands for the idea run. The printed note D stands for the sound D. There is a great deal of danger in converting printed notes to fingerings. A musician must refine the skill of converting printed notes to music."

Inner Ear

Another common problem with students is missing the first note of a phrase. They do not hear this note in their minds and consequently miss the note. The study of pitch recall, the ability to hear a note before its being sounded, is commonly called by musicians the "inner ear" and has nothing to do with with the "inner ear" that maintains balanace.

Often Jacobs will ask a student to sing the first note of a phrase and then play it. Frequently, the student cannot do this. An interesting fact is that holding the instrument is often a precondition to hearing a pitch. It is a good cue, but these skills should developed away from the instrument.

David Brubeck observes, "The first step in developing this inner ear is 'post-hearing'—the ability to continue to hear a note after it has ceased vibrating. Mr. Jacobs develops this ability by playing a note on the piano, and allowing silence after it, not requiring the student to match it but merely letting it sink in. Eventually this leads to the 'pre-hearing' of notes before one plays them. By combining this with an active, creative imagination and past models of excellence, one is able to project an outstanding goal mentally. Post-hearing complements the effects of singing a song in your head as you perform. It allows you to rewind the mental tape and hear how your rendition matched your musical goal, all the while keeping distracting self analysis from cluttering the mind during performance. By imagining the best sound, one will be aided in finding the best way of reaching it."[243]

Roger Rocco remembers an amusing "singing" incident that occurred when he was playing the second tuba part in *Deserts* by Edgar Varese with Jacobs.

"There is a very difficult and treacherous high G [above middle C] in the first tuba part. It is played very softly and without accompaniment. Just before the note was coming up during the first rehearsal, I heard Mr. Jacobs quietly vocalizing the note several times. When the moment for him to play the note came, he pressed the valves on his York tuba and sang the note into the horn! There was an immediate congratulatory shuffle of feet from the members of the orchestra. Nobody knew what he had done!

"He turned to me with a gleam in his eye and said, 'My integrity will not allow me to do that again.' There were several more opportunities for him to play the note again both in rehearsal and performances. He played it beautifully every time! But he was always vocalizing it just before he played it. It was another great Jacobs lesson for me!"

Jacobs concentrated on the pitch as he always does. He passed the proper signal from the brain to the vocal chords of the brass player, the embouchure, and played the pitch to perfection.

During a master class, Jacobs was explaining to a bass trombonist that extremes of range must be a part of daily practice. Jacobs wanted him to play the tenor trombone solo from *Bolero*, starting on a B♭ above middle C. The student could not hit the first note even when playing it an octave lower. Finally, Jacobs took his instrument explaining how he played the trombone in the 1930s, he is old and really had not touched an instrument in several weeks (this was after retirement). He then played a single note, a B♭ above middle C to the amazement of the class! He simply heard the pitch in his brain and sent the proper signal to his body.

"Great players hear the pitch before playing it. Although very few are born with 'perfect pitch,' relative pitch can be developed," Jacobs states.

Analysis

As a part of everyday life, we are constantly analyzing situations. The problem is determining how much analysis is needed. All musicians have had a problem with over-analyzing from time to time.

John Taylor writes, "Musicians, by their nature, are above average in intelligence, which is often a double-edged sword. While they can quickly assimilate difficult material, they also tend to analyze their every move as it relates to playing their chosen instrument.

"Music, as taught by Arnold Jacobs, is primarily the mentalization of the sound the player wants to produce in all its facets, rhythm, pitch, tone quality, dynamic, and then that mental soundtrack is transferred to the instrument. How-ever, by the very nature in which sounds are produced on wind instruments, and largely because this process has historically been one of great micro-analysis by writers of method books and other more contemporary teachers who perpetuate the complex, students often find their attention elsewhere than on solely reproducing the sound they seek.

"In his teachings, Jacobs constantly enjoins the student to 'Sound like me,' or, 'Sound like Herseth.' By repeatedly reinforcing this aural concept in a student, he increasingly brings the student into a purer and simpler approach to the instrument.

"One of the greatest problems of wind instrument players is the desire to analyze each and every problem that they incur. A quick thought that, 'I did not really fill my lungs on that breath,' may stimulate a player to inhale more deeply the next time. But the performer who encounters a problem in sound production and then proceeds to analyze his embouchure, soon finds the problem growing by geometrical proportions, until his entire attention is directed toward his perceived embouchure problem and none toward producing beautiful music.

"Arnold Jacobs once said, 'Embouchure is the result of the musical demands placed upon it.' Those musical demands are generated by the brain—the mental tape recorder—and if the mind directs, the body will follow. Which brings us to that very important point. If the mind wills us to pick up a glass of water, we will. But, if we attempt to analyze the muscle groups, how they interrelate and how they lift the glass to our mouth, we will die of dehydration. Similarly, if a brass player becomes obsessed with the muscle groups of his mouth and the remainder of his face, how they constrict to form the lips to produce a buzz, that individual is headed for trouble. This is not to say that one cannot learn this material in his leisure time, but any application to performance will be deleterious. Conversely, if the mental image of a beautiful sound is strong, and concentrated upon, the body will figure out, *on its own*, how to make that sound. Of course, it may be only one note, but once the mental image is there, it multiplies rapidly."

Although a little analyzing can be harmless, over-analyzing can cause problems. If the mind is flooded with positive thoughts, it will perform in a positive manner. By over analyzing, questions are being asked such as "Am I doing this right?" The mind is flooded with negative thoughts. Jacobs states, "Don't get caught on what not to do, instead, concentrate on what to do."

The mind has the capability for a certain amount of information. If the mind is flooded with too many thoughts, it will overload. Concentration is lost and the note is missed—caused by over-analyzing. Jacobs simply calls this "paralysis by analysis."

Daniel Kohut tells about this situation. "A common error made by instrumental and vocal teachers alike is that they try to teach complex performance tasks like breathing through analysis of physiological function. Merely directing attention to the abdominal muscles, the throat or some other body area usually creates still more muscular tension in that same area. Then, if we also try to consciously control muscular action, things really get bad. The usual result is one of mental overload, thus precluding any real chance of achieving relaxed concentration. Together these muscular tension and mental overload problems bring about what is best described as 'paralysis through analysis.'"[244]

As Jacobs says, "De-emphasize the mechanics of self-analysis and simply play music."

Conditioned Reflexes and Stimuli

A conditioned reflex is a learned or acquired response to an external stimulus. It is an act that we are not born with, but develop through repetition. These repetitions create a neural pathway to the brain and a habit is created.

At the 1995 International Brassfest, Jacobs addressed this.

"One part of the brain will accept what you order as you go through a period of conditioning. In music, we would call this practice—conditioning studies, scales, intervals, drill forms, and so forth. We are actually creating a programming that goes in the brain where these things can be absorbed to become a conditioned reflex—a reflex that we are not born with, but it becomes a reflex simply by the fact that we have repetition.

"From that point on, once you have the reflex, all that it takes to bring it into being is a stimulus, a thought process in the brain that says, for example, 'I want to touch my nose.' You reach up and touch your nose—it's not a big deal. Somebody throws a ball and usually, you catch it and maybe even throw it back.

"These are done without thought of musculatures, or planning of what to do with various parts of your physical structure. They are in response to the stimulus of catching the ball, or touching the nose, or whatever we have to do in a physical factor.

"In playing musical instruments, there are physical factors involved as we all know so well. Some of them are quite complicated, and actually, they are very serious, and we have to do them well. What we are dealing with here, in the art of playing, is the series of developments that come through taking a musical instrument, going through the course of training with the teacher and student relationship.

"Do this. Do that. I want this. I want that. The student listens, the teacher advises and guides. You see that this conditioning starts based on a repetitive type of maneuvering. If you play a C scale, and then you repeat, and play the C scale a second time, then a third time, and maybe in one day you do it five times, then play some music that involves the same notes, you are getting many, many repetitions., and the brain is absorbing it.

"It does not just imprint in the memory banks like it would on our modern computers today—the human biology requires repetitive maneuvers before it becomes a permanent, neural pathway in the brain.

"The reason I am saying this is simply that from the time we start to play, we are actually developing these reflexes whether we realize it or not. If you do this in the study of music, it's a very, very beneficial approach."[245]

Many times Jacobs uses this analogy, "Anything we do that is repetitive is habit forming. Habits are like walking through a field of grass. The first time you walk through the grass, it springs up behind. After continuous walking over the spot, the grass stays down. Eventually, the grass wears down and a path is formed. In the mind, a neural pathway is formed. Once something is learned, it is learned forever."

Forming New Habits to Replace Problem Habits

Much of Jacobs' teachings deals with the breaking of old habits and acquiring new habits. Roger Rocco explains, "Once a correct or incorrect habit has been learned through repetition, it cannot be unlearned. For example after not riding a bicycle for many years, people do not unlearn that skill. The skill may diminish, but it will not be erased. Players are held hostage by the Dr. Jekyll and Mr. Hyde syndrome, where old habits dominate until new habits are formed and dominate the old."

An old habit cannot be discarded. It can only be bypassed by the development of a new habit. "You *renew* an old habit by trying to fight it. Rather, establish a new habit to *replace* it," Jacobs says. It will take time for the new habit to establish itself in the brain. Eventually, the poor habit will diminish as the new one replaces it.

Jacobs uses several psychological processes to achieve desired responses by altering stimuli. Much of this work is done away from music and the instrument because the instrument stimulates old habits. It is also better to play familiar music to help break habits rather than unfamiliar music.

Jacobs uses several psychological tools. Those include:

Strangeness

Anything that is new is strange. Maximum efficiency comes from introducing strangeness to change the perception of a stimulus. It is this "altered" stimulus that is then used to develop the desired response, sidestepping the previously conditioned incorrect response. Introducing strangeness accomplishes change very rapidly and can make learning easier. Often Jacobs will say, "Strangeness is good."

"I like to subject myself and my students to what I call strangeness, the sudden withdrawal of familiar ways of doing things. I take away their instruments and make them sing a piece that they are working on, or have them do things like play while jogging around the studio or doing deep knee bends to demonstrate the irrelevance of crude strength to playing. They find they can play well with diverted strength, because they have to concentrate. I have them hyperventilate or do some exercise to get out of breath and then have them play, to show how a reduced lung capacity, if used efficiently and with concentration, can still supply the amount of air needed to play well.

"Familiar patterns of playing often perpetuate familiar problems, whether with embouchure, breathing, or fingerings. Though I am familiar with them and glad to go into them if a student wants me to, I do not teach methods, because an excellent sound in the mind contains in itself everything necessary to its expression."[246]

An example of strangeness are brass players who commonly switch mouthpieces in trying to get a desired result. "The strangeness of a new mouthpiece may immediately cause better playing. A few weeks later, when more familiar with the mouthpiece, the performer might go back to the old mouthpiece. It is the strangeness of the new mouthpiece that permitted the change in his playing."

Exaggeration
A common analogy for combining two actions together, is to bring black and white into various shades of grey. For example, if walking at a slow speed were represented by the color white and running by black, if we were to walk at a medium speed, the representation would be a mixture of black and white. This would produce shades of grey, the shade depending on speed—the faster the speed, the darker the shade of grey.

If Jacobs would like to move a student towards a different direction, he might have a student move from a shade of dark grey to white. There will be crudities at first, but out of these crudities skills will develop. Eventually, the student will settle on a median point, perhaps a shade of light grey.

David Brubeck observes, "Often the difference between the right way to do something and the student's current attempt is very slight, but the student is unable to recognize the difference. In one particular instance, Mr. Jacobs instructed a student to pronounce Kee-Tee-Yee, then take a breath, followed by Oh-Ah-Ooh and a breath. This illustrates the two extremes of one's oral cavity resistance. The slight difference between an 'A' sound, as in '*day*,' is difficult to distinguish from the syllable Ah, though it marks a significant contrast in one's tone on a brass instrument. However, one can easily feel and hear the vast distinction between Eee and Ooh."[247]

Simplicity
Simplicity, not complexity of knowledge, provides the precise physical control needed to perform.

"If we study the complexities of the body, we lose simplicity and go to complexities that are impossible to comprehend. We must think simply. If I had to handle my physical structures based on my knowledge of anatomy, I would have had to quit the profession years ago. Use an adult's outlook for studying the art form and the emotional content of the artistic matter to communicate, but use a child's outlook for simple physiological approaches. Think like a child, so simplicity comes through. Make simple tasks simple, not complex."

Imitation

"Imitation was, is, and always will be the best method of teaching."

Jacobs first started playing the bugle when he was ten years old. His mother would play bugle calls on the piano and he would imitate her on the bugle. "A young child learns to produce sounds, first by hearing them, then by producing them. So the phenomenon of imitation is one of our very powerful learning tools. The sense of sight is also extremely powerful. Imitation of sounds and sight and both senses reinforcing each other is one of the ways to go."

Frequently, he will play a passage on a student's instrument. "Listen to this carefully. This is what a good note sounds like on your equipment. This is what a bad note sounds like. I have them think about it for a moment to establish recall in silence. Then I ask them to try to sound the way I did. Imitation is like putting a player-piano roll on so that the keyboard knows what to do—the act of trying to sound like a very good player."[248]

Jacobs encourages conceiving what a great artist would sound like and imitating them. "My students come here and they're having trouble, but they're still functional and I'll say, 'Well, how would Herseth sound on this passage?' They will think a moment and they try to play it and they sound better every time. I will tell them 'You see how much better Herseth is than you!' There's your imagery!"[249]

Imitating a player of another instrument [or voice] is another great tool. "If the student hears a great trumpet player play a great solo, he should try to play just as well on the tuba. He should learn phrasing at first by imitation so that he has a base for his own creative thoughts at a later period. But in the elementary aspects, where he is acquiring abilities and developing according to challenges, it is perfectly legitimate to imitate characteristics from a wide variety of fine musicians and absorb their abilities. Your own creativity must be built on top of this as well."[250]

As a student at the Curtis Institute, Jacobs was enrolled in the phrasing class taught by Marcel Tabuteau, at that time principal oboist of the Philadelphia Orchestra. Jacobs would always bring in operatic arias and material from other instruments. By imitating other instrument's phrasings, he rapidly developed as a musician.

"It is perfectly legitimate to imitate characteristics from a wide variety of fine musicians and absorb their abilities. Your own creativity must be built on top of this as well. The point is, you do not consider the tuba, you consider music. I knew nothing about nothing as a youngster, but I was brought up where there was a great deal of music. As a result, I played, on the tuba, music such as the wonderful soprano solo, *One Fine Day* from *Madame Butterfly*, and enjoyed it very much. I was not doing it for the public, I was doing it because I enjoyed playing it. It had similar emotional aspects that the singer would have."[251]

Motivational

It is an understatement to call Jacobs a great motivator. He has a natural positive outlook on life that resonates whenever he speaks. He can always find something good that a student is doing.

Unlike many teachers, he does not dwell on the parts of a student's playing that are not good. Even with a poor player, he always finds something positive. For example, if they played badly and there was nothing good to say about their playing, he might ask, "Do you enjoy playing?" He starts at this point to motivate the student. Luckily, most students play well and he simply tells them that.

"A player must have the attitude that no one should sound better than he does. Since there are people like Adolph Herseth in the world who never play badly, other players must bring themselves up as close as possible to this level."

He is constantly telling students the story that a conductor is outside the door with a $100,000 contract for a major orchestra. "If you play like you deserve it, the position is yours." This is usually sufficient motivation!

Senses

We gather information through our sensory nerves—eyes, ears, and tactile senses. Jacobs stimulates all the senses. David Brubeck writes, "A key element here is Mr. Jacobs' multi-sensory approach. Stated simply, this is the theory that by experiencing something with more than one sensory capacity, or in more than one way, one will achieve a greater understanding."[252]

He will have students do a variety of things with the breath that show results outside the body. Feeling their breath as *wind* passing over their lips, blowing air on the back of their hand, blowing out matches, blowing up paper bags, blowing imaginary paper boats in water and similar acts. While breathing, he has students move a hand in and out as if they were sucking it in and out by the breathing. Since one cannot actually feel one's diaphragm within the body, he will have a student move a hand up and down under the sternum, simulating the movement of the diaphragm inside. These are bringing in another sense to reinforce the sense of feeling within the body.

One of Jacobs' trademarks is the use of external devices. All these tools are used away from the instrument, and while they vary in use and design, the equipment provides a visual stimulus. For a student, seeing a ball or gauge moving gives visual reinforcement to the act of moving air. Some can be adjusted to vary the resistance, some can be used with a mouthpiece, but all introduce strangeness to the student. The skills learned here are then transferable back to the instrument.

During the 1950s, he first assembled the equipment for his studio from various sources. While he continues to use some of the original equipment, he is always expanding his collection. In 1982, he introduced to the music world simple, inexpensive plastic devices [air bag, *Breath Builder, Inspiron,* and *Voldyne®*] that perform some of the same functions as much of the original equipment. Finally, these items are now available to the student to be used on a daily basis {see: The Jacobs' Studio}.

Mouthpiece Practice

When Jacobs was a boy, he was hospitalized for months {see: Retirement}. At that time, he was playing the trumpet, and his mother brought him his mouthpiece. It was here that he first learned the benefit of mouthpiece practice. He was buzzing the mouthpiece all the time. When they finally released him, he went home and picked up his trumpet. After a few moments to reestablish the feeling of the partials, he found that he played better than when he entered the hospital.

By playing only on the mouthpiece, the instrument's acoustic resonation is removed. There is much stimulus involved with the instrument. A player will pick it up, put his hand in position, and a signal is sent from the mind to the embouchure at the mouthpiece. At this point, the instrument resonates.

To introduce change, removing the instrument will force the student into recall and mentalization so that he can immediately concentrate on the musical factor. All of the tissues involved in playing are still involved with the exception of the hands holding and fingering the instrument. When returning to the instrument, the signal being sent to the embouchure is usually improved.

Another method of mouthpiece practice is using a mouthpiece rim [visualizer]. Jacobs does not recommend buzzing without a ring to isolate the embouchure's vibrations that go from the center to the edges of the lip. There is the possibility of deterioration of the lip's muscles without the use of a rim. He recommends that buzzing should only be done in the low and middle range for only two or three minutes at a time.

Jacobs does not encourage practicing long tones or drill forms on the mouthpiece. Instead he encourages practicing music and songs to connect musical thoughts and the lip. "I never give exercises or drills, but challenge students with simple music, such as *Pop Goes the Weasel*."

After studying with Jacobs, Paul Ebbers writes, "Playing on the mouthpiece alone removes the instrument, but it does not remove the need to think. Mouthpiece practice helps connect the ability to hear a pitch in your head with the ability to play the pitch with your lips. Many players do not send a pitch into the instrument—they just blow and use their fingers to find the notes. Invariably, successful players can sing their parts. If you learn to sing using your voice to create the right pitch, sound, and style, the concepts can be transferred to an instrument. The same ideas will apply to the 'vocal chords' of the tuba—your embouchure."[253]

Performance

Jacobs' professional career spans more than seven decades. He has performed as a soloist and in many musical ensembles, most notably fifty-one seasons in professional orchestras. Additionally, he has performed in concert bands, brass ensembles, brass quintets and jazz groups of various sizes. With this vast background, he has many opinions about various aspects of performance.

Procedures

Many elements are needed during performance. Primarily they fall into the categories of pitch, color, and phrase.

Pitch

Pitch must first be conceived in the mind {see: Mental Elements: Conceptual} for the appropriate signal to be sent to the body to initiate motor functions. The mind sets the body to obey the acoustic laws of the instrument.

A part of playing in any musical group is intonation. Musicians must be in tune with themselves and other musicians. While this sounds simple, in practice it can be complex.

Many orchestras tune higher than A=440. During Jacobs' first season with the Chicago Symphony, he had problems adjusting to the pitch of the orchestra.

"Pittsburgh always tuned to A=440. When I came to Chicago, they tuned to A=442, and I had a terrible time getting my instrument to go sharp enough. I was complaining about it to Renold Schilke one day, and he went to his locker, took out a hacksaw and chopped a couple of inches off my main tuning slide and the horn was in tune after that."

A performer must have flexible intonation in ensemble situations. "Do not insist that you are the only one in tune. The pitch of a group constantly changes." In an orchestra, the pitch often rises during performances. The pitch may increase to A=447 or even higher.

The temperature of the stage can also present problems. With the heat generated from lighting systems compounded by one hundred people on stage and several thousand members of the audience, the hall's temperature rises, causing the general pitch to rise.

Often, Jacobs would only play the second half of the performance. While this may not be a problem on many instruments, the size of the tuba compounds the problem, especially during the winter months. He would often leave his instrument on stage during parts of the performance that he was not playing. He could very easily have taken his tuba with him to the dressing room downstairs, but the temperature of this room was often far different from the temperature on the stage. If he came on stage with a tuba that had a temperature five degrees lower than on stage, when the temperature of the instrument rose to the hall's temperature, the pitch would also rise. If he tuned with the orchestra before the temperature adjustment, he would rapidly find himself playing sharp. The solution was simple—leave the instrument on stage so it would be at the ambient room temperature when tuned.

Besides playing in tune with other musicians, performers must play in tune with themselves. All notes in all ranges must be in tune with each other. There are acoustic problems with various valve combinations on brass instruments. Trumpet players are constantly pushing their slides out for valve combinations of the first and third or all three valves. Many tuba players are constantly pushing and pulling various valve slides. Most tubas are made with a fourth valve and many with an additional fifth valve to help with intonation. Other methods are used to correct intonation. Often, if a note is out of tune using the first and second valves, substituting the third valve may solve the problem.

These are all solutions to the intonation problem that involve adjusting the hardware of the instrument to the pitch. No instrument is perfectly in tune. A performer must be familiar with their instrument and how it resonates and its particular intonation strengths and weaknesses. Slides must be set in a position that will help with the adjustment of pitch. Often, they may need to be shortened to enable an instrument to play at a higher pitch.

Although possessing an extremely fine ear, whenever Jacobs would get a new instrument, he would always test the intonation with an electronic tuner in his studio. By the time he used it for performance, he knew the "problem" notes.

Another solution can be used with adjusting the concept of pitch. "If you think a note in tune, you will play it in tune. If a proper signal is sent from the brain, the body will respond. A performer must mentally sing the pitch," Jacobs states.

Commonly a brass player will tune a pitch by adjusting the embouchure to "lip up" or "lip down." While this is a common practice used by all brass players, care must be taken not to affect the tone quality.

Range

Jacobs refers to high and low notes as fast and slow vibrations. To develop range, a performer must simply practice and develop in both the high and low ranges of their instrument. To improve a pitch in the higher register, play the pitch an octave lower three times, then as written, for example G, G, G, g, g, g. "Let the lower notes be the teachers of the higher ones."

Jacobs offers these thoughts, "You cannot immediately have a great sound when you play very high or very low, you develop it just like the mid-range. You establish always the sense that—'I'm elementary in the very highs and in the very lows compared to the norm.' So you start developing these weak areas into excellence. You can take bad sounds and convert them into good sounds, but you cannot take silence and convert it. You have to go through the developmental stages."[254]

Tone Color

Every performer has their own distinct sound. Like a fingerprint, the tone production of no two performers are alike. Jacobs has his own signature tone that separates him from any other musician. This was developed through various influences in his career.

A performer must first develop a concept of the sound that he would like to achieve. In elementary stages, he will probably emulate the sound of a player he admires. Later, other influences such as air stream, embouchure, instrument, mouthpiece, performance hall and other variables will influence his tone. A performer's sound should vary depending on the music being played.

Jacobs constantly alters his tone. In a Mahler symphony, he will use a large tuba with a large, dark tone. In a solo, he might use a smaller instrument with a shallow mouthpiece and, consequently, a smaller sound. Besides the change of equipment, he will change his concept to the desired tone he wants to achieve.

Great care must be used to develop an even tone, and a consistently good quality of sound in all registers. "One of the most important factors in approaching tone building studies, is to do so with a plentiful supply of air in the lungs, and to use a considerable volume level—forte or louder. The tone should not sound forced or strained," Jacobs states.[255]

Dynamics

The velocity of the air stream varies with dynamics. In soft playing, the air stream is slow, for loud playing, the air stream is fast. The tone of the instrument is like a ball riding at the top of water spurting from a fountain. For loud playing the ball rides high on a tall jet of water [a large, fast-moving stream of air]. For soft playing, the ball rides low on a short jet of water. For dynamics, a musician must be concerned with the velocity of the air, not air pressure {see: Physical Elements: Air Flow/Air Pressure}.

As Jacobs explains, "If you were to blow fast air you would get louder. The fortissimo would depend on faster blowing until the amplitude of vibration of your vibrating surfaces increases. If you want an extreme pianissimo, practice diminuendos. Start with the most beautiful mid-dynamic sound, then practice playing softer and softer, and you will find the amplitude of vibration is decreasing as the breath is barely moving. The main thing about the study of dynamics and velocity of air is to tie them together by having a wonderful mid-dynamic sound, and then move it outward to louder and softer extremes, while still carrying the quality of tone by carrying the excellence of the sound so it is not just a loud blat or a useless sound. Always do it based on the product of the sound itself."[256]

At the Curtis Institute, Marcel Tabuteau used a numbering system to teach the concept of controlling dynamics {see: Curtis Institute: Marcel Tabuteau}. For example, a crescendo from pianissimo—one on the scale—to forte—in this case, five on the scale—would have to pass through the other dynamic ranges between.

There should be consistency with tone in a wide variety of dynamics, ranging from piano to forte or fortissimo."Think of dynamics as like the control knob on a radio. You turn it down, but you do not lose the qualities of the sound. The same thing occurs when you play softer. You should keep the quality of sound all the way back to pianissimo. You learn to play a louder sound with excellence of tone, not by great physical effort," Jacobs says.[257]

A common problem among students is determining the extremes of dynamics. Jacobs says, "The average dynamic would be a sound that can be heard comfortably in a nice room, a nice auditorium, where the performer does not have to strain. He should be able to make a diminuendo from it and crescendo from it."[258]

"The point half way between dynamic extremes is the norm for general playing. Establish quality at the norm, and keep this quality while working toward the extremes," he explained.

Vibrato

Vibrato is a fluctuation of frequency, amplitude, or a combination of both. It will show on an oscilloscope as pitch averaging. On a decibel meter it will show as amplitude averaging. Frequency and amplitude variations in combination produce the resultant tone quality. Vibrato should be more a conceptual thought than the realization of specific physiological functions coordinated for the purpose.

To teach vibrato, Jacobs suggests first demonstrating the sound to students. At first only the jaw or lip vibrato should be used. There should be exaggeration of the physical maneuver of the jaw or hand moving the valve or slide. The sense of sight should be added with the use of an oscilloscope or tuner. However, teaching should be based on the sound of the vibrato rather than the methodology of it.

At times, the vibrato's pitch fluctuation can fool players into playing off the resonant center of their instrument. Playing off the resonant center requires tuning compromises. The resonant center is blurred as a result, and the amplifying power of the instrument is lost. Use vibrato to search for the best, most resonant pitch center. Another important consideration is how much vibrato to use and most important, when and when not to use it. Above all, vibrato must be controlled.

Phrasing

Just as a group of words forms a sentence to form a statement, a musical phrase consists of a series of notes put together to form a phrase. Jacobs says, "Audiences hear phrases—artists build them. Don't play phrases, build them." While playing a phrase, a performer should bypass no note. "Play a phrase of notes like walking up a flight of stairs—don't skip any, step on each note." Phrases must have a musical message and tell a story—a performer must be a storyteller of sound.

"Just as a sentence is made of individual words, a musical phrase is made of individual notes. A written word represents something as musical ink spots represent pitch, color, and phrase," Jacobs states.

While playing, Jacobs is always singing in his mind. He encourages students to put words to music conceptually—like a singer. Vocalists have an advantage by using words with their phrases. "Wind players must look at the phrase, think about it, put words to it if it helps. I am not telling you what your musical message should be, I'm only saying that you must have one," Jacobs says.[259]

A phrase does not make a distinction with the lung capacity of the performer. Two players require roughly the same amount of air to play a specific phrase on the same instrument. A smaller person with only a three-liter lung capacity would have to take a full breath to get what a larger colleague with a six-liter capacity gets in a partial breath {see: Physical Elements: Vital Capacity}.

For those with smaller lung capacities, especially young players, aim for the quality of the phrase, not the length of the phrase. "Don't do a long bow task with a short bow," Jacobs states. The quality of the phrase should not be sacrificed for the length. If possible, break up the phrase into smaller segments.

Jacobs says, "Extension of phrase should never be at the expense of quality of tone. Quality of tone should be achieved before the long phrases. I have a constant influx of players who are running into trouble by trying to extend phrases too long. So they keep playing softer and softer. It is all right to play soft. But it can become extreme."[260]

Most players breathe for the first notes of a phrase. Instead, it is better to breathe for the last notes of a phrase to ensure its quality. Be comfortable at phrase ends. The ends of phrases must be protected, more so than the beginnings, which are begun with full breaths.

A performer must know the capabilities of their air supply. Jacobs suggests the following exercise:

Measure the time [in seconds] of a phrase of music played on one breath. Play a long tone in various stages for the same number of seconds. Become familiar with the flow rate to produce a given loudness in a given register for a specific length of time.

Mistakes

Jacobs feels all musicians are allowed a quota of mistakes. "Don't be afraid of making mistakes. I have never heard a brass player in my life who did not make them," he said.

The question is how many mistakes are allowed. In baseball, if a player has a lifetime batting average of .400, he would instantly be in the Hall of Fame although he has failed 60 percent of the time. As a musician, if only 98 percent of the notes are played correctly, there may be a chance of being fired.

All performers occasionally make mistakes, including Adolph Herseth. Once, Jacobs said that he kept track of errors that Herseth made. "He made a mistake about once every three years—perfection all the time!"

For students, having a good sound is more important than playing everything correctly. "Learning is an excuse for missing notes, but it is not an excuse for poor playing. Students must be allowed to develop excellence in conceptual thoughts. It is important that the mind is flooded with great musical thoughts. Mistakes are allowed, but, one must ask what were the thoughts when the mistake was being made," Jacobs stated.

A performance must be as error-free as possible. Most missed passages are a result of lapsed concentration. He offers this suggestion, "When you miss a note, keep going with a positive attitude to improve the next notes. Flood the brain with models of best notes—make the next notes even better than your norm."

Performance Medium

Musicians do not always perform in public. Besides practice and rehearsals with an ensemble, there are many other parts of the performance medium.

Warm-up

All musicians have their own particular warm-up routine that is unique to themselves. Jacobs recalls his colleague, the late Philip Farkas, former CSO principal horn.

"Phil used an hour warm-up before each concert. He would sound as good on the first note of the warm-up as he would sound at the end of the hour. If he would arrive too late for the complete warm-up, he would still sound great in the concert. His warm-up was really to become comfortable with the concert environment rather than to 'warm-up' the embouchure."

John Taylor tells about Jacobs' warm-up. "He never espoused a warm-up like so many teachers do. He said, 'If you played correctly, you didn't need to warm-up, just get the horn and brain together on the same page.' I never recall a single time when he didn't just pick up his tuba and play throughout the entire range without so much as a formal anything."

Jacobs prefers to start the warm-up on only the mouthpiece as, in certain cases, using the instrument may promote bad habits.

Concerning warm-ups, Jacobs states, "Being professional players, full-time players, we never cool off. Warm-up is coupling ourselves to the instrument at the start of the day. My philosophy is to always return to the norms and search out my finest quality of tone based on conceptual thought. I try to sound my very best at the very first note in my brain. I have worked for very high standards of musical concepts and sounds, and I start with the norms and maneuver them into the extremes."[261]

"If you are always thinking musically you should be able to pick up your horn at any time and get your best sound. The first sound after silence should always be your best."[262]

"The first notes should be the very best sounds as you remember them from the day before—the recreation of one's finest sounds. These notes should be in the mid-dynamic level, not too loud or soft. Start with slurs and long tones and as little tongue as possible. Gradually increase range and dynamics.

"If you play a lot, you are always in shape and ready to play. You do not need to have an athlete's warm-up to promote blood flow. The embouchure always has a great blood supply. Once the brain and the embouchure are connected, you are ready to go."

Warming up on stage is forbidden by some conductors. For example, during the era of Jean Martinon with the Chicago Symphony, it was not allowed. Jacobs further advises, when warming up on stage, do not use it as an opportunity to practice trouble spots. "If you are unprepared, there is little that can be done—it gives a bad message to the audience. Use the warm-up to get used to the acoustics of a particular hall; this is especially useful when in a strange hall."

Practicing

Individual practice is where skills are developed. A musician must enjoy practicing no matter how difficult it is. "If an individual gets satisfaction out of personal practice rather than just ensemble playing, or if his satisfaction comes only from the ensemble situation, he is handicapping himself," Jacobs said.[263]

In master classes, Jacobs is commonly asked about practice techniques. While there is no precise answer for all musicians, he tells them, "Don't practice with mediocrity." He encourages playing for an imagined audience.

He tells about his days at the Curtis Institute. "My practice studio was situated along a corridor where people had to walk to get to other parts of the building. All the fine musicians like Leopold Stokowski, Fritz Reiner and musicians from the Philadelphia Orchestra walked past my studio. There was no way I was going to sound bad by taking music I could not play and making it obvious that I couldn't play it. Whatever I practiced at the studio I had to sound good. I was only fifteen years old at the time, but my instincts told me, 'Don't sound bad.' I attribute whatever success I have had to the conditioning I had by being forced to practice where I could be heard by people like Reiner and Stokowski. I could not see them, but I knew they could hear me."

Part of daily practice requires preparing music for performance and daily drill forms such as scales and arpeggios. Although the importance of these drills are not a high priority for many players, Jacobs believes they should be a part of daily practice.

"Playing a scale is like a fighter punching a bag and jumping rope, but it should be more than that. It should be a cadenza from Mozart or Brahms, something that can be put into the art form of music."

There must be a balance as too much practicing of drills will not create a well-rounded musician. "A prize fighter has to go through conditioning. He does a great deal of bag-punching, rope jumping, and road work. Now, he could be excellent in all of this, but when he enters the ring, he would get his head knocked off because he has to have a great deal of experience in actual fighting. He has to build on that basis. There is similarly a balance between what the student must respond to in the way of development. There must be considerable development in drill forms—scales, interval studies, and slurs—the great variety of challenges that we do go through in the drill form. I like to put it to students in this manner—40 percent of their practice should be in the conditioning studies—the bag punching and rope jumping—but 60 percent should be in the interpretive aspects of music."

That balance may change depending on the instrument and musician. "Basically the tuba is an accompanying instrument. Rarely does it go out and carry the melodic line. We are usually accompanying somebody else. As a result, because we are getting a great deal of challenge in accompaniment, we fail very frequently to develop as the soloist—as the one who interprets for the audience. So we have to make up for the lack by putting it into the studio practice. I like to put it this way, 40 percent [interpretive] verses 60 percent [conditioning].

"If a man is on a job and he is out playing all night, he may want to put 80 percent into the drill forms in his personal practice because he is interpreting constantly. The first horn player in a major orchestra is always the soloist. He may want to put a great deal more time on the drill forms. The tuba player puts in equal time on the drill forms, but he does not have equal time on the stage."[264]

"Practicing is 85 percent *making statements* and 15 percent *asking questions*. When starting to practice, it is better to make a statement and practice what is right rather than to ask a question and practice what is wrong."

Music should be worked up by playing short sections. In a long piece, it is not necessary to always start working at the beginning. Start wherever work is needed.

For difficult sections, Jacobs suggests slowing the music, playing it note by note. If needed, change ranges—play it an octave higher if it is too low or an octave lower if it is too high.

To improve the first note of a phrase, first play the first notes of the phrase [1,2,3,4,5]. Next play those notes in reverse order [5,4,3,2,1]. Remember the quality

of sound of the opening note from playing the phrase in reverse order. Play the phrase again in its normal sequence, but match the tone quality learned from playing in reverse. He tells students, "Make each note worth $500, not $5."

Daily practice must be in all ranges with most work done in the mid-range of the instrument. The extreme upper and lower ranges must not be ignored, and should be developed. However, these developmental areas should be approached from the aspect of moving from the mid-range to the extremes, rather than as distinct areas that are practiced away from the familiar mid-range. This concept of moving from the familiar to the unfamiliar is especially important for younger players.

Jacobs states, "Young players try for extremes before they develop their norms. Always the development should be for quality of tone or tonal characteristics according to their own advancement. It doesn't hurt to delve moderately into extremes as long as a 5-10 percent limitation is put on it. That means 90 percent would be in the normal range. After wonderful playing of mid-range work—great development and the ability to play a song, an *Ave Maria*, an adagio, a polka, a little jazz—then 5 or 10 percent can be in the high range."[265]

A practice routine should include time spent in lyric playing or the bel-canto style to develop the best tone qualities. Begin lyric playing with vibrato, then retain the style without vibrato. Be able to play a song with and without vibrato. Keep the lyric quality when adding articulation to the sound. Maintain a lyric quality at all speeds. Practice the lyric song both on the mouthpiece and on the instrument.

Professional players must practice to retain skills. "The more advanced you are, the more practice time you need because you have to keep up with material, and cover more and more ground as a player. You really have to challenge your abilities in all directions, otherwise you begin to lose your repertoire. What was easy one year, will be much more difficult a few years later. At a certain point, you do not need the muscles so much as a fresh image," Jacobs says.

While with the Chicago Symphony, Jacobs would normally practice three hours a day plus rehearsals and performances. This would, of course, vary with the program played. If there was a heavy program, such as Mahler's *Symphony No. 6*, he would practice less.

"I usually keep three programs alive constantly. One is a constant conditioning program of scales and finger drills. Another is a long-term program of a recital, where I spend one to two years developing maybe five or six numbers." Of these, he says, "Usually you can read them or they are developed after a few weeks, but you spend the time after that refining them, interpreting them and tearing them apart and seeing if you can improve them. These studies refine all the neuromuscular patterns because of the connection between thought and physical response. You are going into detail. It becomes more and more a mentalization, which I think is very important."

His third program is a short-term period of solo and orchestral work, involving maybe one to four weeks on specific studies and general reading. In this period he prepares his parts for the upcoming programs if they have not already been incorporated into his long-term program.[266]

Stage Fright

Many fine performers suffer from a form of hysteria—stage fright. While a bit of nervousness helps put a performer in a proper state of mind, a great deal of nervousness can cause severe problems. Music is an art that is performed for others and the performer must develop an ease in performing for an audience. "The more you play in public, the easier it is," Jacobs states.

To help overcome stage fright, the performer must be prepared and have a thorough knowledge of the music. He must be secure in his conceptual thought and flood the brain with positive examples of music making.

Stage fright usually results in an elevated pulse rate and shallow breathing. To help slow the pulse rate, taking slow, deep breaths to a count of six [at sixty beats per minute] for six to eight repetitions is helpful.

"The brain influences the body and the body influences the brain. So if the brain is in turmoil, then put the body in a calmer situation. If we start with slow, measured inhalations, the pulse starts to slow up a little bit. Normally, in anxiety, breathing becomes rapid and shallow. The pulse goes up. Blood pressure goes up. So you try to create the opposite conditions,"Jacobs suggests.[267]

Auditioning

The audition process for symphony orchestras has changed considerably during Jacobs' career. Years ago, there was less competition between players and the conductor had the ultimate choice of personnel. Many auditions were held in a conductor's hotel room, and it was common for a conductor to appoint a player to a position.

Today there are several hundred applicants for a major position and the orchestras have set up audition committees. Auditions are held behind a screen to keep the identity of the applicant from the committee, and the conductor joins the panel only for the finals. Often consideration is given on how to eliminate an auditionee and often the best candidate is not selected to fill the position.

To be successful, a musician must be prepared to play musically despite the circumstances. "An audition can be used to show what you can do. On the negative side, you have to fight nerves. Many things can go wrong and you must 'run or fight for your life.' To counter this, you must have a positive mental attitude.

"The worst thing to do in an audition is to analyze yourself and your playing. You are asking questions rather than issuing statements to the audition committee," Jacobs states.

There is no set method to prepare for an audition. The individual must use his own judgement. All parts of a composition must be prepared, not just the most popular phrases. Part of the preparation is learning how the individual instrument's part fits within the ensemble.

Many musicians over-practice and do not play their best at their appointed time. When arriving, warm-up but do not practice. The purpose of an audition is to show your best playing for the audition committee—not to impress other applicants.

Jacobs does not really care for the auditioning process. "They are poor, especially for the player, and I think it is very difficult to have auditions and find a suitable way to judge, because we have a great many talented players to choose from. This means a lot of heartbreak for people who are very capable."[268]

Hall Acoustics

All concert halls have their own idiosyncracies. For example, in Chicago's Orchestra Hall, hearing other sections of the orchestra is difficult {see: Chicago Symphony Orchestra: Orchestra Hall}.

Jacobs learned to adapt to the acoustics of a room with a tuba whose bell points up, not out. John Taylor writes, "Mr. Jacobs was always very sensitive to being placed with his bell facing a wall or another performer at close proximity. He would never allow himself to be placed so that he was blowing into something, primarily because it disturbs the resonance and overtones."

When playing in a strange room, Jacobs would shift his position to find the optimum angle and avoid acoustical problems. From a tonal aspect, he feels that large halls seem to lose a considerable amount of the instrument's overtones, emphasizing the fundamental. The musician must be prepared to adapt both himself and, if necessary, his equipment to the concert hall.

Recording Sessions

Recording sessions are much different from live performances. Very rarely is a work recorded in its entirety. Instead, it is recorded in sections, then spliced into a final version of the entire work. While this can produce a better recording, sessions can be grueling and last for hours. One of the longest sessions, lasting fifteen hours, was Fritz Reiner's legendary recording of *Ein Heldenleben* with the CSO {see: Chicago Symphony Orchestra: Recordings}.

Before actually recording, microphones are placed and levels are aligned. Frequently, the seating position of the orchestra is changed from it's normal concert seating. Microphone placement is important. If a microphone is positioned too close to a particular performer or section, balance problems occur. If the microphone is too far away, playing louder than normal may be required.

Jacobs tells about one of Reiner's sessions. "Quite often in a recording, I would have to force—I could not play comfortably. When they would want the tuba to be picked up, Reiner would say, 'play louder.' And many times this was not practical. I was already playing quite loud, and either it would not be picked up, or I would have to change position, somehow try to get the bell pointing toward a microphone."[269]

Doubling

While a student at the Curtis Institute, Jacobs would play the tuba during the day and play trumpet and trombone at night. Later, he had a highly successful career doubling on string bass.

About doubling Jacobs says, "It is not for elementary musicians. Always keep artistry in the foreground while playing the secondary instrument. Keep a program of practice that includes both primary and secondary instruments. Play the second instrument at least two or three times a week."

Instruments

Because a musical instrument is an inanimate object and it requires a human to feed it musical information, Jacobs calls it, "A hunk of brass." "The horn has no brain," he states, "It doesn't give you anything, you have to give a message to the horn."

To produce a musical sound, there must be motor activity, pitch vibration, and resonance. Unlike a wind instrument, a piano only requires motor activity as the other elements are built in.

Jacobs says, "When a piano is sent from the factory, it already contains pitch vibration and resonance. It only requires motor function. A cat can run down the piano keyboard, and, although it's not great music, the piano will sound. All that is required from the player is motor function."

All instruments provide resonance. However, to make a sound on any instrument, motor activity must be applied to vibrate the pitch to be played. On a piano, a key is pressed. On a wind instrument, a valve or key must be pressed, individually or in a series. Some woodwind instruments furnish limited pitch vibration in comparison to a brass instrument. However, on all wind instruments, the vibrating surface is stimulated through the breath, causing either a reed or reeds to vibrate, or, in the case of brass instruments, the performer's lip surfaces. A brass instrument is, therefore, only a resonator as pitch vibration must come from the lips. The instrument then amplifies these sound waves according to its acoustical properties. This could be as much as twenty decibels depending upon the pitch.

"We cannot just blow into an instrument and press buttons. An instrument doesn't give pitch, the player does," Jacobs states.

Brasses

Brass instruments are manufactured with a slide, valves or a combination of both. However, these do not provide pitch, they only modify the instrument as they are depressed, singly, in combination, or the slide is extended, so that the instrument will then provide the proper length to resonate the pitch introduced by the player. The player must provide the motor activity and pitch vibration [from the embouchure] for the instrument to resonate according to the laws of acoustics.

Unlike those woodwind instruments that use a wooden reed, brass instruments require the flesh of the lips to provide vibration. As the lips vibrate from air passing through them, the brain sends a signal to the vibrating lips through

162

the seventh cranial nerve to adjust their vibration to the pitch to be sent to the instrument {see: Physical Elements: Embouchure}. The simplest analogy is that brass players use their lips in the same way a singer uses his or her vocal chords.

Beyond the principals of pitch vibration, stimulated by the brain, there are variables in a brass instrument, itself, that can be varied to alter the sound.

Jacobs states, "In playing a brass instrument, you have three basic variables—one, the instrument, second is the mouthpiece, and the third variable is the player. It is very important that we understand that we do have these three variables and the problems of one affects the others."

Many players are overly concerned with varying the instrument and mouthpiece. While these can create change, the major force is the musical message or signal that must be sent to the instrument from the player.

"While the instrument is important, it is still an extension of the person, and it should not become so all-consuming that all one thinks about are mouthpieces and horns. The music that you make with the instrument has to really be dominant."[270]

All brass instruments share common parameters. They all have mouthpieces of various sizes, and the designs of the instrument themselves are similar. Differences occur in the playing of these instruments and their physical requirements, most notably in the amount of air required. In the late 1950s, Jacobs conducted tests at the University of Chicago with the four major orchestral brass instruments using the principal players of the Chicago Symphony {see: Physical Elements: Air Flow/Air Pressure}.[271]

Of the three variables in playing a brass instrument, the easiest to vary is the player, as the signals being sent to the instrument from the brain are constantly adjusted. However, often there is a need to also adjust the "hardware" in order to produce a particular sound, style or to enhance the sound.

Trumpet players commonly use several differently pitched instruments during a performance. Occasionally Jacobs used two tubas, but, more commonly, used only one tuba but several different mouthpieces. "It's cheaper to have one tuba and many mouthpieces than one mouthpiece and many tubas," he often states.

Within the variable of the mouthpiece, the rim and cup are the two most common variables. Players most often prefer to retain one rim but will vary the cup. Jacobs varied both, seeming not to notice the feel of different rims, but instead, concentrated on the mental musical aspects to the exclusion of all other stimuli. When changing mouthpieces, the rule of thumb is that playing with a deeper cup mouthpiece will strengthen the fundamental, while a shallower cup will decrease the fundamental and enhance the overtones. Therefore, modifying the mouthpiece serves to change the sound without changing instruments. Although Jacobs used, as his everyday mouthpiece, a 1930-vintage Conn Helleberg during his entire career {see: York Tuba: Arnold Jacobs Mouthpiece}, he used many different mouthpieces as the situations dictated. His suggestion is, "Play different roles using different equipment to fully explore your potential."

Tuba

A fourth valve is added to a tuba for two reasons, to correct intonation problems related to valve combinations with the first and third valves and to facilitate the lower range.

Many instruments are further equipped with a fifth valve operated by the right thumb or left hand. The fifth valve is configured for various valve combinations, most commonly a flat half [second valve] or whole-step [first valve] but also as a flat two-step [second and third]. This allows for improved intonation in the mid and low range. An additional note [DD♭ on a CC instrument] can be sounded on instruments equipped with a fifth valve.

Some musicians feel that the addition of a fifth valve has a negative affect on the response of an instrument. Jacobs states, "Many people feel that any time you add a valve you moderately deteriorate the tone production of the instrument. I suppose this is true up to a point, but if the instrument is tight and the valves are well made, I think it is so minimal, that I don't even consider it. I use CC tubas with five valves so I can have proper intonation and can play throughout the full range of the instrument. I feel that any loss would be so slight and what I gain would more than outweigh it, so I recommend the use of added valves when necessary for register and intonation."

During the latter part of Jacobs' career, he played many notes in the low range using non-conventional fingerings. These are called "privileged notes," or, as Jacobs, tongue-in-cheek, calls them, "underprivileged notes."

For example, using a four-valve CC tuba, the conventional fingering for a low E would be with the second, third and fourth valves. However, using these "privileged notes," depending on the actual instrument, this note can also be played using only the second valve. Other notes can be sounded with various fingering combinations, which require experimentation and practice to achieve.

Many players have difficulty with these notes since they must mentally hear the very low pitch before playing. There is also less control over the pitch than when using conventional fingerings, but when compared using a decibel meter, there is a greater output of sound. A player with a small lung capacity can benefit from these notes, and Jacobs uses them extensively.

Many instruments are manufactured with valve slides that are too long. Jacobs says, "Most BB♭ tubas seem to have a compromise type of intonation in which first valve slides are a little longer than we would really want for the proper use. The third slides are usually a little longer and you get a compromise tuning where the low B and C are only moderately sharp, but then the upper range is usually moderately flat. It is better that you can tune accurately for both.

"Players constantly miss upper F♯ on the BB♭ tuba, simply because the note is flat. If they have good pitch recognition they are reaching for a higher note than actually exists on that instrument, and very frequently will overshoot it and wind up with one of the notes above it. This is easily corrected by having the tubing the proper length."

Depending on the music being played, Jacobs also used different tubas, including a BB♭ tuba and the smaller F tuba. Primarily, he used his York CC tuba and altered the sound by switching mouthpieces, often using several mouthpieces in a single concert to achieve the proper sound for particular compositions.

"I own fourteen tubas and forty different mouthpieces. Within our trombone section and in our hall, we have quite a large range of dynamics, so my choice of instrument and mouthpiece are equated together. It is based on whether I need a certain strength in the fundamental of the tone. If I use a mouthpiece that makes a horn too bright, then the trombones intrude into the overtones, I am not left with anything—I tend to disappear. So I have to find a mouthpiece that brings out the fundamental and lessens the overtones a little bit. Otherwise the balance in the sections would be lost." [272]

"There are certain established rules such as a very large tuba played with a very large mouthpiece is going to have a very strong fundamental in the tone and rather weak overtones, a phenomenon that can be measured by electronic analysis.

"If we have the same situation of a very large tuba, and the player is put into a situation where he needs to lighten the tone, this could be done very easily by using a shallow-cup mouthpiece. If he has to do a solo or play some very sprightly music where actually too much weight in the tone would be in the way, the smaller cup mouthpiece would dramatically alter the quality of tone coming out of the tuba. If the player played with somewhat the same embouchure and with the same tuba, the introduction of a shallower cup will immediately enhance the overtones and decrease the amount of fundamental in the tone. I use this procedure a great deal myself when I am playing with a large tuba, one that would be very adequate for a Prokofieff Symphony and the *Ring* operas of Wagner, but if I have to go on the stage with that tuba to play a French work, Berlioz or something very spirited and light, I immediately will switch to a shallower cup mouthpiece, and the difference in the quality of tone is amazing. We are simulating the change to smaller equipment, even though we are still using the same tuba, we very definitely have an altered quality due to the mouthpiece.

"As soon as I would use the smaller cup mouthpiece, I would gain tremendous projection to the audience because of the increased overtone content and weakened fundamental, but it would be much more recognizable because I would be the soloist. I would not be fighting all sorts of sounds intruding in my overtones. The weakened fundamental would be of no disadvantage and the enhanced overtones would give much more soloistic character to the tone," Jacobs concluded.

The Tuba in Performance

Until recently, the tuba has not been regarded as a solo instrument. "It has always been my experience that audiences are much more receptive to high pitches than to low pitches, even in the vocal family. The basso profundo is probably the least-used voice of the vocal school. In the tradition of thought, everything was such that bass clef was always shunted aside, compared to the treble clef. What the psychological reasons for that are, I am not so sure. How receptive they are in terms of actual quality of sound, I do not know," he stated.[273]

Tuba players seem to be drawn toward the instrument from other brass instruments. "These people are going to have well-developed musical abilities that they are transferring to an instrument that does not always require as much as they have to offer."[274]

"Composers traditionally write for tuba as an accompanying instrument, which means it is a limited challenge that will produce a limited player, unless he learns to overcome that.[275]

"Recognize that the orchestral portion of your life is just one phase. For a tuba player, or for any instrument that is primarily an accompanist to others or an ensemble instrument, you must have the proper amount of playing alone, of inspiration. I always tell my tuba students, 'You are a soloist when you practice at home,' and then you accept the variety of challenges of being a fine symphonic soloist. So when you interpret music at home and when you are on the stage, you are simulating as best you can the conditions of performance. You always have material that you are not just reading for yourself, but are performing for others. Whenever you have a chance to play for somebody else, it's very important to do so, but the main thing is that you have a constant challenge that keeps you trying to play better. Otherwise, as you get older, you are going to play worse. So we slow it up a little by constantly trying to improve. That means that part of the practice, say, 60 percent of the time should be interpretive and stylistic rather than the orchestral parts, and 40 percent in routine drill forms. If you do a scale, it could have been a scale out of Brahms, it could have been a scale that you would use in a rock group, it doesn't matter, it's still a performance situation. So practice for us [tuba players] is always extroverted."[276]

Much of the contemporary writing for tuba is in the middle and upper range, and less for the low register. Jacobs says, "I always get a kick out of tuba players who want to end a piece on C above high C on the tuba, which comes to the audience's ear as just a normal mid-range note. A fellow tuba player will appreciate C above high C, and will recognize and enjoy the extremely high note, but the audience in general is merely going to hear midrange sounds, and unless they see you turning red or blue they will not appreciate it. But end on a very low note, and you will have the exact reaction that the trumpet player will have on a very high note, lots of applause and amazement.[277]

"The tuba, of course, is a fine solo instrument. I think that it already can be considered a solo instrument. It is obviously being made that way by Harvey Phillips, Roger Bobo and many other fine players. I think that it is possible to have an audience that is conditioned to hearing piano, violin, flute, and voice to be equally responsive to the tuba—there are people who love to listen to brass instruments.

"We are going through a period, thanks primarily to Harvey Phillips—we must give him tremendous credit for this—where there is this search for material for the tuba. There is also a great conditioning going on to having people listening to tubas. Always, when you deal with the phenomenon of conditioning, you can predict that there will be an awakening of interest. I cannot say how far it will go in competition to the soprano and alto sounds. However, I love to hear tubas, but I still say that when you put a tuba player in front of an audience, they will enjoy a great artist playing whether it is a tuba or any other instrument. Whether they would like to hear it constantly is another story. I leave that wide open for another generation."[278]

Other Brass Instruments

The trombone is the only modern-day brass instrument that does not primarily use valves to adjust pitch. Jacobs advises, "Slide movements must be fast so the embouchure does not have to compensate by going flat or sharp."

Today, the bass trombone is actually a large bore B♭ tenor trombone. Jacobs encourages bass trombone players to perform a wide range of music including music for, and in the range of the tenor trombone. "The bass trombone is really a large-bore tenor adapted for low-register playing. Bass trombone players should be fluent throughout the full range of their instrument. They should be capable of an F above high B♭ as well as all the low notes."

A horn section in an orchestra is usually scored for two or four parts. The first horn player is primarily a soloist and the fourth horn player is usually a low range specialist. Both players are equally important to the section, but they must practice the skills that they do not use every day in the orchestra. Otherwise, their overall competence will diminish. By constantly playing in the low range, a fourth horn player may lose proficiency in the high range. The opposite can be true for the principal player.

As the playing position of the horn is across the body, great care must be taken not to hold the instrument tightly to the body. Jacobs once had a student who came to him complaining of a lack of breath. This person played with the left shoulder raised and was bending toward the right, with the bell of the instrument tight against the body. The ribs were being held so tightly that their movement was restricted and the right lung did not have room to fully expand during inhalation.

The solution was to change the playing position so that the instrument was not tight against the body. The change enabled the right lung to expand, allowing the student to inhale much larger amounts of air.

The trumpet is a low flow rate instrument requiring less air but under higher pressure compared to the trombone and tuba. Based on his early experiments Jacobs states, "In an extreme pianissimo on a low C on a trumpet, with a fine player playing, you have a flow rate as low as four liters per minute. In loud playing, the flow rate might go up to maybe fifteen liters per minute. At the maximum fortissimo, the trumpet player's flow rate is forty to forty-eight liters per minute."[279]

For those trumpet players who have problems in the upper range, Jacobs offers these suggestions:

"In the low register, use a thick column of air. The small embouchure of the high register trumpet also uses a thick stream of air. High notes are fast vibrations, low notes are slow vibrations. Don't make a big deal out of the number of vibrations. Approach range as a performer and always strive for high quality.

"The small embouchure surface needed for high pitch and the big push needed for amplitude makes a delicate situation. Danger lies in pushing against resistance. Instead of hard blowing, move toward a bigger sound based on the buzz of the embouchure. Zero in on the buzz of the lips in a lower octave then keeping the same feeling for buzz, play in the upper octave."

Woodwinds

Woodwind players constantly come to Jacobs for advice. He admits that he does not know about the technical aspects of playing a woodwind instrument, so he primarily works with these players as musicians, in specialized areas.

Unlike other woodwind instruments, the flute requires a large quantity of air. Like the tuba, the air pressure required on the flute is low while the flow rate is high.

"Some players with extremely small lung capacities are perceived to be handicapped with a high flow rate instrument like the tuba or the bass trombone. Therefore teachers will frequently assign women to play flute, an equally high flow-rate instrument requiring a fairly large lung capacity. While it is a small instrument, very petite, easy to carry, and so forth, the flute presents a challenge because so frequently smaller women just do not have the lung volumes to complete the phrases that the flute traditionally plays."[280]

During his experiments at the University of Chicago, Jacobs learned about the Venturi Principle. One definition states that if a small air stream is centered in a hole, outside air will also rush in from the edges of the hole.

Air Stream

Outside Air

Tube to air bag

Jacobs demonstrates this with a six-liter air bag. With a vital capacity below six liters, he cannot fill a six-liter bag with one breath. By not putting the tube in his mouth and blowing a steady stream of air in the center of the tube, outside air is pulled in and the six-liter bag is easily filled on one breath.

"I noticed with some flute players that the tone is occasionally increased by several decibels. It has something to do with the Venturi Principle. Where you put the Venturi affects how much outside air will enter the flute and at a certain point you get a huge volume of air. The characteristic sound of that burst of volume sounds more like a very loud trumpet. When this huge volume of air is uncontrolled, the characteristic sound is more like a freight train going around a curve in a tunnel. I have a feeling that if it is recognized and controlled, it could be of great value to the player because of the enormity of the dynamic range."

Single reed instruments such as the clarinet and saxophone are low flow-rate instruments although the lower pitched members of these families require more air than their higher pitched members.

Woodwind mouthpieces that fit inside the oral cavity can create problems during inhalation as the air passage is somewhat blocked. Jacobs does not see a problem with taking air into the mouth with the mouthpiece blocking the passageway. He suggests simply breathing through the corners of the mouth. "Open the corners of your mouth to allow more air in with the mouthpiece in the oral cavity."

The tuba requires the highest air flow with the least amount of air pressure. On the opposite end of the spectrum, the oboe requires the least air flow with the highest pressure of all the winds. It is interesting that oboe students constantly come to Jacobs for advice. Throughout his career, Jacobs has been exposed to fine oboists, beginning with Marcel Tabuteau at the Curtis Institute, and continuing with the CSO's now-retired principal oboe, Ray Still.

Still says, "I send most of my students to Jacobs for at least a few lessons. His world-class reputation among musicians is based on what he knows about breathing, as well as about the psychology of making music. He is on my official resume as my most influential teacher, and no two instruments, in terms of the amount of air needed to make them sound, are farther apart than the tuba and oboe. They use, respectively, five liters per second and three to five liters per minute, yet the principles of efficient breathing that determine the excellent playing of both are the same, and of these principles he is the most effective teacher in the world, the guru, the mentor."[281]

While Jacobs admires oboe players, he has mixed feelings. He says, "I am glad I was not an oboe player! We lived with another couple for a while, and he played the oboe. Gizella and I used to go out dancing while he stayed home working on his reeds!"

"Oboists think they need a breath and start sucking in more air when they have not released the residual air in their lungs. The feeling of having too much air is an incorrect feeling. What you have is too much pressure. You can be easily relieved by sensing the air pressure in the mouth instead of in the chest. Pressure is higher in the thoracic cavity than in the oral cavity. If you can, put the pressure up in the mouth or at the reed and back off in the chest. This can be easily done through the corner of the mouth, or quickly breathing out the nostrils."

"Double reed instrumentalists have a problem getting rid of air. I remember Ray Still showing me a small tube he made that he put in the corner of his mouth to help him get rid of stale air."

A common problem among oboists occurs in playing long passages. In the orchestral repertoire, an oboe solo may last as long as forty-five to sixty seconds on a single breath. With an instrument that requires between three to five liters a minute and a player with a vital capacity in that range, in theory, playing a long phrase should not be a problem.

Inside the body, the carbon dioxide level is increasing in the blood stream {see: Physical Elements: Hyperventilation/Hypoventilation}. Although the lungs are full of air [mostly carbon dioxide], the brain is sending a signal to get more oxygen by breathing. This is hypoventilation [the lack of oxygen], and it occurs in oboists during a long passage.

Jacobs suggests that during the rests before the passage, the player should take three or four deep breaths. This would increase the oxygen level in the blood stream [reducing the carbon dioxide level], temporarily causing hyperventilation. Starting the passage with an increased oxygen level in the blood stream will allow playing a long passage without the brain signaling the respiratory system to breathe.

The Jacobs Studio

Paul Haugan observed, "Those among us who have passed through the south Chicago basement or the Michigan Avenue studio know the side of Arnold Jacobs that has become his trademark—the steady flow of students seeking further progress on their musical performance."[282]

Normal Avenue

The Jacobs Studio was first located in the basement of his home at 8839 South Normal Avenue, on Chicago's South side. Upon arrival, either Mrs. Jacobs, or her mother, Mrs. Valfy, would greet students and frequently serve them coffee and cookies while waiting for their lesson. Mrs. Jacobs commonly calls many of those students "my boys."

John Taylor tells about the studio, "The basement never changed. My first

The Normal Avenue Studio
Photo from the collection of Arnold Jacobs

time there, April 1962, Mr. Jacobs said, 'I should fix this up, but I'm not too handy at that kind of thing.' Once down the stairs, there was a vast sea of things to the left, a slight kink in the path for the washer and dryer and then though the big door into the studio. I recall a skeleton, a flip chart that added or subtracted layers of the body depending upon which way you turned the pages [Jacobs calls this the 'Thin Man'], a string bass standing in the corner, and several tubas.

"He had a good bit of stereo equipment, a couple of tape recorders and an antique highboy that was located under the telephone. He had a huge tuba mouthpiece of European manufacture, turned black with tarnish, that he used to knock on the pipes whenever the telephone was for Mrs. Jacobs. Opposite the door from the telephone, were the two chairs, his a swivel chair, the

171

Student's a straight model, both of aluminum—they even matched. There was also a desk over which was a bathroom medicine cabinet filled with mouthpieces.

"It was a wondrous place, I can still see it in my mind's eye. I have a lot of sentimental attachments to 8839 South Normal, it literally was home to his two or three local tuba students of the day."

Fine Arts Building

In 1973, the studio was moved from Normal Avenue to Room 428 of the Fine Arts Building, located two blocks south of Orchestra Hall at 410 South Michigan Avenue.

Solon S. Bemen designed the building which was completed in 1885 as a showroom to display carriages for the Studebaker company of South Bend, Indiana. Converted in 1898 to studios for artists, tenants have included musicians, sculptors, painters, cartoonists, writers, architects, and organizations ranging from the *Daughters of the American Revolution* to the *Cook County Women's Suffrage Party*. The Studebaker Theater which was for years one of the centers of theater in Chicago and later converted to movie theaters, is located on the ground floor. Since the 1970s, the fourth floor has also been home for several schools including

Fine Arts Building
410 S. Michigan Ave
Photo by Author

the American Conservatory of Music, Harrington Institute of Interior Design, Art

Institute of Chicago and the University of Chicago.[283]

With its proximity to Orchestra Hall and therefore, the ability to teach between rehearsals and concerts, several members of the Chicago Symphony have maintained studios in the building, most notably Edward Kleinhammer who had a tenth-floor studio.

Entering the building is like going back to the turn of the century. With high ceilings, plaster walls and hard floors, the rooms are very live acoustically. The outside casing of the elevators are cast in bronze and the elevators are still run by human operators.

Entry to the Fine Arts Building
Photo by John Taylor

Although the content of the teaching was the same at the Fine Arts Building, those who only had lessons downtown in the Fine Arts Building were missing something.

Roger Rocco comments, "It is my opinion that if you were not fortunate enough to have had your lessons at his home on Normal Avenue, you did not

The Jacobs studio in the Fine Arts Building
Photo by Author

receive the total experience of studying with him. Although I had several lessons after he moved to his downtown studio, it did not seem the same.

"The Normal Avenue studio was crammed with the breathing apparatus and electronic instruments that are now familiar in the downtown studio. However the psychological impact of that equipment was much greater in the small basement where there was just enough room to sit in a chair with your instrument. It was like being in the space shuttle or a cramped doctor's office. I was surrounded by blinking lights, meters, gauges, and anatomical charts. Even though he rarely used any of that equipment with me, its presence still had an intimidating effect. I was well aware of the importance of what was occurring during my lesson time. This was serious business! I was there to he cured by the great doctor."

Equipment

Jacobs had studied pulmonary function in well-equipped laboratories such as those at the University of Chicago. He observed that some of the mechanical devices used in pulmonary research could be used with musicians to develop in minutes and days habits that it would otherwise take weeks and months to accomplish.

In the early 1960s, the cost of the equipment needed was more than $20,000, which was beyond the means and needs of Jacobs. To the great relief of his wife, he decided to experiment with alternate types of laboratory equipment rather than purchasing high-priced medical equipment.

Investing about $5,000, a great deal of money in 1960, he put together the equipment necessary for his studio. His equipment came from such diverse sources as friends in the medical field, gauges bought from heating and air-conditioning companies, and other devices including kitchen utensils borrowed from his wife. He used devices as simple as drinking straws and as complex as a spirometer.

John Taylor studied with Jacobs during this time and said, "During my years of intense study, 1962-1966, we, his regular students, joked that about every fourth or fifth lesson was 'devoted to science.' Mr. Jacobs was still refining and developing equipment at that date, although much was in place by 1962. Often we got to try a new gadget or device while he adjusted it. Those lessons were usually long, because somewhere toward the end he would realize that we had spent quite a bit of time working on the equipment, and we would go on to our musical needs.

173

Arnold Jacobs: *Song and Wind*

"I especially remember the time he got a set of pneumograph tubes—the same as they use on a lie detector. One went around the chest just at the armpits, the second further down and the third around the belt. All I could think of was that I was in an episode of Perry Mason (very popular just then) with Hamilton Berger asking the questions. I am afraid that try as he might, I never responded to the stimuli Arnold gave me.

"Although we joked about 'donating a lesson to science,' Arnold Jacobs never gave us anything but his total effort, and if I ever had counted the hours beyond the one hour he charged, I would owe him for lessons into the next century. To prove a point, one day—it was a holiday—I actually had a lesson that actually lasted all day!"

During this time several physicians visited his studio and complimented him on the equipment he had assembled, telling him that, basically, his equipment yielded the same results as their far more costly laboratory equipment.

Over the years the equipment that Jacobs has used has evolved and changed. For example, in 1982, he introduced many inexpensive disposable devices [Air Bag, *Breath Builder, Inspiron*, and *Voldyne*®] that perform for musicians many of the same functions as the very expensive laboratory-style equipment.

Much has been made over the years of Arnold Jacobs' approach. While primarily teaching music, he divorced remedial function matters from the actual playing of the instrument, and using a variety of external devices away from the instrument, sought to develop new habits of breathing and air usage with his students.

Here is some of that equipment from the Jacobs' Studio.

Air Bags

Air bags come in many shapes and sizes ranging from ordinary paper or plastic bags to black-rubber five or six liter anesthesia bags. In use, a tube is tightly inserted into the bag, the tube in then placed between the teeth on top of the tongue so as not to obstruct the airway.

Six-liter air bag
Photo by John Taylor

Uses of the bags include:

Measuring vital capacity - For those with lung capacities equal or less than the capacity of the bag, the air bag is a rough gauge of that person's vital capacity.

Inhalation and exhalation - Practice emptying and filling the lungs by slowly rebreathing air several times in a row. In this exercise the muscles of enlargement will learn to work apart from the muscles of reduction. It is important that the lungs go from extremes, empty to full. Since the same air is breathed in and out, carbon dioxide, rather than oxygen, is transferred to avoid hyperventilation. Rebreathing from a breathing bag can be done repeatedly for about twenty seconds without discomfort.

With the instrument - Inhale to full capacity, exhale into the bag filling it as much as possible on one breath. Then hold the air in the bag with a finger over the tube. After positioning the instrument for playing take back air from the bag [making sure that it is completely deflated], then using this "old air" start playing the instrument. The bag gives a visually known quantity of air.

Rather than starting with an empty bag, a variation is to fill the bag [with multiple breaths if needed] and put a finger over the bag's opening. Next, inhale as much as possible and start the inhalation/exhalation cycles. For some, the psychology of starting with an inhalation rather than an exhalation may be beneficial.

With the mouthpiece - After placing the mouthpiece in the air bag's tube, buzz on the mouthpiece. All air used buzzing will remain in the bag. This is for demonstrating using more air while playing. By increasing the air flow, more of the bag will expand.

Performing these exercises in front of a mirror is important so as to observe the body motions. Remember the look and feel of a full breath. The bag gives a visual account of how much air is used in a full breath.

Breath Builder

The Breath Builder is a device used to feel the sensation of inhaling and exhaling. It is a tube of plastic [at least six inches tall] with a ping-pong ball inside. The bottom is sealed and the top has three holes drilled to vary the resistance.

To use the Breath Builder, place the tube between the teeth on top of the tongue. Next, get the ball to the top of the tube by either inhaling or exhaling, [which is easier]. Then hold the ball at the top of the tube while slowly inhaling and exhaling. The Breath Builder requires fourteen ounces of pressure to hold the ping-pong ball at the top of the column.

In use, visualize a string player bowing from frog to tip. Keep the motions of inhalation and exhalation as long as possible, increasing the length of the bow. Find the minimal function to keep the ball at the top. Look in the mirror and observe the body's motions to keep the wind moving with minimal effort. Exaggerate inhalation [expansion of the body] and exhalation [contraction of the body].

Breath Builder
Photo by John Taylor

175

Next, lower the resistance by closing more of the holes on the top of the tube. Go for length of breath and mentally increase the length of the imaginary string player's bow.

Another use of the Breath Builder is to first attach a small funnel to the tube. Hold it parallel to the floor with the tube three inches from the mouth. Blow into the tube moving the ball to the rear of the chamber. Next, inhale and try to move the ball to the front of the chamber, keeping the tube three inches from the mouth.

Remembering that oxygen is being breathed in is important because hyperventilation can easily occur. Do only three or four inhalation/exhalation cycles in a row. When dizziness starts, rest for a few minutes and let the oxygen content of the blood return to normal levels.

Decibel Meter

Many professions use decibel meters. Most meters have two controls, one for speed of reaction time, and another for decibels [in tens] with a VU or digital meter for the single digits.

There are several uses of the decibel meter:

To gauge dynamics - If a student's conception of loud and soft are not of sufficient contrast, the decibel meter can provide a visual gauge. For example, if the student is playing fortissimo and generating ninety decibels of sound and his concept of a pianissimo is eighty decibels, it should become obvious to the student that he needs to develop more dynamic contrast.

Mouthpiece practice - Many brass players have difficulty with loud mouthpiece buzzing. With the meter, find the decibel level at which they are currently playing. Increase the meter a few decibels and challenge the student to play a little louder. Repeat as often as possible.

Vibrato - Vibrato will show on a decibel meter as intensity variation. For this operation, set the reaction time control to fast.

A draft meter connected to a funnel will help challenge a student to control air volume. A decibel meter can be used in a similar manner. Rather than measuring the amount of air passing through it, as the draft meter does, the decibel meter measures how much sound is generated as air passes over the microphone.

Decibel Meter
Photo by John Taylor

Draft Meter

Draft Meter for Inhalation
Photo by John Taylor

Borrowed from the heating and air-conditioning industries, Jacobs has adapted these for his own use.

One gauge has a meter that moves as air is sucked in. He has the student form an "O" with their lips and places a tube outside the lips within the air stream. As the student inhales, the meter moves. This is used to give a visual clue that air is moving during inhalation.

While one meter is used for inhalation, the other is for exhalation. To focus the air, a common kitchen funnel is added. When exhaling into the funnel, the meter moves. Jacobs varies the distance from the student's mouth encouraging them to move the meter. Of course the further away from him the meter is, more air volume is needed to move the meter.

Draft Meter for Exhalation
Photo by John Taylor

Dynalevel

Conn Dynalevel
Photo by John Taylor

This is a sound-level measuring device made by the C. G. Conn Corporation, that has a series of ten lights. As one plays louder, more lights illuminate. To make more of a contrast, different colored Christmas-tree lights are used [that is why Jacobs calls it the "Christmas tree"]. In use, the Dynalevel provides a visual representation of dynamic ranges in highly visual light form rather than the numeric form of the decibel meter.

Gauges

Another air-conditioning industry gauge Jacobs uses is attached to a pipe with four holes of increasing diameters. The gauge has a positive and negative area for inhalation and exhalation. First, he covers the largest hole and has the student inhale and exhale until the meter shows four. After resting a few minutes to avoid

Air Gauge
Photo by John Taylor

hyperventilation, he then has them perform the same maneuver until the meter reads eight. Finally, the three smaller holes are covered, exposing the largest [adding resistance], and the inhalation/exhalation cycle is repeated, first to four then eight.

In 1998 Jacobs worked with WindSong Press to reproduce this vintage gauge as the *Variable Resistance Compound Gauge*.

Inspiron [Inspirx®]

Inspiron
Photo by John Taylor

The incentive spirometer, or Inspiron [Inspirx®], is a device used in hospitals to give respiratory patients a visual demonstration of how much air they can inhale. While the instrument was designed for inhalation, if it is turned upside down, it can also be used for exhalation. There is a gauge to measure resistance, with the most open position providing the most resistance.

Place the tube between the teeth and on top of the tongue so as not to obstruct the air passage. With the gauge set to maximum resistance, inhale and move the ball to the top. If there is a problem, lower the resistance. Just before exhalation, turn the Inspiron upside down and when exhaling, move the ball to the top. Continue the inhalation/exhalation series. On the minimum setting, hyperventilation is difficult. On other settings, to avoid hyperventilation, only three or four inhalation / exhalation cycles should be performed in a row.

Keep inhalations and exhalations as slow as possible and exaggerate. Next, lower the resistance and keep the cycles as long as possible. Reduce suction and control the ball. Observe the body motions in a mirror.

Another use is in conjunction with mouthpiece practice. Remove the large hose at the base, replace with a four-inch rubber hose, and place a mouthpiece in the other end. The Inspiron must be upside down [the exhalation position]. Adjust the resistance so the ball can remain in the up position while buzzing several notes on the mouthpiece. Imagine that the air supporting the ball is a fountain of water—its height will vary but it should not hit the bottom between notes. The object is to play throughout the range of the instrument while keeping the ball suspended. When moving into the high range any attempt to increase pressure while decreasing the rate of air flow will cause the ball to drop. One of the most important uses of the incentive spirometer is to teach the relaxed low pressure/high flow rate concept of playing.

It is important to remember that hyperventilation can easily occur. When dizziness starts, rest for a few minutes and let the oxygen content of the blood return to a normal level.

Keyboard

A piano or electronic keyboard has several uses. The most obvious is playing a phrase on the keyboard to hear the intervals. Other uses are to establish pitch recognition and to help develop absolute pitch by playing a note and then mentalizing that note. Check your memory of the note by later singing it and check the accuracy by playing it on the keyboard. Repeat often. Eventually, the pitch should be in the mind and can be reproduced whenever needed.

Mirror

Perhaps the simplest tool that Jacobs uses is a full-length mirror. In his studio, it is found in front of the student's chair. He encourages students to observe motions of the body while playing the instrument. This enhances learning by adding sight to the other senses.

Mouthpiece Rim

A part of Jacobs' clothing is a mouthpiece rim. He always has one in his shirt pocket along with pencils, pens and a flashlight. He would feel naked without them!

Many mistakenly call these "embouchure visualizers," but they have more uses than to observe the placement of one's embouchure.

Mouthpiece Rims
Photo by John Taylor

The mouthpiece rim removes the stimuli of an old [normally bad] habit by temporarily eliminating the mouthpiece and instrument. It is helpful to stimulate the "buzz," and to some extent, refine pitch. The real value in the mouthpiece rim, is to isolate the lip's muscle fibers while buzzing. Jacobs cautions students not to buzz their lips without the use of a rim. The lip's muscles must be isolated. Buzzing without a rim involves many more muscles than if the lips are supported with a rim. He recommends that buzzing should only be performed in the lower mid-range and for very short periods—two or three minutes maximum.

Oscilloscope

There is a variation of an oscilloscope in Jacobs' studio. It was made by CSO trombonist James Gilbertsen using a microphone connected to a modified television set. In the center of the screen is a dot. As the sound level increases, the dot lengthens turning into a line above and below the center dot.

Jacobs often uses this device to demonstrate the speed of an attack, and for the study of vibrato.

Jacobs' Oscilloscope
Photo by John Taylor

The pulses of the vibrato become apparent on the screen and the student is encouraged to keep the line on the screen long between pulses.

Pneumograph

Three pneumograph bands are placed on the body. The first is placed high around the chest at the armpits. The second is placed on the bottom edge of the ribcage around the tenth rib and the third is placed at the navel. Each band is connected to a gauge that shows any expansion or contraction in body size.

While inhaling, a correct breath would cause motion in all three areas and would register on the gauge. This visual demonstration of an inhalation is very useful for students who are having problems by either breathing only from the upper chest or lower chest.

Spirometer

Drum Spirometer
Photo by John Taylor

Spirometer
Photo by John Taylor

During a first lesson, Jacobs usually has the student take a full breath and exhale into the spirometer. This is a laboratory device that has a storage tank of water with a chamber on top that raises as air enters. Pens are attached to the movable chamber and a graph is written showing air volume movement over carefully calibrated time measurements. This is the most accurate method of measuring vital capacity, and is usually the first time a student becomes aware of his lung capacity.

Tuners

Jacobs has owned a variety of tuners, from the original twelve-window Conn Stroboconn, to the modern battery-operated compact tuners.

For his personal use, Jacobs would use a tuner to set the slides of any new instrument. In his teaching, he uses an electronic tuner for pitch recognition, as it gives the student a visual representation of the correct pitch {see: The Teacher: Greatest Teaching Problems}.

Conn Stroboconn
Photo by John Taylor

180

Tape Recorder

Jacobs always encourages students to practice with a tape recorder. By recording and immediately listening to it, one becomes their own audience.

Tubes

Jacobs has students inhale and exhale through various tubes. The sizes range from 3/4" diameter to common drinking straws—the most inexpensive tool in Jacobs' studio.

He places a tube in the student's mouth between the teeth over the tongue and instructs the student to breathe through it. With the reduced airway, the student is forced to take long deep breaths during inhalation and exhalation. He then instructs the student to observe the strangeness of the reduced passageway.

To open the passageway and reduce resistance, Jacobs gradually adds more straws [or cuts the straw repeatedly in half]. An easier method to control resistance is to add a valve to a 3/4" diameter tube.

Ideally, the student becomes aware of the freedom of motion to the air he should experience during playing.

Voldyne®

A Voldyne® is used to measure the amount of air inhaled [up to five liters]. There are two chambers—the larger [right] is to measure the air volume and the smaller [left] for air pressure.

To use, place the tube between the teeth over the tongue so as not to obstruct the air passageway. Inhale with a fast breath, keeping the ball in the pressure chamber as close to the top as possible.

Watch the main chamber for the amount of air inhaled indicated by the top of the disk. There is a marker to manually mark the amount of air previously inhaled. Use a mirror and observe the body motions while breathing in.

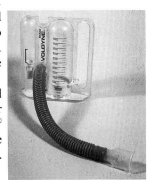

Unlike the air bag, *Breath Builder*, and *Inspiron* [Inspirx®], the Voldyne® is used only for inhalation. Use these in conjunction with the Voldyne® to discover the total vital capacity. Perform only three or four inhalations at a time to avoid hyperventilation.

Voldyne®
Photo by John Taylor

York Tuba

When Jacobs auditioned for the Curtis Institute, he had a Conn E♭ tuba. By taping the fourth valve down and pulling the slides, he played the tuba as a BB♭ instrument {see: Curtis Institute}. Upon entering the Curtis Institute, he played on the school's Italian-made CC tuba, which he recalls was not a very good instrument. When he initially used the CC tuba, he wrote the fingerings in the music—especially when performing and rehearsing with Reiner.

During this period, Leopold Stokowski was the conductor of the Philadelphia Orchestra. In keeping with his aural concept of orchestra sound, Stokowski requested a true contrabass tuba that would supply an organ-like quality to the Philadelphia Orchestra. In answer to this request, Philip Donatelli contacted the J.W. York Band Instrument Company of Grand Rapids, Michigan, and ordered a very large CC tuba.

James Warren York was born on November 24, 1839, in Exeter, New Hampshire. He first worked for the Boston Musical Instrument Manufactory and in 1882 moved to Grand Rapids, Michigan where he first played in a music pit. He then owned his instrument manufacturing company until his retirement to California in 1917. He died in Los Angeles on February 9, 1927.

York manufactured a full line of brass instruments, both under its own name and proprietary brand names. York briefly participated in two partnerships, Smith & York (1883) and York & Holton (1885). In 1884 the company was known as J.W. York and Company. In recognition of his infant son Charles E. York, he renamed the company York & Son in 1887. York further changed the company's name to York & Sons in 1898 to include his other son, Frank W. York. Both sons were active with the company until about 1913.

In 1897, Alfred J. "Bill" Johnson became the company's foreman. In 1913, Johnson, along with John and James Duffy, formed a stockholding company, and when the York family relinquished all interest in the company in 1926, Johnson became a co-owner. The company was then known as the York Band Instrument Company. In December 1940, York was sold to Carl Fischer Musical Instruments and Johnson left the company. During World War II the company manufactured munitions. After the war, York produced student-line instruments. In 1971, Tolchin Instrument Company who then owned York, closed the factory.[284]

Arnold Jacobs and his York Tuba
Photo by John Taylor

In 1933, in answer to Donatelli's request for a true contra-bass tuba, Bill Johnson designed and built two large CC tubas, one was given to Philip Donatelli and the second was retained by the factory, later being sold.

York of the 1930s built premium-quality tubas, and, during the time Jacobs' tuba was manufactured, York was highly selective with the quality and composition of the metals used in their instruments. This tuba has a .750-inch bore at the valves, but unlike traditional European designed tubas, it flares rapidly, especially at the bottom bow terminating in a twenty-inch bell. The four piston valves are augmented by a fifth rotary valve operated by the thumb that adds a flat whole step.

Characteristic of all 1930-vintage Yorks, this tuba has a short leadpipe going directly into the first valve, with the tuning slide located between the fourth and fifth valves. Fortunately, or unfortunately, depending upon one's perspective, the short leadpipe created problems for Donatelli. Being of portly stature, whenever he breathed, his body would push the tuba away from him, making playing this instrument nearly impossible. One day Donatelli, knowing that Jacobs needed to purchase a tuba, called him into his studio and offered to sell his large York for $175, an enormous amount of money in the 1930s. However, Jacobs had a payment plan, $5 a week until paid, with no carrying charges.

When Jacobs first brought the tuba to orchestra rehearsal at the Curtis Institute, Fritz Reiner liked the sound of the tuba so much that he sent his chauffeur to bring Jacobs and his tuba to each rehearsal {see: Curtis Institute: Fritz Reiner}. Jacobs used this tuba throughout his career. At one point, he traveled to Grand Rapids and toured the York factory where he met the tuba's designer, Bill Johnson. York advertisements in the 1930s featured a photograph of Jacobs, then with the Indianapolis Symphony Orchestra.

Later, as chance would have it, Philip Donatelli was on tour with the Philadelphia Orchestra and performing at the University of Oklahoma. There, he saw the second York tuba on stage, and informed Jacobs. Jacobs immediately called the dean of the school of music to attempt to buy or trade for the York tuba. They finally struck a deal. In return for the York, he sent them two tubas, a brand new Alexander F and an overhauled Conn BB♭.

When the second York arrived, it was badly dented, full of dirt, deceased insects and other assorted problems, but it had the same sound as Jacobs' original York. Jacobs sent the tuba to T. M. (Ted) Koeder in Naperville, Illinois for repair. Koeder had, before opening his own business, been a valve maker for Holton. Koeder's initial assessment was that the valves were bad. He offered Jacobs the choice of replating the valves for $15 each, or replacing them with new valves for the same price. Jacobs chose new valves. Afterwards, he took his other tubas to Koeder for new valves.

Both York tubas were reunited—and Jacobs owned both of them! Over the years, he used both instruments with the Chicago Symphony.

At one point, York number one developed a problem. "I was playing the Powerama [a large exposition displaying America's technological achievements], and between shows took my horn to Lyon-Healy. I asked them to patch the leadpipe, as it was leaking. When I returned, they had *replaced* the leadpipe. They looked for the old one, but it had already gone out with the trash."[285]

This replacement leadpipe was a smaller one from a Conn tuba and York number one retains this leadpipe. The fifth valve was removed after being judged unrepairable and replaced by another valve. To his dismay, Jacobs later saw the original valve installed on another tuba.

In the early 1980s, York number one was almost destroyed in shipment to be copied at the Hirsbrunner factory in Switzerland. The tuba was shipped in a cardboard box, rather than a wood crate, and something fell on the box, severely damaging the tuba. Jacobs was to have had the tuba returned within three months, but additional time was required to rebuild it. During this time, work needed to be done on York number two requiring him to use his Holton tuba with the CSO. Eighteen months later, the repaired York number one was returned complete with a new fifth-valve.

This is not the only case of damage to Jacobs' Yorks. In the 1960s, on the eve of a tour, Jacobs received a call from one of the CSO's stagehands. While moving instruments from a recording session at one of Chicago's hotels, the cable of an exterior elevator snapped. A bass, a harp and several other large instruments, including York number two, plunged seven floors into an excavation pit filled with water. The tuba was in a shipping trunk made for the tuba by orchestra members Fred Boos and Johnny Klima. Luckily, the trunk protected the tuba. "Sand got into the valves and several solder joints were knocked open—that was all," recalled Jacobs. There was also a storage area on the top of the trunk for Jacobs' concert clothing. Because the orchestra was beginning their tour the next day, the late-night phone caller instructed Jacobs to bring both his other tuba and another set of tails for the tour. When the instrument was repaired, the bill was $150. Inexpensive in comparison to the repairs on both the harp and bass.

During the mid 1970s, York number two, which was more than showing its years, was overhauled by Jerry Lechniuk who worked for Renold Schilke's company.

When he retired in 1988, Jacobs sold York number two to the Chicago Symphony. Gene Pokorny chooses to use the York daily. Pokorny writes, "Mr. Jacobs has never twisted my arm into insisting which instrument I use. The York is a beautiful instrument and one that is very difficult to copy—ask any tuba designer, because they have all seemed to try at one point or another."

Jacobs sold York number one to the CSO in 1996.[286]

Copies

Over the years there have been several manufacturers who have tried, some more successfully than others, to copy this particular York tuba.

Carl Fisher Inc. owned the York company from 1940-1971, and briefly sponsored Jacobs at various clinics. Carl Fisher sold tubas trademarked "York" but made by Boehm & Meinl in West Germany. These tubas were much smaller in size than Jacobs' York tuba.

During the 1950s, the Chicago Symphony Brass Quintet began their affiliation with the Holton company. During this time, the quintet members played Holton instruments {see: Chicago Symphony Orchestra: Chicago Symphony Brass Quintet}. However, at that time Holton made only a BBb tuba. Therefore, Jacobs lent Holton his York tuba for three weeks. Arnold Westphal of Holton measured the tuba, but because Holton did not have the proper mandrels, the resulting tuba was a BBb tuba, modified to CC. While this tuba is actually larger than the York, it lacked some qualities possessed by the original York.

Fred Marzan, who had marketed several tubas over the years, at one time imported a York copy from Boehm & Meinl of Germany. They did not measure the original tuba. By this time [1971] the original York mandrels had been sold for scrap.

In 1979, during the Chicago Symphony's tour of Europe, Jacobs traveled to Sumiswald, Switzerland, and visited the factory of Peter Hirsbrunner. As a result of this visit, he permitted Hirsbrunner's representatives to ship his original York to Switzerland to be measured for a copy. However, shipping this tuba halfway around the world nearly turned into a disaster, as the tuba was crushed and nearly destroyed in shipment. Jacobs was upset about his prized tuba and made nothing from the ordeal. The resulting Hirsbrunner copy is a fine instrument played by many tubists of the world's major orchestras.[287]

One of Jacobs' students, Robert Rusk was the long-time tubist of the Milwaukee Symphony, has taken a different approach to copying the York tuba. He has taken old York tubas and used many original parts such as the bell and larger tubing often adding only a new valve section. Because of the original York parts being used, especially the bell, these "recycled Yorks" retain much of the characteristic York sound.

When cleaning Jacobs' studio, an old three-valve York E♭ tuba was found. Rusk was given the tuba and converted it into a fine F tuba that he used with the Milwaukee Symphony. He converted another York for Charles Daellenbach of the Canadian Brass. A copy of this instrument is in production, by the Canadian Brass Musical Instruments and later Getzen (Elkhorn, Wisc.).

During the 1992-93 season, Floyd Cooley substituted in the Chicago Symphony {see: Chicago Symphony Orchestra: Other tubists of the CSO}. That season he played the CSO's tuba, York number two. He carefully measured the tuba and copies are being produced by Walter Nirschl in Germany.

Photo from the collection of Arnold Jacobs

Other Tubas

Although Jacobs is most associated with his York CC tuba, at one time he owned seventeen tubas. There have been many occasions when he has chosen to use another instrument, and one tuba that was not of his choosing.

Arnold Jacobs: *Song and Wind*

For the 1951 recording of *Pictures at an Exhibition*, Raphael Kubelik requested that Jacobs be prepared to play the solo in the *Bydlo* movement. Jacobs found a double tuba [BB♭ and F] and started preparing for the solo. To his surprise, he found the solo worked better on the BB♭ side of the tuba than on the F side. The solo is often played on a euphonium. He played it [as written] on the larger [BB♭] side of the tuba, pitched a full octave below the euphonium {see: Chicago Symphony Orchestra: Recordings}.[288]

Although Jacobs had experimented with F tubas, he never considered using one until Fritz Reiner guest conducted the Vienna Philharmonic in 1956, Reiner's third year with the CSO. During his visit in Vienna, Reiner decided that he would like to incorporate some of the sound characteristics from the Vienna Philharmonic into the Chicago Symphony.

"Reiner wrote to Herseth about using rotary valve trumpets, and to our principal bass about using gut strings and five-string basses. He wrote to me about using a little Viennese tuba. Everybody turned him down except me. I wrote to him and said, 'I would be glad to play the little horn.' I figured he had always given me good advice. My relationship with Reiner was in a musical sense, quite close. I grew up playing under his guidance, and his advice to me was always right."[289]

With an Alexander F Tuba
From CSO Archives

What Reiner had heard was a smaller bass tuba in F made by Anton Dehmal. Bob Tucci was a Jacobs student prior to moving to Europe and tells about these tubas. "The true Viennese F tuba was not built by Dehmal, but by a company that went out of business in the early 1920s. The true Viennese tubas were very small, even smaller than the Dehmal that the CSO had."

The Dehmal F tuba that Reiner brought back from Vienna was a six-valve freak—three valves in the right hand and three in the left. In addition, fingerings were not standard to conventional tubas! Jacobs said, "I took it over to Carl Geyer who just shook his head. The thing wasn't even soldered up right. The valves were

187

not set up like ours so when I had to play fast I had to cross my hands." Jim Palacek, a bass player in the orchestra, dubbed it *The brass accordion.*[290]

"In addition to having to transpose fingerings from one key to another, which by itself is no great problem, you add the transference of right-hand technique to the left hand. This makes it a little hairy, especially when the instrument arrives in the middle of the season, and you have to start playing it immediately in some very difficult works, There was no learning to swim gradually with Reiner, you got thrown in the pool, and you would sink or swim."[291]

Jacobs used this tuba on the Reiner recording of Tchaikovsky's *Symphony No. 6, "The Pathetique."*

"Finally, I figured Reiner's eyesight wasn't getting any better, and I began bringing my old York into rehearsals. One day Reiner said he liked the sound of the horn I was using—my York. I found a good hiding place for the Viennese F and made sure no other conductor ever saw it again." Jacobs concluded with a chuckle.

Long after the Reiner days, during one of the restorations of Orchestra Hall, they finally found the instrument somewhere in the basement. It has never been used since in the Chicago Symphony.[292]

Not all was lost as Jacobs became more proficient on the F tuba. He later purchased an Alexander F tuba that was larger and more resonant and has, on occasion, used this and other F tubas with the CSO.

For his performances and recordings of the Vaughan Williams *Concerto for Bass Tuba and Orchestra* during the 1978 season {see: Chicago Symphony Orchestra: As a Soloist}, Jacobs used an F tuba made by Boosey and Hawkes, the instrument for which Vaughan Williams composed the Concerto.

Arnold Jacobs Mouthpiece

During the 1930s while Jacobs was a student at the Curtis Institute, he purchased a Conn Helleberg mouthpiece for $2.50. August Helleberg was the original tubist of the Chicago Symphony {see: Chicago Symphony Orchestra: Other Tubists of the CSO} and is generally credited with developing the funnel-shaped style of mouthpiece that bears his name. In the 1960s Jacobs was at the Conn factory and was shown the cutter for this mouthpiece, which had not been made since the mid 1930s.

Canadian Brass -
Arnold Jacobs Mouthpiece
Photo by Author

The Conn Helleberg was one of the primary mouthpieces that Jacobs used during his career. Later, Renold Schilke modified one of his Hellebergs and, in December 1993, the Canadian Brass Musical Instrument Company reproduced the modified Conn Helleberg mouthpiece as the *Arnold Jacobs Model.*

Jacobs constantly uses different mouthpieces depending on the sound characteristics he was looking for in a particular composition {see: Instruments: Mouthpieces}. One of the more interesting mouthpieces that Jacobs often used has an adjustable-cup that was made for him by Renold Schilke. The cup is in two parts that are precisely fitted to each other. Both parts are threaded and by turning the outer portion, the depth of the cup can be adjusted.

Passing the Torch

Arnold Jacobs: Song and Wind was first released in September 1996. Since then, Mr. Jacobs continued teaching on Wednesdays and Saturdays but did no masterclasses other than Northwestern University during July 1997 and 1998.

October 7, 1998 began as a teaching day. Dallas Jacobs describes the morning's events. "Dad got up at 7:30 and we talked briefly. He said he did not feel good and was going to take some asprin and lay back down for an hour (the alarm was always set for 8:30 on teaching days). I told him that I was going out to breakfast and would back well before he was to leave.

"I got home about 9:15 and heard the alarm ringing and went to the bedroom. I found Dad there looking just like he was asleep, quiet and peaceful. I touched him and he was very cold, no pulse. He was gone from us.

"Mom was still asleep at his side. I thought she had died too because she slept thru the alarm for at least 45 minutes of ringing - she had never slept through a minute of it before. God must have protected her from finding him alone. I woke her up and told her, then got hysterical myself. About 10:15, our neighbor, Mark Morrisey came over to drive Dad downtown. Instead, he called 911 for us and took care of all that he could."

Dallas informed me, and since I was in downtown Chicago, was assigned the task of contacting the Chicago Symphony and the Fine Arts Building to cancel lessons. The CSO was assembling for their morning rehearsal when I arrived. CSO Executive Director Henry Fogel announced the news to the orchestra and after a moment of silence, they began playing - just like Arnold would have wanted. The staff at the Fine Arts Building was stunned and the morning's first student was in shock having fitted a lesson in en route to Germany.

I returned home on an early train and it was during that trip that I talked with a very upset Gizella - she wanted a fitting memorial, but had no firm plans. Symphony Center was suggested and the CSO was contacted. Then the phone calls started - Henry Fogel contacted Gizella, Bernard Droboski, Dean of the School of Music, offering Northwestern University as a cosponsor and the December 1998 *Tribute to Arnold Jacobs* was born.

Finally, the music world had to be informed and messages were posted on all of the brass lists on the Internet. Word spread rapidly and tributes came in from all corners of the world. Some called this, *"The end of an Era,"* while many wrote, *"Although I never met Arnold Jacobs, I consider him the most influential person in my life."* Gizella was deeply touched by all the tributes and wanted to personally thank everyone, but because of the scope of the job, she was never able to.

Less than a month later, on November 6, 1998, more bad news arrived when Arnold's long time colleague and friend, Frank Crisafulli passed away. For many years we would go to the Crisafulli's for lunch following the final session of the Northwestern masterclass. The previous July, less than four months, Arnold and Frank were together and now both were gone.

On December 17, 1998, Symphony Center was nearly filled to capacity for the *Tribute to Arnold Jacobs.* Students, friends and colleagues arrived from all over the world. Sitting in the center box was the Jacobs family with Gizella Jacobs and her long time friend, Dorothy Crisafulli in the first row.

For the tribute's program, Gizella wrote:

The Arnold Jacobs family greatly appreciates your presence today at this wonderful tribute for our loved one. We thank Henry Fogel and the Chicago Symphony members, colleagues, students, and all who participate.

We are grateful for the variety of sentiments bestowed upon us from so many of you. The plants, flowers, cards, letters and phone calls we received - and are still receiving - from all over the world are happy reminders of love, affection, admiration, and friendship so many had for our dear Arnold, and in some ways for his family.

Letters from many who studied with him say that when they are playing or teaching, Arnold seems to be right therewith them, his voice guiding them. We must believe this is not the "end of an era" but through them, the contribution of the Arnold Jacobs tradition and method of teaching will exist for generations to come.

Arnold's sudden death left the family and the world stunned, shocked and heartbroken, but our memories will keep him alive. While we have tearful moments, we must also rejoice for him, for the new life he entered is free from pain and he has perfect vision again. That grand orchestra in heaven needed another tuba player, and Arnold quickly answered the call, joining his old buddies in a joyful musical reunion.

We know Arnold is with us in spirit right now, and it is time to say "goodbye." He wants to leave us his favorite quote: "Be good to each other - until we meet again."

Henry Fogel read portions of a prayer that was read at a small family final viewing written by a friend of Gizella's for 77 years, Alva Guntner. *". . . He's playing his tuba in God's Heavenly Orchestra and telling all the others how to breathe right. I am sure there are plenty there who didn't have the opportunity to take lessons from the master. . . Arnold was a very special person, who will be remembered all over the world. Those of us who were privileged to know him personally have always considered it an honor. He wasn't just a famous tuba player and teacher. He was a friend and a kind and generous individual. . . . "*

Mr. Fogel added his own comments, *". . . I had never thought of the tuba as a bel canto instrument until I started regularly hearing Jake play – and now I know its possibilities. And on top of that, I had the pleasure to know the man –*

Arnold Jacobs: *Song and Wind*

generous, warm, caring, sensitive, witty – all of the things that made him a unique colleague. If one's goal in life is to make a difference, I can assure you that Arnold Jacobs made a difference . . . "

Norman Schweikert read a statement by retired CSO Bass Trombonist, Edward Kleinhammer, *". . . Countless are the times that I had a 'key hole peek' into heaven playing next to Arnold in a world class orchestra, and countless are the teachings I learned from him in so doing. We had a great understanding and respect between us . . . "*

Adolph Herseth, Principal Trumpet of the CSO said, *". . . It was a great experience to have a colleague like Jake. We enjoyed so many things together, musical things, personal things, social things, shared a lot of experiences - even a sip or two. And I only want to say, it was a pleasure and a privilege to know him and to work with him."*

Harvey Phillips, Distinguished Professor Emeritus from Indiana University stated, *"Into the next millennium, ad infinitum, Arnold Jacobs will stand as an icon of music pedagogy for all teachers and performers of vocal, wind, and brass instruments . . . As a master teacher, I believe it can be said that Arnold Jacobs never met a musician he couldn't improve; his teaching and personal example inspired a better understanding of themselves, their art, and their instrument. He provided logical comprehension and artistic application of his 'Song and Wind' philosophy and pedagogy."*

CSO tubist and Jacobs' successor, Gene Pokorny added, *"The way he chose to teach this material is also worth examining . Although he would teach the subject through instruction and by example, he never forgot that he was not so much teaching the subject as he was teaching the student. . . Even towards the end when his eyes were failing him and his legs were refusing to walk, his attitude was always positive. No matter what he was struggling with physically, he always seemed to be able to smile. And nobody did that better."*

Rex Martin, Tuba instructor at Northwestern University remembered, *". . . My greatest inspiration as a player comes from remembering his tone quality . . . He had the most crystalline clarity to his tone, and the first time I heard it, I knew that I had just listened to the most beautiful sound of my life. I can still hear those few notes, as if he had just played them for me this morning . . . I know that he influenced not only my generation and generations before mine. I also know that he will leave his mark on generations after mine, for many teachers and players of brass instruments subscribe to his approach to music."*

Bernard Droboski, Dean of Northwestern's School of Music stated, *"During his over forty-five years on the faculty of Northwestern University, Arnold Jacobs was responsible for influencing the lives of thousands of our students, regardless of their instrumental or vocal specialization . . .*

Arnold Jacobs' artistry and teaching leave those of us who carry on after him better musicians, better educators, but most importantly — better human beings. I speak for hundreds of his students when I pledge to Gizella that we stand as living memorials to Jake as we will continue to strive for the standards that he

192

established. Mr. Jacobs, we will never forget you. The world cannot help to be a better place because you were once among us. Jake, you are loved. Jake, you will be missed."

During the preparation for the tribute, Gene Pokorny emerged as *the* person who did more to honor his predecessor, possibly more than any other symphony musician. Days prior to the tribute he worked with me nearly seven hours for the Tribute's slide presentation - a true challenge! While he chose to be low keyed, those of us who worked on the memorial would like to recognize him.

Tributes appeared in various brass journals including *TUBA JOURNAL, ITA JOURNAL, ITG JOURNAL,* and the *NEW YORK CONFERENCE FOR BRASS SCHOLARSHIPS.* Worldwide, several concerts were dedicated to Mr. Jacobs including the Chicago Symphony who opened a concert with Gabrieli *Canzonas* dedicated to Jacobs. In April 1999, the *Millar Brass Ensemble,* lead by retired CSO trumpeter Vincent Cichowiz dedicated a concert to Frank Crisafulli and Arnold Jacobs. Special guests were Dallas Jacobs, Gizella Jacobs and Dorothy Crisafulli.

Following his passing, it was obvious that Gizella missed Arnold tremendously. Her health deteriorated rapidly and she was admitted to the hospital in the Spring of 1999. She told me several times that she was only waiting for Arnold to come and take her away. Gizella wanted to be at home, not in a hospital or nursing home so Dallas remained with her nearly ten months and, with the help of his wife Dorothy and caregivers (especially Rebecca Clausen), Gizella remained home with only a few hospital stays. Arnold would have been proud of Dallas and Dorothy!

Finally, on November 26, 1999, Arnold and Gizella were again reunited after a little more than a year apart, Arnold playing in an orchestra and Gizella dancing, just as when they first met more than sixty years earlier.

Christine Querfeld, Harvey Phillips and Gene Pokorny at TubaChristmas, Chicago 2001
Photo by Tom Phillips

Perhaps the highest honor for a symphony musician is the endowment and naming a chair in their honor. In the 1940's, Christine Querfeld accompanied Arnold Jacobs {see: CSO: As a Soloist} and endowed the principal tuba chair.

On October 12, 2001 the Chicago Symphony dedicated the *Arnold Jacobs Principal Tuba Chair, Endowed by Christine Querfeld* with a reception. Dale Clevenger, Gene Pokorny and Edward J. Buckbee, (CSO's former Director of Planned Giving) spoke of Arnold Jacobs and Christine Querfeld {see: Awards}. Due to illness, Christine Querfeld was unable to attend. TubaChristmas - Chicago was dedicated to Christine Querfeld on December 20, 2001. Here she was presented with a plaque by Henry Fogel, Harvey Phillips and Gene Pokorny. Christine Querfeld passed away on April 21, 2002.

Shortly after Mr. Jacobs' passing, Bob Tucci stated, *"Arnold Jacobs did not pass away, he only changed his address."* One time Roger Rocco commented to Mr. Jacobs, *"You will live forever because you taught your students well."* I am sure that all Jacobs student would agree—we were fortunate enough to work with the master himself. The torch has passed to the his students to continue his work and teach future generations.

During the summer of 1998, former CSO trumpeter and Jacobs student William Scarlett asked Mr. Jacobs about sharing the studio in the Fine Arts Building.. After Mr. Jacobs' passing, Scarlett persuaded the building's management to lease the studio to him. After Scarlett's retirement, in 2002 the studio is occupied by John Hagstrom and Charles Vernon. Sounds of aspiring students can still be heard from room 428. As a remembrance, many of Mr. Jacobs are still there including the chair he taught from for twenty five years proudly displayed above the closet.

Another Jacobs student and member of The Marine Band, Frank Byrne, assembled a 77-minute Compact Disc, *Portrait of an Artist* for Summit Records. The goal of this project was to preserve Arnold Jacobs' legacy for future generations by presenting an audio time capsule of his voice, magnificent playing, and teaching philosophy. After an absence of thirty years, in 2002 the Chicago Symphony Trombone and Tuba Section LP was re-released on CD.

The Jacobs family realizes the importance of preserving material Mr. Jacobs used over the years. The problem is that assembling a final collection could take years. During the summer of 1999, Gizella and Dallas allowed me to take Mr. Jacobs' medical books with the idea of creating a *Arnold and Gizella Jacobs Collection*.

Masterclass videos are the major part of the collection. These have been edited and Mr Jacobs returned with his masterclasses with *Arnold Jacobs Almost Live*. Five segments were premiered in Melbourne, Australia in 2004 and was expanded to a three day workshop of ten segments in 2005.

Gizella stated, *"Many who studied with him say that when they are playing or teaching, Arnold seems to be right there with them, his voice guiding them."* Worldwide, concert halls and music studios of those touched by Mr. Jacobs continue to resonate the words *Song and Wind*. All who knew Arnold Jacobs recognize that his true legacy will always live through his students passing his pedagogy and musicianship to their students who will in turn pass the torch to future generations.

Bravo Mr. Jacobs! You will be missed but not forgotten.

Brian Frederiksen, January 2006

Appendix A: Arnold Jacobs Discography[293]

Pittsburgh Symphony Orchestra

Composer	Composition	Conductor	Date	Notes
Berlioz	Hungarian March	Fritz Reiner	11/15/41	
Debussy	Iberia	Fritz Reiner	11/15/41	
R. Strauss	Don Juan	Fritz Reiner	1/9/41	
	Don Quixote	Fritz Reiner	1/15/41	Soloist: Gregor Piatigorsky
Wagner	Die Meistersinger(Prelude to Act I)	Fritz Reiner	3/14/40	Not Released
	Die Meistersinger(Prelude to Act I)	Fritz Reiner	1/9/41	
	Die Meistersinger(Prelude to Act III)	Fritz Reiner	1/9/41	
	Die Meistersinger(Dance of the Apprenticies)	Fritz Reiner	1/9/41	
	Die Meistersinger(Procession of the Masters)	Fritz Reiner	1/9/41	
	Die Valkyrie (Ride of the Valkyries)	Fritz Reiner	3/14/40	
	Lohengrin (Introduction to Act I)	Fritz Reiner	11/15/41	Not Released
	Lohengrin (Introduction to Act III)	Fritz Reiner	3/14/40	
	Lohengrin (Introduction to Act III)	Fritz Reiner	1/9/41	

Arnold Jacobs: *Song and Wind*

Composer	Composition	Conductor	Date	Notes
Wagner (cont.)	*Siegfried (Waldweben)*	Fritz Reiner	3/14/40	Not Released
	Siegfried (Waldweben)	Fritz Reiner	1/9/41	
	Tannhauser (Venusberg Music)	Fritz Reiner	3/14/40	Not Released
	Tannhauser (Venusberg Music)	Fritz Reiner	1/9/41	Not Released
	Tristan Und Isolde (Prelude & Love Death)	Fritz Reiner	3/14/40	Not Released

All-American Youth Orchestra

Composer	Composition	Conductor	Date	Notes
Bach	*Chorale "Ein Feste Burg"*	L. Stokowski	7/3-11/41	
	"Little" Fugue in G Minor	L. Stokowski	7/3-11/41	
	Passacaglia and Fugue in C Minor	L. Stokowski	7/3-11/41	Arr: Stokowski
	Song "Komm Susser Tod"	L. Stokowski	7/3-11/41	Arr: Stokowski
	Toccata and Fugue in D Minor	L. Stokowski	7/3-11/41	Arr: Stokowski
Cowell	*Tales of Our Countryside*	L. Stokowski	7/3-11/41	Henry Cowell,Piano
Creston	*Scherzo from Symphony, Op. 20*	L. Stokowski	7/3-11/41	
Gould	*Guaracha from*	L. Stokowski	7/3-11/41	
	Latin - American Symphoette No. 4			
Mendelssohn	*Midsummer Night's Dream (Scherzo)*	L. Stokowski	7/3-11/41	
Mussorgsky	*Pictures at an Exhibition*	L. Stokowski	7/3-11/41	Arr: Stokowski
	Symphonic Synthesis from Boris Gounov	L. Stokowski	7/3-11/41	Arr: Stokowski

Composer	Composition	Conductor	Date	Notes
Strauss	*Death and Transfiguration*	L. Stokowski	7/3-11/41	
Stravinsky	*Firebird Suite*	L. Stokowski	7/3-11/41	
Tchaikovsky	*Solitude (Again as Before, Alone)*	L. Stokowski	7/3-11/41	Arr: Stokowski

Philadelphia Orchestra

Composer	Composition	Conductor	Date	Notes
Thompson	*Louisiana Story Suite*	Eugene Ormandy	5/49	
Ravel	*Daphnis and Chloe Suite No. 2*	Eugene Ormandy	5/49	

Chicago Symphony

Composer	Composition	Conductor	Date	Notes
Albeniz	*Iberia: "Fete-Dieu a Seville"*	Fritz Reiner	4/26/58	
	Iberia: "Triana"	Fritz Reiner	4/26/58	
	Navarra	Fritz Reiner	4/26/58	
Auber	*Masaniello Overture*	Fritz Reiner	1966	
Barber	*School for Scandal (Overture)*	Thomas Schippers	10/22/55	
Bartok	*Concerto for Orchestra*	Fritz Reiner	1969	
	Concerto for Orchestra	Seiji Ozawa	1/81	Chicago Symphony Release
	Concerto for Orchestra	Georg Solti		Chicago Symphony Release

197

Arnold Jacobs: *Song and Wind*

Composer	Composition	Conductor	Date	Notes
Bartok (cont.)	*Dance Suite*	Georg Solti	1981	
	Hungarian Sketches	Fritz Reiner	12/29/58	
	Miraculous Mandarin	Antal Dorati	1/30/54	
	Miraculous Mandarin	Jean Martinon	1967	
	Miraculous Mandarin	Istvan Kertesz	1968	Chicago Symphony Release
	Piano Concerto No. 2	Claudio Abbado	1977	Soloist: Maurizio Pollini
	Piano Concerto No. 3	Seiji Ozawa	1965	Soloist: Peter Serkin
Berlioz	*Benvenuto Cellini (Overture)*	Fritz Reiner	1957	Chicago Symphony Release
	Damnation of Faust	Georg Solti	1981	Soloist: von Stade, Riegel, Van Dam, King Second Tuba: James Johnson
	Judges of the Secret Court Overture	Georg Solti	1974	
	Romeo and Juliet (Excerpts)	Carlo M. Giulini	1969	Laserdisc
	Romeo and Juliet (Excerpts)	Georg Solti	1977	Second Tuba: Roger Rocco
	Symphonie Fantastique	Georg Solti	1972	Second Tuba: Rex Martin
	Symphonie Fantastique	Claudio Abbado	1983	
Borodin	*Prince Igor: March*	Fritz Reiner	3/14/59	
	Prince Igor: Overture	Georg Solti	1982	Video Cassette
	Prince Igor: Polovetsian Dances	Seiji Ozawa	1969	
	Prince Igor: Polovetsian Dances	Daniel Barenboim	1977	
	Symphony No. 2	Desire Defauw	1947	
Brahms	*A German Requiem*	Georg Solti	1978	Soloist: Kiri Te Kanawa, Weikl
	Academic Festival Overture	Paul Hindemith	1963	Chicago Symphony Release

Arnold Jacobs: *Song and Wind*

Composer	Composition	Conductor	Date	Notes
Brahms (cont.)	*Academic Festival Overture*	Georg Solti	1978	Chicago Symphony Release
	Academic Festival Overture	Eugene Ormandy	1982	
	Symphony No. 2	James Levine	1976	
	Symphony No. 2	Georg Solti	1979	
	Tragic Overture	Fritz Reiner	12/14/57	
	Tragic Overture	Georg Solti	1978	
Britten	*Young Person's Guide to the Orchestra*	Seiji Ozawa	1967	
	Young Person's Guide to the Orchestra	Georg Solti	1979	Not Released
Bruckner	*Symphony No. 4 ("Romantic")*	Daniel Barenboim	1972	
	Symphony No. 4 ("Romantic")	Georg Solti	1981	
	Symphony No. 5	Daniel Barenboim	1977	
	Symphony No. 5	Georg Solti	1980	
	Symphony No. 6	Daniel Barenboim	1977	
	Symphony No. 6	Georg Solti	1979	
	Symphony No. 6	Georg Solti	1979	Laserdisc - Not Released
	Symphony No. 7	Daniel Barenboim	1979	
	Symphony No. 7	Georg Solti	1986	Sub Tuba (Portions): Rex Martin
	Symphony No. 8	Daniel Barenboim	1980	
	Symphony No. 9	Daniel Barenboim	1975	
	Symphony No. 9	Carlo M. Giulini	1976	
Bruch	*Violin Concerto No. 1*	Claudio Abbado	1980	Soloist: Shlomo Mintz
Copland	*Dance Symphony*	Morton Gould	1965	

Arnold Jacobs: *Song and Wind*

Composer	Composition	Conductor	Date	Notes
Creston	Fantasy for Trombone and Orchestra	Georg Solti	1976	Chicago Symphony Release Soloist: Jay Friedman
Debussy	Images for Orchestra No. 2: "Iberia"	Fritz Reiner	3/4/57	
	La Mer	Fritz Reiner	2/27/60	
	La Mer	Georg Solti	1976	Chicago Symphony Release
	La Mer	Erich Leinsdorf	1978	Chicago Symphony Release
	Nuages			
Defalla	Love the Magician Suite	Fritz Reiner	1963	Soloist: Leontyne Price
	La Vida Breve: Interlude and Dance	Fritz Reiner	4/26/58	
	Three Cornered Hat, Suite No. 2	Fritz Reiner	4/26/58	
	Three Cornered Hat, Suite No. 2	Earnst Ansermet	1968	Chicago Symphony Release
Dohnanyi	Variations on a Nursery Air	Georg Solti	1985	Soloist: Andras Schiff
Dvorak	Carnival Overture	Fritz Reiner	1/7/56	
	Cello Concerto	Daniel Barenboim	1970	Soloist: Jacqueline du Pre
	Symphony No. 8	Carlo M. Giulini	1978	
	Symphony No. 9 ("New World")	Rafael Kubelik	11/21/51	
	Symphony No. 9 ("New World")	Fritz Reiner	11/9/57	
	Symphony No. 9 ("New World")	Carlo M. Giulini	1977	
Elgar	Enigma Variations	Georg Solti	5/74	
	Violin Concerto	Daniel Barenboim	1981	Soloist: Itzhak Perlman
Finzi	New Year Music (Nocturne)	Leonard Slatkin	1983	Chicago Symphony Release
Franck	Le Chasseur Maudit	Desire Defauw	1946	

Arnold Jacobs: *Song and Wind*

Composer	Composition	Conductor	Date	Notes
Frank (cont.)	*Psyche: Three Excerpts*	Desire Defauw	1945	
	Redemption, Symphonic Interlude	Desire Defauw	1946	
	Symphony in D Minor	Pierre Monteux	1961	
Gould	*Spirituals*	Morton Gould	1965	
Hindemith	*Cello Concerto*	Fritz Reiner	1957	Chicago Symphony Release
				Soloist: Janos Starker
	Nobilissima Visione Suite	Jean Martinon	1968	
	Symphonic Metamorphosis of Themes by Weber	Rafael Kubelik	4/4/53	
Hovhaness	*Symphony No. 2* *("Mysterious Mountain")*	Fritz Reiner	4/28/58	
Ives	*Orchestra Set No. 2*	Morton Gould	1967	
	Robert Browning Overture	Morton Gould	1967	
	Symphony No. 1	Morton Gould	1965	
	Three Places in New England *("Putnam's Camp")*	Morton Gould	1967	
	Variations on "America"	Morton Gould	1966	
Janacek	*Sinfonietta*	Seiji Ozawa	1970	
Kabalevsky	*Colas Breugnon Overture*	Fritz Reiner	3/14/59	
Khachaturian	*Gayne Ballet Suite No. 1*	Arthur Rodzinski	11/18/47	
	Symphony No. 3	L. Stokowski	1968	
Lalo	*Le Roi D'ys Overture*	Jean Martinon	1966	

Arnold Jacobs: *Song and Wind*

Composer	Composition	Date	Conductor	Notes
Lalo (cont.)	Symphonie Espagnole	2/28/59	Walter Hendl	Soloist: Henryk Szeryng
Liebermann	Concerto for Jazz Band and Orchestra	12/6/54	Fritz Reiner	Soloist: Sauter - Finegan Band
Liszt	Les Preludes	1977	Daniel Barenboim	
	Mephisto Waltz (Episode No. 2)	12/10/55	Fritz Reiner	
	Symphonic Poem No. 7 ("Festklange")	1977	Georg Solti	Chicago Symphony Release
	Todtentanz	2/23/59	Fritz Reiner	Soloist: Byron Janis
Lutoslawski	Concerto for Orchestra	1970	Seiji Ozawa	
Mahler	Das Lied von der Erde	11/9/59	Fritz Reiner	Soloist: Forrester, Lewis
	Das Lied von der Erde	1972	Georg Solti	Soloist: Minton, Kollo
	Four Songs from Des Knaben Wunderhorn	1970	Georg Solti	Soloist: Yvonne Minton
	Songs from Ruckert	1981	Claudio Abbado	Soloist: Hanna Schwarz
	Symphony No. 1 ("Titan")	1971	Carlo M. Giulini	
	Symphony No. 1 ("Titan")	1981	Claudio Abbado	
	Symphony No. 2 ("Resurrection")	1976	Claudio Abbado	Sub Tuba (Portions): Russell Ward
	Symphony No. 2 ("Resurrection")	1980	Georg Solti	Soloist: Marilyn Horne, Neblett
	Symphony No. 3	1975	James Levine	Soloist: Buchanan, Mira Zakai
	Symphony No. 3	1983	Georg Solti	Soloist: Mayilyn Horne
	Symphony No. 5	5/70	Georg Solti	Sub Tuba (Portions): Rex Martin
	Symphony No. 5	1980	Claudio Abbado	Soloist: Helga Dernesch
	Symphony No. 5	1986	Georg Solti	Laserdisc

Arnold Jacobs: *Song and Wind*

Composer	Composition	Conductor	Date	Notes
Mahler (cont.)	*Symphony No. 6*	Georg Solti	1970	
	Symphony No. 6	Claudio Abbado	1979	
	Symphony No. 7	Georg Solti	1971	
	Symphony No. 7	James Levine	7/15/80	Sub Tuba (Portions): Rex Martin
	Symphony No. 7	Claudio Abbado	1984	
	Symphony No. 7	Georg Solti	1986	Various Soloists
	Symphony No. 8 ("Symphony of a Thousand")	Georg Solti	1971	Various Soloists
	Symphony No. 8 ("Symphony of a Thousand")			
	Part 1: Hymnus: Veni, Creator Spiritus			
	Symphony No. 9	James Levine	1979	Chicago Symphony Release
	Symphony No. 9	Carlo M. Giulini	1976	
	Symphony No. 10 (Deryck Cooke Version)	Georg Solti	1982	
Martinon	*Overture pour une Tragedie Grecque*	Jean Martinon	1966	Chicago Symphony Release
	Symphony No. 4 ("Altitudes")	Jean Martinon	1967	Chicago Symphony Release
Mendelssohn	*Midsummer Night's Dream(Incidental Music)*	Jean Martinon	1967	
	Midsummer Night's Dream(Incidental Music)	Georg Solti	1976	Laserdisc - Not Released
	Midsummer Night's Dream(Incidental Music)	James Levine	1984	
	Midsummer Night's Dream(Overture)	Georg Solti	1976	Chicago Symphony Release
	Midsummer Night's Dream(Overture)	Daniel Barenboim	1979	
Mennin	*Symphony No. 7*	Jean Martinon	1967	

Arnold Jacobs: *Song and Wind*

Composer	Composition	Conductor	Date	Notes
Miaskovsky	*Symphony No. 21*	Morton Gould	1968	
Mussorgsky	*Night on Bald Mountain*	Fritz Reiner	3/14/59	
	Night on Bald Mountain	Seiji Ozawa	1968	
	Night on Bald Mountain	Daniel Barenboim	1977	
	Pictures at an Exhibition	Rafael Kubelik	4/24/51	*Bydlo:* Arnold Jacobs
	Pictures at an Exhibition	Fritz Reiner	12/7/57	
	Pictures at an Exhibition	Seiji Ozawa	1967	*Bydlo:* Arnold Jacobs
	Pictures at an Exhibition	Carlo M. Giulini	1976	
	Pictures at an Exhibition	Georg Solti	5/80	
	Pictures at an Exhibition	Georg Solti	1986	Laserdisc - Not Released
Nielsen	*Helios Overture*	Jean Martinon	1966	
	Symphony No. 2 ("Four Temperments")	Morton Gould	1966	
	Symphony No. 4 ("Inextinguishable")	Jean Martinon	1966	
Orff	*Carmina Burana*	James Levine	1984	Soloist: Anderson, Creech, Weikl
Prokofiev	*Alexander Nevsky*	Fritz Reiner	3/9/59	Soloist: Rosalind Elias
	Lieutenant Kije Suite	Fritz Reiner	3/2/57	
	Lieutenant Kije Suite	Claudio Abbado	1977	
	Romeo and Juliet (Excerpts)	Georg Solti	1982	
	Scythian Suite	Desire Defauw	1945	
	Scythian Suite	Claudio Abbado	1977	
Rachmaninoff	*Symphony No. 5*	Fritz Reiner	1958	
	Isle of the Dead	Fritz Reiner	4/13/57	Chicago Symphony Release

Arnold Jacobs: *Song and Wind*

Composer	Composition	Conductor	Date	Notes
Rachmaninoff				
(cont.)	*Piano Concerto No. 2*	Fritz Reiner	1/9/56	Soloist: Arthur Rubinstein
	Piano Concerto No. 2	Fritz Reiner	1962	Soloist: Van Cliburn
	Piano Concerto No. 3	Georges Pretre	1967	Soloist: Alexis Weissenberg
	Rhapsody on a Theme by Paganini	Fritz Reiner	1/16/56	Soloist: Arthur Rubinstein
Ravel	*Alborada Del Gracioso*	Fritz Reiner	4/13/57	
	Alborada Del Gracioso	Jean Martinon	1968	
	Bolero	Jean Martinon	1966	
	Bolero	Georg Solti	5/76	
	Daphnis and Chloe Suite No. 2	Jean Martinon	1964	
	La Valse	Jean Martinon	1967	
	Rapsodie Espagnole	Fritz Reiner	11/3/56	
	Rapsodie Espagnole	Jean Martinon	1968	
	Valses Nobles et Sentimentales	Fritz Reiner	4/15/57	
Respighi	*Pines of Rome*	Fritz Reiner	10/24/59	
	Fountains of Rome	Fritz Reiner	10/24/59	
Rimsky-Korsakov	*Capriccio Espagnol*	Daniel Barenboim	1977	
	Russian Easter Overture	L. Stokowski	1968	
	Russian Easter Overture	Daniel Barenboim	1977	
	Scheherazade	Fritz Reiner	2/8/60	
	Scheherazade	Seiji Ozawa	1969	

Arnold Jacobs: *Song and Wind*

Composer	Composition	Conductor	Date	Notes
Rimsky-Korsakov (cont.)				
	Symphony No. 2 ("Antar")	Morton Gould	1968	
Rossini	*La Gazza Ladra*	Fritz Reiner	11/22/58	
Roussel	*Bacchus and Ariadne, Suite No. 2*	Jean Martinon	1964	
	Bacchus and Ariadne, Suite No. 2	Charles Munch	1966	Chicago Symphony Release
Saint-Saens	*Symphony No. 3 ("Organ")*	Daniel Barenboim	1975	
Schoenberg	*Five Pieces*	Rafael Kubelik	4/4/53	
	Piano Concerto	Seiji Ozawa	1967	Soloist: Peter Serkin
	Variations for Orchestra	Georg Solti	1975	
Scriabin	*Poem of Ecstasy*	Daniel Barenboim	1984	Chicago Symphony Release
Shostakovich	*Age of Gold Ballet Suite*	L. Stokowski	1968	
	Symphony No. 1	Georg Solti	1977	Laserdisc - Not Released
	Symphony No. 1	Leonard Bernstein	6/1988	Sub Tuba (Portions): Rex Martin
	Symphony No. 4	Andre Previn	1977	Second Tuba: Dave Fedderly
	Symphony No. 5	Andre Previn	1977	
	Symphony No. 6	L. Stokowski	1968	
	Symphony No. 7 ("Leningrad")	Leonard Bernstein	6/1988	Sub Tuba (Portions): Rex Martin
	Symphony No. 10	L. Stokowski	1966	Chicago Symphony Release
Smetana	*Ma Vlast (Complete)*	Rafael Kubelik	12/6/52	
	Ma Vlast (Moldau)	Daniel Barenboim	1977	
Johann Strauss	*Morning Papers*	Fritz Reiner	4/15/57	
	On the Beautiful Blue Danube	Fritz Reiner	4/15/57	

Arnold Jacobs: *Song and Wind*

Composer	Composition	Conductor	Date	Notes
J. Strauss(cont.)	*Thunder and Lightning Polka*	Fritz Reiner	4/26/60	
	Mein Lebenslauf	Fritz Reiner	4/26/60	
Richard Strauss	*Also Sprach Zarathustra*	Arthur Rodzinski	11/17/47	Second Tuba: Michael Perrone
	Also Sprach Zarathustra	Fritz Reiner	3/8/54	Second Tuba: Daniel Corrigan
	Also Sprach Zarathustra	Fritz Reiner	1962	Second Tuba: Charles Guse
	Also Sprach Zarathustra	Georg Solti	1975	Second Tuba: James Johnson
	Also Sprach Zarathustra	Georg Solti	1982	Video Cassette
				Second Tuba: Dave Fedderly
				Chicago Symphony Release
	Death and Transfiguration	Desire Defauw	1947	
	Der Rosenkavalier: Waltzes	Fritz Reiner	4/15/57	
	Don Juan	Fritz Reiner	12/6/54	
	Don Juan	Fritz Reiner	2/6/60	
	Don Juan	Georg Solti	1972	
	Don Juan	Georg Solti	1977	Laserdisc - Not Released
	Don Quixote	Fritz Reiner	4/11/59	Soloist: Janigro, Preves
	Ein Heldenleben	Fritz Reiner	3/6/54	
	Elektra: Monologue, Duet & Recognition	Fritz Reiner	4/16/56	Soloist: Borkh, Yeend,
	Four Last Songs	Georg Solti	1977	Soloist: Lucia Popp
				Laserdisc - Not Released
	Salome (Selections)	Fritz Reiner	3/6/54 & 12/10/55	
	Symphonia Domestica	Fritz Reiner	11/5/56	
	Till Eulenspiegels Lustige Streiche	Georg Solti	1975	Portions: James Johnson

Arnold Jacobs: *Song and Wind*

Composer	Composition	Conductor	Date	Notes
R. Strauss (cont.)	*Till Eulenspiegels Lustige Streiche*	Georg Solti	1977	Laserdisc - Not Released
Stravinsky	*Firebird (Suite - 1919)*	Carlo M. Giulini	1969	
	Fireworks	Desire Defauw	1946	
	Fireworks	Seiji Ozawa	1968	
	Petrouchka (Suite - 1947)	Carlo M. Giulini	1969	
	Petrouchka (Complete)	James Levine	1977	
	Rite of Spring	Seiji Ozawa	1968	Second Tuba: Clyde Bashand
	Rite of Spring	Georg Solti	5/74	Second Tuba: James Johnson
	Song of the Nightingale	Fritz Reiner	11/3/56	
	The Fairy's Kiss: Divertimento	Fritz Reiner	4/28/58	
Tchaikovsky	*1812 Overture*	Fritz Reiner	1/7/56	
	1812 Overture	Daniel Barenboim	1981	
	Marche Slave	Fritz Reiner	3/14/59	
	Marche Slave	Daniel Barenboim	1981	Sub Tuba (Port):Dave Fedderly
	Nutcracker: Excerpts	Fritz Reiner	3/21/59	
	Nutcracker: Waltzes	Morton Gould	1966	
	Romeo and Juliet	Antal Dorati	1/30/54	
	Romeo and Juliet	Daniel Barenboim	1981	
	Sleeping Beauty	Morton Gould	1965	
	Symphony No. 4	Rafael Kubelik	11/20/51	
	Symphony No. 5	Seiji Ozawa	1968	
	Symphony No. 5	Georg Solti	1975	

Arnold Jacobs: *Song and Wind*

Composer	Composition	Conductor	Date	Notes
Tchaikovsky (cont.)	*Symphony No. 5*	Morton Gould	1966	
	Symphony No. 5	Georg Solti	1988	
	Symphony No. 6 ("Pathetique")	Rafael Kubelik	4/22/52	
	Symphony No. 6 ("Pathetique")	Fritz Reiner	4/16/57	
	Symphony No. 6 ("Pathetique")	Georg Solti	1976	
	Symphony No. 6 ("Pathetique")	James Levine	7/16/84	
	Symphony No. 6 ("Pathetique")	Claudio Abbado	1986	
	Swan Lake: Valse Bluette, Waltz, Waltz of the Swans			
	Swan Lake (Suite)	Morton Gould	1966	
		Georg Solti	1988	
Tippett	*Suite in D Major, a Suite for the Birthday of Prince Charles*	Georg Solti	1981	Euphonium: Tim Meyers
Vaughan Williams	*Symphony No. 4*	Georg Solti	1979	
	Concerto for Bass Tuba and Orchestra	Daniel Barenboim	3/27/1977	Soloist: Arnold Jacobs
	Concerto for Bass Tuba and Orchestra	Henry Mazer	10/1978	Soloist: Arnold Jacobs Chicago Symphony Release
Varese	*Arcana*	Jean Martinon	1966	Second Tuba: John Taylor
Verdi	*Four Sacred Pieces*	Georg Solti	1978	Soloist: Jo Ann Pickens
	Requiem Mass	Georg Solti	1977	Soloist: Price, Baker, Van Dam, Luchetti

Arnold Jacobs: *Song and Wind*

Composer	Composition	Conductor	Date	Notes
Wagner	Die Meistersinger (Prelude to Act 1)	Fritz Reiner	4/18/59	
	Die Meistersinger (Prelude to Act 1)	Georg Solti	1972	
	Die Meistersinger (Prelude to Act 1)	Georg Solti	1976	Laserdisc
	Die Meistersinger (Prelude to Act III)	Fritz Reiner	4/18/59	
	Flying Dutchman (Complete)	Georg Solti	1976	Soloist: Bailey, Martin, Talvela
	Flying Dutchman (Overture)	Georg Solti	5/76	Laserdisc
	Gotterdammerung: Siegfried's Rhine Journey	Fritz Reiner	4/18/59	
	Gotterdammerung: Funeral Music	Fritz Reiner	4/18/59	
	Parsifal: Good Friday Spell	Fritz Reiner	1958	Chicago Symphony Release
	Rienzi (Overture)	Fritz Reiner	1958	Chicago Symphony Release
	Tannhauser (Overture)	Georg Solti	5/77	
	Tristan and Isolde (Prelude to Act III)	Arthur Rodzinski	11/17/47	
	Tristan and Isolde (Prelude & Liebestod)	Arthur Rodzinski	12/13/47	
	Tristan and Isolde (Prelude & Liebestod)	Fritz Reiner	1958	Chicago Symphony Release
	Tristan and Isolde (Prelude & Liebestod)	Georg Solti	5/76	Laserdisc
	Tristan and Isolde (Prelude & Liebestod)	Georg Solti	5/77	
Webern	Six Pieces	Fritz Reiner		Chicago Symphony Release
Weinberger	Schwanda Polka and Fugue	Fritz Reiner	1/7/56	
Weill	Three Penny Opera	Erich Leinsdorf	1985	Chicago Symphony Release
	Suite Kleine Dreigroschenmusik for Wind Orchestra	Erich Leinsdorf	1985	Chicago Symphony Release

Chicago Symphony Brass Quintet

Bach	*Sarabande and Minuet*	1954
Beethoven	*Quartet, Op.18, No. 2*	1954
Gabrieli	*Canzona per Sonare, No. 2*	1954
Haines	*Toccata*	1954
Hindemith	*Morgen Musik*	1954
Lebow	*Suite for Brass*	1954
Reiche	*Sonata No. 15*	1954
Weelkes	*A Gay Tune*	1954
Zindars	*Suite for Brass*	1954

Philadelphia, Cleveland, Chicago Brass Ensembles

Gabrielli	*Canzon a 12 in Echo*	1968
	Sonata Oavi Toni	1968
	Canzon Quarti Toni	1968
	Canzona per Sonore No. 2	1968

Gunnison Music Camp - Director's Band

Composer	Composition	Date	Conductor	Notes
Bell	*The Elephant's Tango*	1961	Robert Hawkins	Soloist: Bill Bell, Tuba
Bennett	*Flute Fresco*	1961	Glen C. Bainum	Soloist: Jervis Underwood, Flute
Berlioz	*Roman Carnival Overture*	1963	Robert Hawkins	
Brahms	*Symphony No. 3*	1962	Robert Hawkins	
	Tragic Overture	1962	Robert Hawkins	
Butterfield	*Toccata / Archaic Portrait*	1961		Arnold Jacobs, Bill Bell
Catozzi	*Beelzebub*	1961	Robert Hawkins	Soloist: Arnold Jacobs, Tuba
Delius	*The Walk to the Paradise Garden*	1963	Robert Hawkins	
Dvorak	*Symphony No. 5 ("from the New World")*	1961	Robert Hawkins	
Frank	*Psyche Symphonic Poem*	1963	Robert Hawkins	
	Symphony in D Minor	1963	Robert Hawkins	
Gabrieli	*Canzon Duodecemi Toni*	1961		
Kleinsinger	*Tubby the Tuba*	1962	Robert Hawkins	Soloist: Bill Bell, Tuba and Narrator
Liszt	*Les Preludes*	1963	Robert Hawkins	
Mozart	*Bassoon Concerto*	1962	Robert Hawkins	Soloist: Leonard Sharrow, Bassoon
	O Isis and Osiris from The Magic Flute	1961	Robert Hawkins	Soloist: Bill Bell, tuba
	Horn Concerto No. 4	1963	Robert Hawkins	Soloist: Milan Yancich, Horn
Paganini	*Moto Perpetuo*	1963	Robert Hawkins	Soloist: Arnold Jacobs, Bill Bell,

Arnold Jacobs: *Song and Wind*

Harvey Phillips, Tubas

Composer	Composition	Conductor	Date	Notes
Prokofieff	*Peter and the Wolf*	Robert Hawkins	1963	Bill Bell, Narrator
Rachmaninoff	*Piano Concerto No. 2*	Robert Hawkins	1961	Soloist: Rodney Ash, Piano
Rimsky-Korsaskav				
	Trombone Concerto	Robert Hawkins	1963	Soloist: Lawrence Wiehe
Rossini	*Overture to La Cenerentola*	Robert Hawkins	1962	
Rozsa	*Ben Hur Overture*	Robert Hawkins	1961	
Saint-Saens	*The Swan*	Robert Hawkins	1962	Soloist: Earle Louder, Euphonium, Carol Peebles, Harp
	Introduction and Rondo Capriccioso	Charles Brendler	1961	Soloist: Paul Todd, Violin
	Piano Concerto No. 2	Robert Hawkins	1962	Soloist: Rodney Ash, Piano
	Morceau de Concert	Robert Hawkins	1961	Soloist: Milan Yancich, Horn
Strauss, Richard	*Horn Concerto No. 1*	Robert Hawkins	1962	Soloist: Arnold Jacobs, Tuba
Stravinsky	*Concerto for Piano and Wind Orchestra*	Robert Hawkins	1963	Soloist: Rodney Ash, Piano
Tchaikovsky	*Symphony No. 4*	Robert Hawkins	1962	
	Francesca da Rimini	Robert Hawkins	1963	
Thomas	*Polonaise from Mignon: Jesuist*	Robert Hawkins	1961	Soloist: Richard Waller, Clarinet
Verdi	*Fors E Lui from La Traviata*	Robert Hawkins	1961	Soloist: Richard Waller, Clarinet
Weber	*Clarinet Concerto No. 1*	Robert Hawkins	1962	Soloist: Richard Waller, Clarinet
Zindars	*The Brass Square*	Gabriel Bartold	1963	Soloist: Richard Waller, Clarinet

Dick Schory's Percussion and Brass Ensemble
Runnin' Wild (The Sound your Eyes can Follow)

Composer	Composition	Date	Notes
Dick Schorey-W. Charkovsky	*Brass Jockeys*	1961	
Rose-Jolson-Dreyer	*Me and My Shadow*	1961	
W. Charkovsky	*Portrait in Jazz*	1961	
Peter Boccage-A.J. Piron	*Mama's Gone, Goodbye*	1961	
George and Ira Gershwin	*But Not for Me*	1961	
Cole Porter	*Love for Sale*	1961	
Grey-Wood-Gibbs	*Runnin' Wild*	1961	
Mercer-Charmichael	*Lazy Bones*	1961	
Roger Lewis-Wilbur Sweatman	*Down Home Rag*	1961	
Spec. Arr Dick Schorey	*Greensleeves*	1961	
M. Simpson	*Bully*	1961	Soloist: Arnold Jacobs, tuba
			William Babcock, trumpet
Richard Rogers-Lorenz Hart	*Thou Swell*	1961	

recorded in Orchestra Hall, Chicago

Chicago Symphony Trombone and Tuba Sections

Composer	Composition	Conductor	Date	Notes
Berlioz	Excerpt from *Damnation of Faust: Rakoczy March*	Joseph Kreines	7/71	
Brahms	*Ein Ist Ein Ros'entsprungen*	Joseph Kreines	7/71	
Bruckner	Excerpt from *Symphony No. 8* (Fourth Movement)	Joseph Kreines	7/71	
	Excerpt from *Symphony No. 4* (First Movement)	Joseph Kreines	7/71	
Gliere	Excerpt from *Symphony No. 3* (First Movement)	Joseph Kreines	7/71	
Holst	Excerpt from the *Planets: Mars*	Joseph Kreines	7/71	
Kreines	*Chorale Variations*	Joseph Kreines	7/71	
Mahler	Excerpt from *Symphony No. 3* (First Movement)	Joseph Kreines	7/71	
	Excerpt from *Symphony No. 2* (Fifth Movement)	Joseph Kreines	7/71	
Smetana	Excerpt from *The Moldau*	Joseph Kreines	7/71	

Arnold Jacobs: *Song and Wind*

Composer	Composition	Conductor	Date	Notes
Tchaikovsky	Excerpt from *1812 Overture*	Joseph Kreines	7/71	
	Excerpt from *Symphony No. 6* (Fourth Movement)			
Tomasi	*To Be or Not to Be*	Joseph Kreines	7/71	
Verdi	Excerpt from *Nabucco*	Joseph Kreines	7/71	
Wagner	Excerpt from *Tannhauser: Overture*	Joseph Kreines	7/71	
	Excerpt from *Die Valkyrie:*	Joseph Kreines	7/71	
	Wotan's Fire and Magic Fire Music	Joseph Kreines	7/71	
	Excerpt from *Lohengrin: Prelude to Act III*	Joseph Kreines	7/71	
	Excerpt from *Die Valkyrie: Ride of the Valkyries*	Joseph Kreines	7/71	

Appendix B: Brass Personnel

Indianapolis Symphony Orchestra Brass Personnel 1937-39[294]

	1937-38	1938-39
Principal Horn	Frank Brouk	
Asst. Principal Horn	Myron Barber	
Horn 2	W. Frederick Schaub	
Horn 3	Norman Pickering	
Horn 4	Harry M. Michels	
Trumpet 1	Max Woodbury	
Trumpet 2	Louis Ruth	
Trumpet 3	F. Kessler	
Trumpet 4	Charles Munger	
Trombone 1	Guy Boswell	
Trombone 2	Charles Payne	
Trombone 3	A. Worth	Robert Harper
Euphonium	Noble Howard	
Tuba	Arnold Jacobs (A)	

Pittsburgh Symphony Orchestra Brass Personnel 1939-44[295]

	1939-40	1940-41	1941-42	1942-43	1943-44
Principal Horn	Wendell Hoss		Tibor Shik	Leonard Klein (F)	Mary Patricia Quinn
Asst PrinHorn	Mario Grilli		Martin Noliboff	Allan Fuchs	Morris Secon (H)
Horn 2	Frank Gorell	Ginesio Lecce	Jack Kirksmith	William Brown	William Miller
Horn 3	Attilio DePalma	Tibor Shik	James Chambers	Hugh Cowden (F)	
Horn 4	Ginesio Lecce	Frank Gorell			
Extra Horn			August Fischer(E)	Robert Hare (G)	
Trumpet 1	Murray Karpilovsky			James Tamburini (F)	Irving Sarin (H)
Trumpet 2	James Morrow				Max Gershunoff
Trumpet 3	William Post				Karl Wennerberg
Trumpet 4	Joseph Nirella	James Parella	John Harmaala (D)	Guy Borrelli	Vacant
Trombone 1	Neal Di Biase				Howard Cole (H)
Trombone 2	Donato Cerilli (A)				Donald Emberg (H)
Trombone 3	Howard Cole (B)				Louis Counihan
Tuba	Arnold Jacobs (C)			Arnold Jacobs	
Personnel Mgr	Frank Panella	John Harmaala (D)			Chauncey Brown

All-American Youth Orchestra - 1941[296]

Principal Horn	Edward Murphy
Asst. Prin. Horn	Americus Tomei
Horn 2	James Chambers
Horn 3	Helen Kotas (A)
Horn 4	Hilbert Moses
Trumpet 1	Saul Caston (B)
Trumpet 2	John Clyman
Trumpet 3	Lloyd Geisler
Trombone 1	Charles Gusikoff (C)
Trombone 2	Robert Marsteller
Trombone 3	Howard Cole (D)
Tuba	Arnold Jacobs (E)

Arnold Jacobs: *Song and Wind*

Chicago Symphony Trumpet Personnel 1944-88[297]

Season	Music Director	Principal Trumpet	Second Trumpet	Third/Asst. Principal Trumpet	Fourth Trumpet
1944-45	Desire Defauw (A)	Gerald Huffman (B)	Ed Masacek (C)	Renold Schilke (D)	Frank Holz (E)
1945-46		Huffman/Baker (F)			
1946-47		Sydney Baker	Gerald Huffman		
1947-48	Arthur Rodzinski				
1948-49	Guest Conductors	Adolph Herseth (G)			
1949-50					
1950-51	Raphael Kubelik		Rudolph Nashan	Gerald Huffman	Renold Schilke
1951-52				William Babcock	Robert Grocock
1952-53					Vincent Cichowicz
1953-54	Fritz Reiner				
1954-55					
1955-56					
1956-57					
1957-58					
1958-59				Frank Kaderabek	
1959-60					
1960-61			Vincent Cichowicz		
1961-62					Rudolph Nashan
1962-63					(H)
1963-64	Jean Martinon				Vacant (H)

220

Arnold Jacobs: *Song and Wind*

Season	Music Director	Principal Trumpet	Second Trumpet	Third/Asst. Principal Trumpet	Fourth Trumpet
1964-65					William Scarlett
1965-66					
1966-67				William Scarlett	Charles Geyer (I)
1967-68					
1968-69	Irwin Hoffman (J)				
1969-70	Georg Solti				
1970-71					
1971-72					
1972-73					
1973-74					
1974-75			Charles Geyer		Philip Smith (K)
1975-76					
1976-77					
1977-78					
1978-79			George Vosburgh(L)		Timothy Kent (M)
1979-80					
1980-81					
1981-82					
1982-83					
1983-84					
1984-85					
1985-86					
1986-87					
1987-88					

221

Chicago Symphony Trombone Personnel 1944-88[298]

Season	Music Director	Principal Trombone	Assist Principal Trombone	Second Trombone	Bass Trombone
1944-45	Desire Defauw	Frank Crisafulli (A)	Richard Schmitt(B)	David Anderson(C)	Elmer Janes (D)
1945-46		Richard Schmitt (E)	Vacant		Edward Kleinhammer (F)
1946-47		Frank Crisafulli	Vacant		
1947-48	Arthur Rodzinski		Joseph Bejcek		
1948-49	Guest Conductors				
1949-50					
1950-51	Raphael Kubelik		Vacant		
1951-52			Joseph Bejcek		
1952-53					
1953-54	Fritz Reiner				
1954-55			Robert Rada (G)		
1955-56		Robert Lambert		Frank Crisafulli	
1956-57					
1957-58			John Swallow		
1958-59					
1959-60			Byron Peebles		
1960-61					
1961-62					
1962-63					
1963-64	Jean Martinon		Jay Friedman		

Arnold Jacobs: *Song and Wind*

Season	Music Director	Principal Trombone	Assist Principal Trombone	Second Trombone	Bass Trombone
1964-65		Jay Friedman (H)	Glenn Dodson		
1965-66					
1966-67					
1967-68					
1968-69	Irwin Hoffman		James Gilbertsen		
1969-70	Georg Solti				
1970-71					
1971-72					
1972-73					
1973-74					
1974-75					
1975-76					
1976-77					
1977-78		(I)			
1978-79		(I)			
1979-80					
1980-81					
1981-82					
1982-83			(J)		
1983-84					
1984-85					
1985-86					Vacant
1986-87					Charles Vernon
1987-88					

Chicago Symphony Horn Personnel 1944-88[299]

Season	Principal Horn	Associate Principal Horn	Assistant Principal Horn	Second Horn	Third Horn	Fourth Horn
1944-45	Helen Kotas(A)	Vacant	Charles Jackson(B)	Clyde Wedgwood(C)	Harry Jacobs(D)	Max Pottag(E)
1945-46			William Verschoor (F)			Joseph Mourek (G)
1946-47						
1947-48	Philip Farkas	Helen Kotas (H)	Milan Yancich			
1948-49		Vacant				
1949-50					John Henigbaum	
1950-51						
1951-52			Hugh Cowden		Gail Weimer	
1952-53			Cowden / Arthur Goldstein (I)			
1953-54			Cowden / Alan Fuchs (J)			
1954-55			Alan Fuchs		Wayne Barrington	
1955-56		Louis Stout				
1956-57		Vacant	Louis Stout			
1957-58						
1958-59	Christopher Leuba		Arthur Krehbiel		Barrington / Louis Stout (K)	
1959-60					Barrington / Louis Stout (K)	
1960-61		Frank Brouk (L)			Wayne Barrington	
1961-62		Arthur Krehbiel				
1962-63	Frank Brouk		Vacant			
1963-64	C. Van Norman	Frank Brouk	Richard Oldberg (M)			

Arnold Jacobs: *Song and Wind*

Season	Principal Horn	Associate Principal Horn	Assistant Principal Horn	Second Horn	Third Horn	Fourth Horn
1964-65	Brouk/Clevenger(N)	Frank Brouk	Nancy Fako		Richard Oldberg	
1965-66						
1966-67	Dale Clevenger					
1967-68						
1968-69			Vacant (O)			
1969-70		David Babcock	Frank Brouk (P)	Wedgewood /Brouk (P)		
1970-71		Thomas Howell (Q)	Norman Schweikert (R)			
1971-72		Thomas Howell	Norman Schweikert			
1972-73						
1973-74						
1974-75						
1975-76			Daniel Gingrich	Norman Schweikert		Frank Brouk
1976-77						
1977-78						
1978-79			Gail Williams (S)			Daniel Gingrich
1979-80						
1980-81						
1981-82						
1982-83						
1983-84						
1984-85		Gail Williams (T)	Thomas Howell (T)			
1985-86						
1986-87						
1987-88						

225

Indianapolis Symphony Orchestra Personnel Notes

(A)   Jacobs replaced Harry Brown from the 1936-37 season. Robert Barr replaced Jacobs in the 1939-40 season.

Pittsburgh Symphony Orchestra Personnel Notes

(A)   Donato Cerilli replaced Ottavio Ferrara from the previous season.

(B)   Howard Cole replaced Davis Shuman from the previous season. Cole played with Jacobs in the All-American Youth Orchestra and the England-Scotland tour of the Philadelphia Orchestra.

(C)   Arnold Jacobs replaced Michael J. Hickly from the previous season. Jacobs was replaced by Louis Chassagne in 1944-45.

(D)   John Harmaala was a student at the Curtis Institute graduating in 1936 with Jacobs.

(E)   August Fischer was an extra and removed from the roster October 18, 1941.

(F)   Hugh Cowden later played in the Chicago Symphony with Jacobs.

(G)   Robert Hare was an extra player and not on the regular roster.

(H)   In service with the United States Armed Forces.

All-American Youth Orchestra Notes

(A)   Helen Kotas played in the Chicago Symphony with Jacobs.

(B)   Saul Caston was the assistant conductor and played in the Philadelphia Orchestra. He taught at the Curtis Institute while Jacobs was there.

(C)   Charles Gusikoff was in the Philadelphia Orchestra and was with Jacobs on the England-Scotland tour.

(D)   Howard Cole played in the Pittsburgh Symphony with Jacobs.

(E)   The tubist during the 1940 tour was Philip Cadway [ne:Silverman].

226

Chicago Symphony Trumpet Notes

(A) Desire Defauw was Music Director starting in the 1943-44 season.

(B) Gerald Huffman joined the orchestra on second in the 1939-40 season and was moved to principal in the 1942-43 season.

(C) Edward Masacek joined the orchestra in the 1938-39 season on third and was moved to second in the 1943-44 season.

(D) Renold Schilke joined the orchestra in the 1936-37 season on third, played second (1938-39), principal (1939-41), second (1942-43), and third in the 1943-44 season.

(E) Frank Holz joined the orchestra in the 1926-27 season playing (from 1926-33) third or fourth trumpet and on occassion second trumpet. He also played in the violin section (1926-45).

(F) He played third starting in 1933 and played bass trumpet (1931-44).

(G) Sydney Baker was principal for the 1941-42 season and returned from military service in January, 1946.

(H) Adolph Herseth joined the orchestra at Ravinia in June, 1948.

(I) Rudolph Nashan resigned his position in the orchestra in January 1963, when he was elected Vice President of the Chicago Federation of Musicians. Phyllis Bleck substituted from that time through the 1964 Ravinia season.

(I) Charles Geyer joined the orchestra in December, 1966.

(J) Irwin Hoffman was Acting Music Director for the 1968-69 season. He started as Associate Conductor in the 1964-65 season.

(K) Philip Smith arrived in January, 1975. Vincent Chicowicz filled in on fourth, September through December 1974.

(L) George Vosburgh joined the orchestra at Ravinia in June, 1979.

(M) Timothy Kent joined the orchestra in January, 1979.

Chicago Symphony Trombone Notes

(A) Frank Crisafulli joined the orchestra as assistant first in the 1938-39 season and was moved to principal in the 1939-40 season.

(B) Richard Schmitt joined the orchestra in 1944.

(C) David Anderson joined the orchestra in the 1929-30 season on second and played third from 1938-40 before being moved to

Arnold Jacobs: *Song and Wind*

second in the 1940-41 season.

(D) Elmer Janes was assistant principal for the 1941-42 season and moved to bass trombone while Edward Kleinhammer was on military duty from 1942-45. He later played with the Detroit Symphony for 35 seasons.

(E) Frank Crisafulli was on military duty during 1945-46. Richard Schmitt moved from assistant first to principal during this time leaving the assistant first position vacant.

(F) Edward Kleinhammer joined the orchestra beginning in the 1940-41 season.

(G) Robert Rada was principal during the 1955 Ravinia season.

(H) Jay Friedman began principal duties in April 1965.

(I) Jay Friedman was on medical leave March 5 through October 24, 1979. James Gilbertsen assumed principal responsibilities.

(J) James Gilbertsen has been Associate Principal since 1982.

Chicago Symphony Horn Notes

(A) Helen Kotas joined the orchestra during the 1940-41 season but was not under contract until the 1941-42 season. She previously played with Jacobs in the All-American Youth Orchestra.

(B) Charles Jackson joined the orchestra in 1944.

(C) Clyde Wedgewood joined the orchestra in 1943 as assistant principal.

(D) Harry Jacobs joined the orchestra in 1944.

(E) Max Pottag joined the orchestra in 1907 playing second. He moved to fourth his last two seasons.

(F) William Verschoor, who had been assistant principal horn, 1937-43, returned from military service in March, 1946.

(G) Joseph Mourek, who had been third horn, 1929-43, returned from military service in 1945 and moved to fourth horn.

(H) Helen Kotas also played third horn during 1947-48.

(I) Hugh Cowden and Arthur Goldstein shared the assistant principal horn position during the 1952-53 season. Cowden played previously in Pittsburgh with Jacobs.

(J) Hugh Cowden and Alan Fuchs shared the assistant principal horn position during the 1953-54 season. Alan Fuchs played previously in Pittsburgh with Jacobs.

(K) Wayne Barrington and Louis Stout shared the third horn position during the 1959-60 season.

(L) Frank Brouk joined the orchestra in January, 1961, as assistant principal horn but was not under contract until the

Arnold Jacobs: *Song and Wind*

1961-62 season. He previously played in the Indianapolis Symphony with Jacobs.

(M) Richard Oldberg played assistant principal horn, 1962-63, but was not under contract until the next season.

(N) Dale Clevenger joined the orchestra in February, 1966, at which time Frank Brouk became the associate principal horn.

(O) Although the assistant principal horn chair was officially vacant, Ethel Merker filled in during the season.

(P) Frank Brouk moved to second horn upon the tragic death of Clyde Wedgwood on December 25, 1969, leaving the assistant principal horn position vacant.

(Q) Thomas Howell joined the orchestra in January, 1971, and moved to associate principal horn in June of that year.

(R) Norman Schweikert joined the orchestra in June, 1971.

(S) Gail Williams joined the orchestra in December, 1978, but was not under contract until January, 1979.

(T) Thomas Howell and Gail Williams exchanged positions in October, 1984.

Endnotes

Preface and Acknowledgements

1.   Stewart, M. Dee, ed. *Arnold Jacobs The Legacy of a Master*.Northfield, Il.:
      The Instrumentalist Company, 1987.

Early Years (1915-1930)

2.   Schwendener, Peter. "The Best Tuba Player in the World." *Chicago Reader*, June 1,1984,1+.
      Copyright ©1984 Chicago Reader, Inc. Used with permission.
3.   Whitman, Dale. "In Memoriam: Joseph Singer." *The Horn Call* 9, no. 2 (April 1979): 21-22.
      reprinted from *The Horn Call*. Used with permission.
      Ravina Festival Programs, Dale Clevenger, June 26-29, 1975
4.   Haugan, Paul. "TUBA Profile - Arnold M. Jacobs Tubist of the Chicago Symphony
      Orchestra." *TUBA Journal* 4, no. 2 (Winter 1977): 2-10. Used with permission.
5.   "Mary Pickford", *Software Toolworks Multimedia Encyclopedia*.
      Novato, Ca.: Software Toolworks, Version 5.1, 1992.
      "Mary Pickford", *Microsoft Cinemania CD ROM*. Bellevue, Washington: Microsoft
      Corporation.
6.   Schwendener, Peter. "The Best Tuba Player in the World." *Chicago Reader*, June 1, 1984,
      1+. Copyright ©1984 Chicago Reader, Inc. Used with permission.
7.   Furlong, William Barry. *Season With Solti: A Year in the Life of the ChicagoSymphony*.
      New York,N.Y.:MacMillan,1974.[267-270, 290-293,297-307,310-311]
      reprinted with permission of Simon & Schuster, Inc., from *Season with Solti:
      A Year in the Life of the Chicago Symphony* by William Barry Furlong.
      Copyright ©1974 by William Barry Furlong.
8.   Meyer, Eileen. "Career Counseling: Interviews With Arnold Jacobs and Frank Crisafulli."
      Journal of the International Trombone Association 13, no. 4 (October 1985): 32-
      33. Used with permission from the *Journal of the International Trombone
      Association.*
9.   Furlong, William Barry. *Season With Solti: A Year in the Life of the ChicagoSymphony*.
      New York,N.Y.:MacMillan,1974.[267-270, 290-293,297-307,310-311]
      reprinted with permission of Simon & Schuster, Inc., from *Season with Solti:
      A Year in the Life of the Chicago Symphony* by William Barry Furlong.
      Copyright ©1974 by William Barry Furlong.
10.   Haugan, Paul. "TUBA Profile - Arnold M. Jacobs Tubist of the Chicago Symphony
      Orchestra." *TUBA Journal* 4, no. 2 (Winter 1977): 2-10. Used with permission.
11.   Whitfield, Edward J. "Remembrances and Recollections of Arnold M. Jacobs." *TUBA
      Journal* 12, no. 4 (May 1985): 7-8. Used with permission.

The Curtis Institute (1930-1937)

12. "Curtis Institute of Music", *Software Toolworks Multimedia Encyclopedia*. Novato, Ca.: Software Toolworks, Version 5.1, 1992.

13. Haugan, Paul. "TUBA Profile - Arnold M. Jacobs Tubist of the Chicago Symphony Orchestra." *TUBA Journal* 4, no. 2 (Winter 1977): 2-10. Used with permission.

14. Haugan, Paul. "TUBA Profile - Arnold M. Jacobs Tubist of the Chicago Symphony Orchestra." *TUBA Journal* 4, no. 2 (Winter 1977): 2-10. Used with permission.

15. Schwendener, Peter. "The Best Tuba Player in the World." *Chicago Reader*, June 1, 1984, 1+. Copyright ©1984 Chicago Reader, Inc. Used with permission.

16. "Josef Hoffman", *Software Toolworks Multimedia Encyclopedia*. Novato, Ca.: Software Toolworks, Version 5.1, 1992.
    Overtones: 50th Anniversary Edition. Vol. 11, no. 1, (October 1974). Philadelphia, Pa.: Curtis Institute, 1974.

17. "Curtis Institute adds Four to its Faculty." *Musical America*, October 25, 1937, 21. Reprinted with permission of K-III Directory Corporation.

18. *Overtones: 50th Anniversary Edition*. Vol. 11, no. 1, (October 1974). Philadelphia, Pa.: Curtis Institute, 1974.

19. Meyer, Eileen. "Career Counseling: Interviews With Arnold Jacobs and Frank Crisafulli." *Journal of the International Trombone Association* 13, no. 4 (October 1985): 32-33. Used with permission from the *Journal of the International Trombone Association*.

20. "Donatelli, Philip." Obituary in *Billboard* 66 (April 17, 1954): 34. reprinted from *Billboard*. © 1954 BPI Communications Inc. Used with permission from *Billboard*.
    "Donatelli, Philip." Obituary in *Variety* 194 (April, 14, 1954): 63.

21. Meyer, Eileen. "Career Counseling: Interviews With Arnold Jacobs and Frank Crisafulli." *Journal of the International Trombone Association* 13, no. 4 (October 1985): 32-33. Used with permission from the *Journal of the International Trombone Association*.

22. Funderburk, Jeffrey L. "The Man and his Horn." *TUBA Journal* 15, no. 4 (May 1988): 43. Used with permission.

23. Meyer, Eileen. "Career Counseling: Interviews With Arnold Jacobs and Frank Crisafulli." *Journal of the International Trombone Association* 13, no. 4 (October 1985): 32-33. Used with permission from the *Journal of the International Trombone Association*.

24. Carter, Elliott. "Letters to the Editor." *Journal of Music Theory* 7, no. 2 (1963): 270-273. Mr. Carter mentions Longy-Miquelle, *Principles of Musical Theory*, Concord Series Number 12, E.C. Schirmer Music Co,Boston, 1925.

25. "Longy, Renee." Obituary in *Central Opera Service Bulletin*. 22, no. 1 (1980): 42-43.

26. Schneider, Richard. "Arnold Jacobs Sounds Off." *Fritz Reiner Society Newsletter* No. 4, n.d. Used with permission.

27. Schneider, Richard. "Arnold Jacobs Sounds Off." *Fritz Reiner Society Newsletter* No. 4, n.d. Used with permission.

28. Schneider, Richard. "Arnold Jacobs Sounds Off." *Fritz Reiner Society Newsletter* No. 4, n.d. Used with permission.

29. Meyer, Eileen. "Career Counseling: Interviews With Arnold Jacobs and Frank Crisafulli." *Journal of the International Trombone Association* 13, no. 4 (October 1985): 32-33. Used with permission from the *Journal of the*

International Trombone Association.

30. "Marcel Tabuteau", Slonimsky, Nicolas, ed. *Baker's Biographical Dictionary of Musicans.* Seventh Edition. New York: Schirmer Books, 1984.
"Tabuteau, Marcel." Obituary in *Opera News*, February 19, 1966,33.
"Marcel Tabuteau", Philadelphia Orchestra Program., December 21, 1951, 265.
Overtones: 50th Anniversary Edition. Vol. 11, no. 1, (October 1974).
Philadelphia, Pa.: Curtis Institute, 1974.

31. Tabuteau, Marcel. "Marcel Tabuteau of Philadelphia Orchestra Summarizes Training." *Musical America*, November 25, 1944, 29. Reprinted with permission of K-III Directory Corporation.

32. Krell, John. *Kincaidiana.*Culver City, Ca.: Trio Associates, 1973

33. Bobo, Roger. "Arnold Jacobs [Chicago, December 3, 1979]: Interview with Roger Bobo." Parts 1, 2. *Brass Bulletin* 33 (1981): 43-50; 34 (1981): 37, 39, 41, 43-44. reprinted from Brass Bulletin. ©1981 by Roger Bobo and Brass Bulletin (Jean-Pierre Mathez, CH-1630 Bulle/Switzerland) used with permission.

34. "Curtis Institute has Second Commencement." *Musical America*, June, 1935, 15.
"Curtis Institute Holds Third Commencement." *Musical America*, June 1936, 31. Reprinted with permission of K-III Directory Corporation.
Overtones: 50th Anniversary Edition. Vol. 11, no. 1, (October 1974). Philadelphia, Pa.: Curtis Institute, 1974.

35. "Julius Baker", Slonimsky, Nicolas, ed. *Baker's Biographical Dictionary of Musicans.* Seventh Edition. New York:Schirmer Books, 1984.

36. "Samuel Barber", *Compton's Interactive Encyclopedia.* Carlsbad, Ca.: Compton's NewMedia, Versions 1.01 VW (1992), 2.01 VW (1993).

37. "Gian Carlo Menotti", *Compton's Interactive Encyclopedia.* Carlsbad, Ca.: Compton's NewMedia, Versions 1.01 VW (1992), 2.01 VW (1993).

38. Furlong, William Barry. *Season With Solti: A Year in the Life of the Chicago Symphony.* New York,N.Y.:MacMillan,1974.[267-270, 290-293, 297-307,310-311] reprinted with permission of Simon & Schuster, Inc., from *Season with Solti: A Year in the Life of the Chicago Symphony* by William Barry Furlong. Copyright ©1974 by William Barry Furlong.

39. Furlong, William Barry. *Season With Solti: A Year in the Life of the Chicago Symphony.* New York,N.Y.:MacMillan,1974.[267-270, 290-293, 297-307,310-311] reprinted with permission of Simon & Schuster, Inc., from *Season with Solti: A Year in the Life of the Chicago Symphony* by William Barry Furlong. Copyright ©1974 by William Barry Furlong.

40. Furlong, William Barry. *Season With Solti: A Year in the Life of the Chicago Symphony.* New York,N.Y.:MacMillan,1974.[267-270, 290-293,297-307,310-311] reprinted with permission of Simon & Schuster, Inc., from *Season with Solti: A Year in the Life of the Chicago Symphony* by William Barry Furlong. Copyright ©1974 by William Barry Furlong.

41. Schwendener, Peter. "The Best Tuba Player in the World." *Chicago Reader*, June 1, 1984, 1+. Copyright ©1984 Chicago Reader, Inc. Used with permission.

42. Furlong, William Barry. *Season With Solti: A Year in the Life of the Chicago Symphony.* New York,N.Y.:MacMillan,1974.[267-270, 290-293, 297-307,310-311] reprinted with permission of Simon & Schuster, Inc., from *Season with Solti: A Year in the Life of the Chicago Symphony* by William Barry Furlong. Copyright ©1974 by William Barry Furlong.

43.   Furlong, William Barry. *Season With Solti: A Year in the Life of the Chicago Symphony.*
      New York,N.Y.:MacMillan,1974.[267-270, 290-293, 297-307,310-311]
      reprinted with permission of Simon & Schuster, Inc., from *Season with Solti:
      A Year in the Life of the Chicago Symphony* by William Barry Furlong.
      Copyright ©1974 by William Barry Furlong.

Gizella Jacobs and Family

44.   "Arnold Jacobs", Chicago Symphony Orchestra Program, January 15,1948.
      reprinted from the *Chicago Symphony Programs.* Copyright ©1948 by The
      Orchestral Association. Used with Permission.
45.   "Valfy, Tereza M." Obituary in *Chicago Tribune*, December 29, 1985, Sec. 3, p. 7.
      © Copyright Chicago Tribune Company. All rights reserved.
      Used with permission.

Professional Experience (1937-1949)

46.   Bobo, Roger. "Arnold Jacobs [Chicago, December 3, 1979]: Interview with Roger Bobo."
      Parts 1, 2. *Brass Bulletin* 33 (1981): 43-50; 34 (1981): 37, 39, 41, 43-44.
      reprinted from Brass Bulletin. ©1981 by Roger Bobo and Brass Bulletin
      (Jean-Pierre Mathez, CH-1630 Bulle/Switzerland) used with permission.
47.   Furlong, William Barry. *Season With Solti: A Year in the Life of the Chicago Symphony.*
      New York,N.Y.:MacMillan,1974.[267-270, 290-293, 297-307,310-311]
      reprinted with permission of Simon & Schuster, Inc., from *Season with Solti:
      A Year in the Life of the Chicago Symphony* by William Barry Furlong.
      Copyright ©1974 by William Barry Furlong.
48.   Bobo, Roger. "Arnold Jacobs [Chicago, December 3, 1979]: Interview with Roger Bobo."
      Parts 1, 2. *Brass Bulletin* 33 (1981): 43-50; 34 (1981): 37, 39, 41, 43-44.
      reprinted from Brass Bulletin. ©1981 by Roger Bobo and Brass Bulletin
      (Jean-Pierre Mathez, CH-1630 Bulle/Switzerland) used with permission.
49.   "Sevitzky to lead Indianapolis Players." *Musical America*, March 25, 1937. Reprinted with
      permission of K-III Directory Corporation.
50.   From Norman Schweikert based on ASCAP directory of 1952.
51.   Indianapolis Symphony Orchestra Programs, December 11, 1938 [performance of
      Dubensky Fantasia]
52.   "Pittsburgh Symphony Orchestra", *Software Toolworks Multimedia Encyclopedia.*
      Novato, Ca.: Software Toolworks, Version 5.1, 1992.
53.   Bobo, Roger. "Arnold Jacobs [Chicago, December 3, 1979]: Interview with Roger Bobo."
      Parts 1, 2. *Brass Bulletin* 33 (1981): 43-50; 34 (1981): 37, 39, 41, 43-44.
      reprinted from Brass Bulletin. ©1981 by Roger Bobo and Brass Bulletin
      (Jean-Pierre Mathez, CH-1630 Bulle/Switzerland) used with permission.
54.   Pittsburgh Symphony Orchestra Programs, Personnel Listing 1938-1939.
      Indianapolis Symphony Orchestra Programs, Personnel Rosters 1939-1940.
55.   Pittsburgh Symphony Orchestra Programs, Personnel Listing 1942-1943.
56.   Schwendener, Peter. "The Best Tuba Player in the World." *Chicago Reader*, June 1, 1984,
      1+. Copyright ©1984 Chicago Reader, Inc. Used with permission.
57.   "Stokowski to Gather New Youth Orchestra." *Musical America*, January 10, 1941, 8.
      Reprinted with permission of K-III Directory Corporation.

58.   Daniel, Oliver. *Stokowski: A Counterpoint of View.* New York: Dodd, Mead and
           Company, 1982.
59.   Tracy, Bruce. "Orchestra Showcase The Chicago Symphony Orchestra." *International
           Trombone Association Newsletter* 7, no. 2 (April 1980): 10-15. Used with
           permission from the *Journal of the International Trombone Association.*
60.   Daniel, Oliver. *Stokowski: A Counterpoint of View.* New York: Dodd, Mead and
           Company, 1982.
           Smith, William Ander, *The Mystery of Leopold Stokowski,*
           Associated University Press, 1990, p. 182
61.   von Rhein, John. "Tuba or not Tuba, After 44 Years, Arnold Jacobs is leaving the CSO."
           Chicago Tribune, September 25, 1988. © Copyright Chicago Tribune Company.
           All rights reserved. Used with permission.
62.   Bobo, Roger. "Arnold Jacobs [Chicago, December 3, 1979]: Interview with Roger Bobo."
           Parts 1, 2. *Brass Bulletin* 33 (1981): 43-50; 34 (1981): 37, 39, 41, 43-44.
           reprinted from Brass Bulletin. ©1981 by Roger Bobo and Brass Bulletin
           (Jean-Pierre Mathez, CH-1630 Bulle/Switzerland) used with permission.
63.   Bobo, Roger. "Arnold Jacobs [Chicago, December 3, 1979]: Interview with Roger Bobo."
           Parts 1, 2. *Brass Bulletin* 33 (1981): 43-50; 34 (1981): 37, 39, 41, 43-44.
           reprinted from Brass Bulletin. ©1981 by Roger Bobo and Brass Bulletin
           (Jean-Pierre Mathez, CH-1630 Bulle/Switzerland) used with permission.
64.   "Philly Cures Tuba-Culosis." *Billboard,* March 19, 1949, 20.reprinted from *Billboard.*
           ©1949, BPI Communications Inc. Used with permission from *Billboard.*
65.   Bobo, Roger. "Arnold Jacobs [Chicago, December 3, 1979]: Interview with Roger Bobo."
           Parts 1, 2. *Brass Bulletin* 33 (1981): 43-50; 34 (1981): 37, 39, 41, 43-44.
           reprinted from Brass Bulletin. ©1981 by Roger Bobo and Brass Bulletin
           (Jean-Pierre Mathez, CH-1630 Bulle/Switzerland) used with permission.
66.   "Philly Orch British Tour Pacted in $400,000 Deal." *Variety,* February 5, 1949, 50.
67.   Tracy, Bruce. "A Conversation with Robert Harper." *Journal of the International Trombone
           Association* 12, no. 3 (July 1984): 15-16, 18. Used with permission from the
           Journal of the International Trombone Association.
68.   Lockspeiser, Edward. "Philadelphia Orchestra Tours Britain." *Musical America,*
           July, 1949, 6. Reprinted with permission of K-III Directory Corporation.

Chicago Symphony Orchestra (1944-1988)

69.   "Chicago Symphony Orchestra", *Software Toolworks Multimedia Encyclopedia.*
           Novato, Ca.: Software Toolworks, Version 5.1, 1992.
70.   Murrow, Richard. "August Helleberg, Sr. Part 1." *TUBA Journal* 10, no. 1
           (Summer 1982): 2-3.
           Comments by Norman Schweikert and John Taylor.
71.   Comments by Norman Schweikert. Obituary in *Chicago Tribune,* October 9, 1914.
72.   Comments by Norman Schweikert. Obituary in *Chicago Tribune,* April 23, 1948.
73.   "Gene Pokorny", Chicago Symphony Orchestra Program, October 17, 1991, p. 14
           reprinted from the *Chicago Symphony Programs.* Copyright ©1991 by The
           Orchestral Association. Used with Permission.
74.   Schneider, Richard. "Arnold Jacobs Sounds Off." *Fritz Reiner SocietyNewsletter*
           No.4, n.d. Used with permission.
75.   Marsch, Robert C. "Kubelik and the Thomas Tradition." Program notes to *Chicago
           Symphony Orchestra: The Kubelik Legacy.* Mercury Records MG 3-4500, 3-

4501, 1973.

Arado, M., Henderson, E. M. , Robinson, W. , Ward, D. "Orchestra Hall Tours Fact Sheet." Chicago Symphony Orchestra, October 7, 1985. Copyright ©1991 by TheOrchestral Association. Used with Permission.

Ryan, Nancy. "Orchestra Hall: Crushing Note" *Chicago Tribune*, May 19, 1995. Section 2, page 1.

76.   Ravinia Festival Assocation. *Ravinia: The Festival at its Half Century*. Highland Park, Il: Ravinia Festival Association in conjuction with Rand McNally, 1985. Used with permission from Ravinia Festival.

77.   Information from Chicago Symphony Archives, after 1971- from Norman Schweikert.

78.   von Rhein, John. "Tuba or not Tuba, After 44 Years, Arnold Jacobs is leaving the CSO." *Chicago Tribune*, September 25, 1988. © Copyright Chicago Tribune Company. All rights reserved. Used with permission.

79.   Arado, M., Henderson, E. M. , Robinson, W. , Ward, D. "Orchestra Hall Tours Fact Sheet." Chicago Symphony Orchestra, October 7, 1985.

80.   Marsch, Robert C. "Kubelik and the Thomas Tradition." Program notes to *Chicago Symphony Orchestra: The Kubelik Legacy*. Mercury Records MG 3-4500, 3-4501, 1973.

81.   Marsch, Robert C.,"Solti in Chicago, a Critical Discography." *Ovation* 5 (December 1984): 26-29, 35.

82.   Bishop, Ronald. "Arnold Jacobs on Record: Its Influence on me." *TUBA Journal*15, no. 4 (May 1988): 27-29. Used with permission.

83.   Schneider, Richard. "Arnold Jacobs Sounds Off." *Fritz Reiner Society Newsletter* No. 4, n.d. Used with permission.

84.   Schneider, Richard. "Arnold Jacobs Sounds Off." *Fritz Reiner Society Newsletter* No. 4, n.d. Used with permission.

85.   These concerts were not performed as part of the regular subscription series. Therefore, the Chicago Symphony Archives has no record of these performances.

86.   *Chicago Symphony Orchestra Repertory*. [95th Season] Chicago: Chicago Symphony Orchestra, 1986, 107. reprinted from the *Chicago Symphony Programs*. Copyright ©1986 by The Orchestral Association. Used with Permission.

87.   "Arnold Jacobs", Chicago Symphony Orchestra Program, October 26-28,1978. [Performance of Vaughan Williams *Tuba Concerto*] reprinted from the *Chicago Symphony Programs*. Copyright ©1978 by The Orchestral Association. Used with Permission.

88.   Bauer, Paul. "Frank Crisafulli." *Journal of the International Trombone Association* 17, no. 4 (Fall 1989): 13-17. Used with permission from the *Journal of the International Trombone Association.*

89.   Based on a letter Audiophile Records wrote to Norman Schweikert on November 8, 1967.

90.   Stoddard, Hope. "Brass Ensembles—Twentieth Century Specialty." *International Musician* [February, 1958]: cover photo, 22-23, 42-45.

91.   From conversations with Roger Rocco, John Taylor, David Fedderly, Rex Martin, Michael Grose, Don Little, Charles Guse.

92.   Bobo, Roger. "Arnold Jacobs [Chicago, December 3, 1979]: Interview with Roger Bobo." Parts 1, 2. *Brass Bulletin* 33 (1981): 43-50; 34 (1981): 37, 39, 41, 43-44. reprinted from Brass Bulletin. ©1981 by Roger Bobo and Brass Bulletin (Jean-Pierre Mathez, CH-1630 Bulle/Switzerland) used with permission.

93.   Bobo, Roger. "Arnold Jacobs [Chicago, December 3, 1979]: Interview with Roger Bobo." Parts 1, 2. *Brass Bulletin* 33 (1981): 43-50; 34 (1981): 37, 39, 41, 43-44. reprinted from Brass Bulletin. ©1981 by Roger Bobo and Brass Bulletin

(Jean-Pierre Mathez, CH-1630 Bulle/Switzerland) used with permission.

94.   Bauer, Paul. "Frank Crisafulli." *Journal of the International Trombone Association* 17, no. 4 (Fall 1989): 13-17. Used with permission from the *Journal of the International Trombone Association.*

"Four Day Mid-West Band and Orchestra Clinic." *School Musician* 35, no. 3 (November 1963): 72-73.

95.   "Edward Kleinhammer", Chicago Symphony Orchestra Programs,March 7-9, 1968. p. 48. reprinted from the *Chicago Symphony Programs.* Copyright ©1968 by The Orchestral Association. Used with Permission.

Yeo, Douglas. "Edward Kleinhammer: A Tribute." *Journal of the International Trombone Association* 8, no. 3 (July 1985). Used with permission from the *Journal of the International Trombone Association.*

96.   "Interview with Arnold Jacobs and Jim Unrath." Broadcast on WFMT-FM, Chicago, Illinois. 1978. Used with permission from WFMT-FM.

97.   Personnel file, CSO Archives. Material submitted by Robert Lambert.

98.   Furlong, William Barry. *Season With Solti: A Year in the Life of the Chicago Symphony.* New York,N.Y.:MacMillan,1974.[267-270, 290-293, 297-307,310-311] reprinted with permission of Simon & Schuster, Inc., from *Season with Solti: A Year in the Life of the Chicago Symphony* by William Barry Furlong. Copyright ©1974 by William Barry Furlong.

99.   Furlong, William Barry. *Season With Solti: A Year in the Life of the Chicago Symphony.* New York,N.Y.:MacMillan,1974.[267-270, 290-293, 297-307,310-311] reprinted with permission of Simon & Schuster, Inc., from *Season with Solti: A Year in the Life of the Chicago Symphony* by William Barry Furlong. Copyright ©1974 by William Barry Furlong.

100.   "Jay Friedman", Chicago Symphony Orchestra Programs, September 24, 1987. p. 56. reprinted from the *Chicago Symphony Programs.* Copyright ©1987 by The Orchestral Association. Used with Permission.

101.   "James Gilbertsen", Chicago Symphony Orchestra Programs, Youth Concert Program, October 19-25, 1983. reprinted from the *Chicago Symphony Programs.* Copyright ©1983 by The Orchestral Association. Used with Permission.

102.   "Charles Vernon", Chicago Symphony Orchestra Programs, January 19, 1989. p. 8. reprinted from the *Chicago Symphony Programs.* Copyright ©1995 by The Orchestral Association. Used with Permission.

103.   "Four Day Mid-West Band and Orchestra Clinic." *School Musician* 35, no. 3 (November 1963): 72-73.

Clark, Keith C. "Trumpet Sections of American Symphony Orchestras: The Chicago Symphony Orchestra." *International Trumpet Guild Journal* 8, no. 2 (December 1983): 17-22. Used with permission of the *International Trumpet Guild Journal.*

104.   Schneider, Richard. "Arnold Jacobs Sounds Off." *Fritz Reiner Society Newsletter* No. 4, n.d. Used with permission.

105.   Furlong, William Barry. *Season With Solti: A Year in the Life of the Chicago Symphony.* New York,N.Y.:MacMillan,1974.[267-270, 290-293, 297-307,310-311] reprinted with permission of Simon & Schuster, Inc., from *Season with Solti: A Year in the Life of the Chicago Symphony* by William Barry Furlong. Copyright ©1974 by William Barry Furlong.

106.   Furlong, William Barry. *Season With Solti: A Year in the Life of the Chicago Symphony.* New York,N.Y.:MacMillan,1974.[267-270, 290-293, 297-307,310-311] reprinted with permission of Simon & Schuster, Inc., from *Season with Solti: A Year in the Life of the Chicago Symphony* by William Barry Furlong.

Copyright ©1974 by William Barry Furlong.
107. Clark, Keith C. "Trumpet Sections of American Symphony Orchestras: The Chicago Symphony Orchestra." *International Trumpet Guild Journal* 8, no. 2 (December 1983): 17-22. Used with permission of the *International Trumpet Guild Journal*.
108. Furlong, William Barry. *Season With Solti: A Year in the Life of the Chicago Symphony.* New York,N.Y.:MacMillan,1974.[267-270, 290-293, 297-307,310-311] reprinted with permission of Simon & Schuster, Inc., from *Season with Solti: A Year in the Life of the Chicago Symphony* by William Barry Furlong. Copyright ©1974 by William Barry Furlong.
109. "Adolph Herseth", Chicago Symphony Orchestra Programs,November 25, 1987, p. 64. reprinted from the *Chicago Symphony Programs.* Copyright ©1987 by The Orchestral Association. Used with Permission.
Clark, Keith C. "Trumpet Sections of American Symphony Orchestras: The Chicago Symphony Orchestra." *International Trumpet Guild Journal* 8, no. 2 (December 1983): 17-22. Used with permission of the *International Trumpet Guild Journal*.
110. "Vincent Cichowicz", Chicago Symphony Orchestra Programs, January 4-6, 1968. reprinted from the *Chicago Symphony Programs.* Copyright ©1968 by The Orchestral Association. Used with Permission.
Clark, Keith C. "Trumpet Sections of American Symphony Orchestras: The Chicago Symphony Orchestra." *International Trumpet Guild Journal* 8, no. 2 (December 1983): 17-22. Used with permission of the *International Trumpet Guild Journal*.
111. "William Scarlett", Chicago Symphony Orchestra Programs,October 13, 1988, p.8. reprinted from the *Chicago Symphony Programs.* Copyright ©1988 by The Orchestral Association. Used with Permission.
Clark, Keith C. "Trumpet Sections of American Symphony Orchestras: The Chicago Symphony Orchestra." *International Trumpet Guild Journal* 8, no. 2 (December 1983): 17-22. Used with permission of the *International Trumpet Guild Journal*.
112. Farkas, Philip. *The Art of Brass Playing.* Bloomington, Ind.: Wind Music Inc., 1962
113. Farkas, Philip, "Oral History Project", Chicago Symphony Orchestra Programs, January 17-22, 1991. reprinted from the *Chicago Symphony Programs.* Copyright ©1991 by The Orchestral Association. Used with Permission.
114. Furlong, William Barry. *Season With Solti: A Year in the Life of the Chicago Symphony.* New York,N.Y.:MacMillan,1974.[267-270, 290-293, 297-307,310-311] reprinted with permission of Simon & Schuster, Inc., from *Season with Solti: A Year in the Life of the Chicago Symphony* by William Barry Furlong. Copyright ©1974 by William Barry Furlong.
115. "Frank Brouk", Chicago Symphony Orchestra Programs,November 23-25, 1967. reprinted from the *Chicago Symphony Programs.* Copyright ©1967 by The Orchestral Association. Used with Permission.
Schweikert, Norman. "Frank Brouk Retires from the Chicago Symphony." *The Horn Call* 9, no. 2 (April 1979): 75-78. reprinted from *The Horn Call.* Used with permission.
116. "Cowden, Hugh—In Memoriam." *The Horn Call* 19, no. 2 (April 1989): 110-111. reprinted from *The Horn Call.* Used with permission.
117. "Norman Schweikert", Chicago Symphony Orchestra Programs, January 9-14, 1992. reprinted from the *Chicago Symphony Programs.* Copyright ©1992 by The Orchestral Association. Used with Permission.
118. From files of Norman Schweikert. Supplied by Wayne Barrington, April 28, 1970.
119. "Richard Oldberg", Chicago Symphony Orchestra Programs,April 7, 1988. reprinted from the *Chicago Symphony Programs.* Copyright ©1988 by The Orchestral

Arnold Jacobs: *Song and Wind*

Association. Used with Permission.

Other Performances

120. "Pablo Casals", *Software Toolworks Multimedia Encyclopedia*. Novato, Ca.: Software Toolworks, Version 5.1, 1992.
121. Brubeck, David and Olah, John. "Connie's Final Toot." *TUBA Journal* 18, no. 1 (Summer 1991): 28-36. Used with permission.

Conductors

122. "Desire Defauw", Chicago Symphony Orchestra Programs, November 14-15, 1943. p. 47. reprinted from the *Chicago Symphony Programs*. Copyright ©1943 by The Orchestral Association. Used with Permission.
Desire Defauw, Slonimsky, Nicolas, ed. *Baker's Biographical Dictionary of Musicans*. Seventh Edition. New York: Schirmer Books, 1984.
123. "Arthur Rodzinski", Chicago Symphony Orchestra Programs, October 14, 1947.reprinted from the *Chicago Symphony Programs*. Copyright ©1947 by The Orchestral Association. Used with Permission.
"Orchestra", *Compton's Interactive Encylopedia*. Carlsbad, Ca.: Compton's NewMedia, Versions 1.01 VW (1992), 2.01 VW (1993).
"Arthur Rodzinsky", Slonimsky, Nicolas, ed. *Baker's Biographical Dictionary of Musicans*. Seventh Edition. New York: Schirmer Books, 1984.
Ravinia Festival Assocation. *Ravinia: The Festival at its Half Century*. Highland Park, Il: Ravinia Festival Association in conjuction with Rand McNally, 1985. Used with permission from Ravinia Festival.
Farkas, Philip, "Oral History Project", Chicago Symphony Orchestra Programs, January 17-22, 1991. reprinted from the *Chicago Symphony Programs*. Copyright ©1991 by The Orchestral Association. Used with Permission.
124. Marsch, Robert C. "Kubelik and the Thomas Tradition." Program notes to *Chicago Symphony Orchestra: The Kubelik Legacy*. Mercury Records MG 3-4500, 3-4501, 1973.
"Wilhelm Furtwangler", *Compton's Interactive Encyclopedia*. Carlsbad, Ca.: Compton's NewMedia, Versions 1.01 VW (1992), 2.01 VW (1993).
125. "Rafael Kubelik", Chicago Symphony Orchestra Programs, October 30, 1975. reprinted from the *Chicago Symphony Programs*. Copyright ©1975 by The Orchestral Association. Used with Permission.
Marsch, Robert C. "Kubelik and the Thomas Tradition." Program notes to *Chicago Symphony Orchestra: The Kubelik Legacy*. Mercury Records MG 3-4500, 3-4501, 1973.
"Raphael Kubelik", Slonimsky, Nicolas, ed. *Baker's Biographical Dictionary of Musicans*. Seventh Edition. New York: Schirmer Books, 1984.
"Raphael Kubelik", *Software Toolworks Multimedia Encyclopedia*. Novato, Ca.: Software Toolworks, Version 5.1, 1992.
126. "Fritz Reiner", Slonimsky, Nicolas, ed. *Baker's Biographical Dictionary of Musicans*. Seventh Edition. New York: Schirmer Books, 1984.
127. von Rhein, John. "Tuba or not Tuba, After 44 Years, Arnold Jacobs is leaving the CSO." *Chicago Tribune*, September 25, 1988. © Copyright Chicago Tribune Company. All rights reserved. Used with permission.

238

128. Schwendener, Peter. "The Best Tuba Player in the World." *Chicago Reader*, June 1, 1984, 1+. Copyright ©1984 Chicago Reader, Inc. Used with permission.

129. Haugan, Paul. "TUBA Profile - Arnold M. Jacobs Tubist of the Chicago Symphony Orchestra." *TUBA Journal* 4, no. 2 (Winter 1977): 2-10. Used with permission.

130. Haugan, Paul. "TUBA Profile - Arnold M. Jacobs Tubist of the Chicago Symphony Orchestra." *TUBA Journal* 4, no. 2 (Winter 1977): 2-10. Used with permission.

131. von Rhein, John. "Tuba or not Tuba, After 44 Years, Arnold Jacobs is leaving the CSO." *Chicago Tribune*, September 25, 1988. © Copyright Chicago Tribune Company. All rights reserved. Used with permission.

132. Doherty, Jim, "For All Who Crave a Horn That Thrills, This Bud's for You", *Smithsonian* 25 no. 6, (September 1994): 94-103.reprinted from *Smithsonian*. ©1995 by *Smithsonian*. Used wirh permission.

133. Haugan, Paul. "TUBA Profile - Arnold M. Jacobs Tubist of the Chicago Symphony Orchestra." *TUBA Journal* 4, no. 2 (Winter 1977): 2-10. Used with permission.

134. Haugan, Paul. "TUBA Profile - Arnold M. Jacobs Tubist of the Chicago Symphony Orchestra." *TUBA Journal* 4, no. 2 (Winter 1977): 2-10. Used with permission.

135. Haugan, Paul. "TUBA Profile - Arnold M. Jacobs Tubist of the Chicago Symphony Orchestra." *TUBA Journal* 4, no. 2 (Winter 1977): 2-10. Used with permission.

136. Schneider, Richard. "Arnold Jacobs Sounds Off." *Fritz Reiner Society Newsletter* No. 4, n.d. Used with permission.

137. "Jean Martinon", Chicago Symphony Orchestra Programs, 1943-1991, September 28-29, 1967. reprinted from the *Chicago Symphony Programs*. Copyright ©1967 by The Orchestral Association. Used with Permission.
"Jean Martinon", Slonimsky, Nicolas, ed. *Baker's Biographical Dictionary of Musicans*. Seventh Edition. New York: Schirmer Books, 1984.

138. "Sir Georg Solti", Chicago Symphony Orchestra Programs, 1943-1991, November 14, 1974. reprinted from the *Chicago Symphony Programs*. Copyright ©1974 by The Orchestral Association. Used with Permission.
"Georg Solti", Slonimsky, Nicolas, ed. *Baker's Biographical Dictionary of Musicans*. Seventh Edition. New York: Schirmer Books, 1984.

139. von Rhein, John. "Tuba or not Tuba, After 44 Years, Arnold Jacobs is leaving the CSO." *Chicago Tribune*, September 25, 1988. © Copyright Chicago Tribune Company. All rights reserved. Used with permission.

140. "Who is Arnold Jacobs?" *TUBA Journal* 15, no. 4 (May 1988): 30-34. Comment by Sir Georg Solti.

141. "Daniel Barenboim", Chicago Symphony Orchestra Programs, October 1-8, 1991, p. 32-34. reprinted from the *Chicago Symphony Programs*. Copyright ©1991 by The Orchestral Association. Used with Permission.
"Daniel Barenboim", Slonimsky, Nicolas, ed. *Baker's Biographical Dictionary of Musicans*. Seventh Edition. New York: Schirmer Books, 1984.
"Daniel Barenboim", *Software Toolworks Multimedia Encyclopedia*. Novato, Ca.: Software Toolworks, Version 5.1, 1992.

142. "Orchestra", *Compton's Interactive Encylopedia*. Carlsbad, Ca.: Compton's NewMedia, Versions 1.01 VW (1992), 2.01 VW (1993).
"Seiji Ozawa", Ravina Festival Programs, June 16, 1964, p. 57

Ravinia Festival Assocation. *Ravinia: The Festival at its Half Century*. Highland Park, Il: Ravinia Festival Association in conjuction with Rand McNally, 1985.Used with permission from Ravinia Festival.

"Seiji Ozawa"Slonimsky, Nicolas, ed. *Baker's Biographical Dictionary of Musicans*. Seventh Edition. New York: Schirmer Books, 1984.

"Seiji Ozawa"*Software Toolworks Multimedia Encyclopedia*. Novato, Ca.: Software Toolworks, Version 5.1, 1992.

143.   "James Levine", Ravina Festival Programs, June 16, 1964, p. 57

Ravinia Festival Assocation. *Ravinia: The Festival at its Half Century*. Highland Park, Il: Ravinia Festival Association in conjuction with Rand McNally, 1985. Used with permission from Ravinia Festival.

"James Levine"Slonimsky, Nicolas, ed. *Baker's Biographical Dictionary of Musicans*. Seventh Edition. New York: Schirmer Books, 1984.

"James Levine"*Software Toolworks Multimedia Encyclopedia*. Novato, Ca.: Software Toolworks, Version 5.1, 1992.

144.   "Claudio Abbado", Chicago Symphony Orchestra Programs, 1943-1991 April 1-5, 1988, p. 45-46. reprinted from the *Chicago Symphony Programs*. Copyright ©1998 by The Orchestral Association. Used with Permission.

"Orchestra", *Compton's Interactive Encylopedia*. Carlsbad, Ca.: Compton's NewMedia, Versions 1.01 VW (1992),2.01 VW (1993).

"Claudio Abbado"Slonimsky, Nicolas, ed. *Baker's Biographical Dictionary of Musicans*. Seventh Edition. New York: Schirmer Books, 1984.

"Claudio Abbado"*Software Toolworks Multimedia Encyclopedia*. Novato, Ca.: Software Toolworks, Version 5.1, 1992.

145.   Ravinia Festival Assocation. *Ravinia: The Festival at its Half Century*. Highland Park, Il: Ravinia Festival Association in conjuction with Rand McNally, 1985. Used with permission from Ravinia Festival.

"Leonard Bernstein", Slonimsky, Nicolas, ed. *Baker's Biographical Dictionary of Musicans*. Seventh Edition. New York: Schirmer Books, 1984.

"Leonard Bernstein"*Software Toolworks Multimedia Encyclopedia*. Novato, Ca.: Software Toolworks, Version 5.1, 1992.

146.   "Fritz Busch", Chicago Symphony Orchestra Programs, 1943-1991, January 26-27, 1950. reprinted from the *Chicago Symphony Programs*. Copyright ©1950 by The Orchestral Association. Used with Permission.

"Fritz Busch", Slonimsky, Nicolas, ed. *Baker's Biographical Dictionary of Musicans*. Seventh Edition. New York: Schirmer Books, 1984.

147.   "Carlo Maria Giulini", Chicago Symphony Orchestra Programs,1943-1991, April 1, 1976. reprinted from the *Chicago Symphony Programs*. Copyright ©1976 by TheOrchestral Association. Used with Permission.

"Carlo Maria Giulini", Slonimsky, Nicolas, ed. *Baker's Biographical Dictionary of Musicans*. Seventh Edition. New York: Schirmer Books, 1984.

"Carlo Maria Giulini", *Software Toolworks Multimedia Encyclopedia*. Novato, Ca.: Software Toolworks, Version 5.1, 1992.

148.   von Rhein, John. "Tuba or not Tuba, After 44 Years, Arnold Jacobs is leaving the CSO." *Chicago Tribune*, September 25, 1988. © Copyright Chicago Tribune Company. All rights reserved. Used with permission.

149.   Ravinia Festival Assocation. *Ravinia: The Festival at its Half Century*. Highland Park, Il: Ravinia Festival Association in conjuction with Rand McNally, 1985. Used with permission from Ravinia Festival.

"Orchestra", *Compton's Interactive Encylopedia*. Carlsbad, Ca.: Compton's NewMedia, Versions 1.01 VW (1992), 2.01 VW (1993).

"Erich Leinsdorf", Slonimsky, Nicolas, ed. *Baker's Biographical Dictionary of Musicans*. Seventh Edition. New York: Schirmer Books, 1984.

"Erich Leinsdorf", *Software Toolworks Multimedia Encyclopedia*. Novato, Ca.: Software Toolworks, Version 5.1, 1992.

150. Ravinia Festival Assocation. *Ravinia: The Festival at its Half Century*. Highland Park, Il: Ravinia Festival Association in conjuction with Rand McNally, 1985. Used with permission from Ravinia Festival.

151. "Orchestra", *Compton's Interactive Encylopedia*. Carlsbad, Ca.: Compton's NewMedia, Versions 1.01 VW (1992), 2.01 VW (1993).

"Pierre Monteux", Slonimsky, Nicolas, ed. *Baker's Biographical Dictionary of Musicans*. Seventh Edition. New York: Schirmer Books, 1984.

"Pierre Monteux", *Software Toolworks Multimedia Encyclopedia*. Novato, Ca.: Software Toolworks, Version 5.1, 1992.

152. "Eugene Ormandy", Chicago Symphony Orchestra Programs, 1943-1991, February 18-20, 1971, p. 29. reprinted from the *Chicago Symphony Programs*. Copyright ©1971 by The Orchestral Association. Used with Permission.

"Orchestra", *Compton's Interactive Encylopedia*. Carlsbad, Ca.: Compton's NewMedia, Versions 1.01 VW (1992), 2.01 VW (1993).

Ravinia Festival Assocation. *Ravinia: The Festival at its Half Century*. Highland Park, Il: Ravinia Festival Association in conjuction with Rand McNally, 1985. Used with permission from Ravinia Festival.

"Eugene Ormandy", Slonimsky, Nicolas, ed. *Baker's Biographical Dictionary of Musicans*. Seventh Edition. New York: Schirmer Books, 1984.

"Eugene Ormandy", *Software Toolworks Multimedia Encyclopedia*. Novato, Ca.: Software Toolworks, Version 5.1, 1992.

153. "Hans Rosbaud", Chicago Symphony Orchestra Programs, 1943-1991, November 8-9, 1962. reprinted from the *Chicago Symphony Programs*. Copyright ©1962 by The Orchestral Association. Used with Permission.

"Hans Rosbaud", Slonimsky, Nicolas, ed. *Baker's Biographical Dictionary of Musicans*. Seventh Edition. New York: Schirmer Books, 1984.

154. "Sevitzky Players in Ninth Symphony." *Musical America*, May 10, 1936, 22.

"Sevitzky to lead Indianapolis Players." *Musical America*, March 25, 1937. Reprinted with permission of K-III Directory Corporation.

"Fabian Sevitsky", Slonimsky, Nicolas, ed. *Baker's Biographical Dictionary of Musicans*. Seventh Edition. New York: Schirmer Books, 1984.

155. "Leopold Stokowski", *Compton's Interactive Encylopedia*. Carlsbad, Ca.: Compton's NewMedia, Versions 1.01 VW (1992), 2.01 VW (1993).

"Leopold Stokowski", Slonimsky, Nicolas, ed. *Baker's Biographical Dictionary of Musicans*. Seventh Edition. New York: Schirmer Books, 1984.

"Leopold Stokowski", *Software Toolworks Multimedia Encyclopedia*. Novato, Ca.: Software Toolworks, Version 5.1, 1992.

156. von Rhein, John. "Tuba or not Tuba, After 44 Years, Arnold Jacobs is leaving the CSO." *Chicago Tribune*, September 25, 1988. © Copyright Chicago Tribune Company. All rights reserved. Used with permission.

157. "Orchestra", *Compton's Interactive Encylopedia*. Carlsbad, Ca.: Compton's NewMedia, Versions 1.01 VW (1992), 2.01 VW (1993).

Ravinia Festival Assocation. *Ravinia: The Festival at its Half Century*. Highland Park, Il: Ravinia Festival Association in conjuction with Rand McNally, 1985. Used with permission from Ravinia Festival.

"Georg Szell", Slonimsky, Nicolas, ed. *Baker's Biographical Dictionary of Musicans*. Seventh Edition. New York: Schirmer Books, 1984.

"Georg Szell", *Software Toolworks Multimedia Encyclopedia*. Novato, Ca.: Software Toolworks, Version 5.1, 1992.

158.   "Orchestra", *Compton's Interactive Encylopedia*. Carlsbad, Ca.: Compton's NewMedia, Versions 1.01 VW (1992), 2.01 VW (1993).

"Bruno Walter", Slonimsky, Nicolas, ed. *Baker's Biographical Dictionary of Musicans*. Seventh Edition. New York: Schirmer Books, 1984.

"Bruno Walter", *Software Toolworks Multimedia Encyclopedia*. Novato, Ca.: Software Toolworks, Version 5.1, 1992.

Retirement

159.   "Spinocerebellar Diseases", Berkow, Robert, ed. *The Merck Manual*. Rahway, N.J.: Merck Sharp & Dohme Research Laboratories, 1982, 1368.

160.   Trusheim, William H., *Mental Imagery and Musical Performance: An Inquiry into Imagery Use by Eminent Orchestral Brass Players in the United States*, Rutgers The State University of New Jersey - New Brunswick, 1987, used with permission

161.   Schwendener, Peter. "The Best Tuba Player in the World." *Chicago Reader*, June 1, 1984, 1+. Copyright ©1984 Chicago Reader, Inc. Used with permission.

162.   Bobo, Roger. "Arnold Jacobs [Chicago, December 3, 1979]: Interview with Roger Bobo." Parts 1, 2. *Brass Bulletin* 33 (1981): 43-50; 34 (1981): 37, 39, 41, 43-44. reprinted from Brass Bulletin. ©1981 by Roger Bobo and Brass Bulletin (Jean-Pierre Mathez, CH-1630 Bulle/Switzerland) used with permission.

163.   "Arnold Jacobs: Lecture at International Brassfest, Bloomington, Indiana, June 1, 1995." Joe Hughes, transcriber. Brian Frederiksen, editor. Parts 1,2 3. *Atlanta Brass Society Journal*. Volume 7, #1 (Fall, 1995), #2 (Winter,1996), #3 (Spring, 1996). Copyright 1995. Used with permission.

164.   von Rhein, John. "Tuba or not Tuba, After 44 Years, Arnold Jacobs is leaving the CSO." *Chicago Tribune*, September 25, 1988. © Copyright Chicago Tribune Company. All rights reserved. Used with permission.

165.   "Arnold Jacobs: Lecture at International Brassfest, Bloomington, Indiana, June 1, 1995." Joe Hughes, transcriber. Brian Frederiksen, editor. Parts 1,2 3. *Atlanta Brass Society Journal*. Volume 7, #1 (Fall, 1995), #2 (Winter,1996), #3 (Spring, 1996). Copyright 1995. Used with permission.

Awards

166.   Bannon, Lorraine. "City to Have Traditional 4th of July—on July 5th." *Evanston Review*, July 1, 1982.

167.   "Del Segno Brunch." *Intermezzo*. [Newsletter of the Chicago Federation of Musicians] (June 1988)

A biography was in *Intermezzo*. (April 1988)

168.   For more information see:
Reich, Howard. "The Honor is All Theirs." *Chicago Tribune*, September 18, 1994,

Section 13, 16-17.

Reich, Howard. "LAMA Night Made for City's Musicians." *Chicago Tribune*, September 19, 1994, Section 1, back page.

The Teacher

169.   Schwendener, Peter. "The Best Tuba Player in the World." *Chicago Reader*, June 1, 1984, 1+. Copyright ©1984 Chicago Reader, Inc. Used with permission.
von Rhein, John. "Tuba or not Tuba, After 44 Years, Arnold Jacobs is leaving the CSO." *Chicago Tribune*, September 25, 1988. © Copyright Chicago Tribune Company. All rights reserved. Used with permission.

170.   Walters, Rick. *The Canadian Brass Book*. Milwaukee: Hal Leonard Publishing Corporation, 1992. [:27-28, 92]

171.   Clevenger, Dale. "Mentors." *Chicago Tribune Magazine*, January 27, 1985.© Copyright Chicago Tribune Company. All rights reserved. Used with permission.

172.   Schwendener, Peter. "The Best Tuba Player in the World." *Chicago Reader*, June 1, 1984, 1+. Copyright ©1984 Chicago Reader, Inc. Used with permission.

173.   "Sir Georg Solti", "Who is Arnold Jacobs?" *TUBA Journal* 15, no. 4 (May 1988): 30-34.

174.   Whitfield, Edward J. "Remembrances and Recollections of Arnold M. Jacobs." *TUBA Journal* 12, no. 4 (May 1985): 7-8. Used with permission.

175.   Maldonado, Luis. "A Conversation with Abe Torchinsky." *TUBA Journal* 16, no. 4 (Summer 1989): 17-21.

176.   Northwestern University. Press Release, "NU School of Music Names Eleven CSO Professors," January, 11, 1972.

177.   "Arnold Jacobs", Chicago Symphony Orchestra Programs, 1943-1991, October 26-28,1978 [Performance of Vaughan Williams *Tuba Concerto*]. reprinted from the *Chicago Symphony Programs*. Copyright ©1978 by The Orchestral Association. Used with Permission.

178.   Bobo, Roger. "Arnold Jacobs [Chicago, December 3, 1979]: Interview with Roger Bobo." Parts 1, 2. *Brass Bulletin* 33 (1981): 43-50; 34 (1981): 37, 39, 41, 43-44. reprinted from Brass Bulletin. ©1981 by Roger Bobo and Brass Bulletin (Jean-Pierre Mathez, CH-1630 Bulle/Switzerland) used with permission.

179.   Schwendener, Peter. "The Best Tuba Player in the World." *Chicago Reader*, June 1, 1984, 1+. Copyright ©1984 Chicago Reader, Inc. Used with permission.

180.   Bobo, Roger. "Arnold Jacobs [Chicago, December 3, 1979]: Interview with Roger Bobo." Parts 1, 2. *Brass Bulletin* 33 (1981): 43-50; 34 (1981): 37, 39, 41, 43-44. reprinted from Brass Bulletin. ©1981 by Roger Bobo and Brass Bulletin (Jean-Pierre Mathez, CH-1630 Bulle/Switzerland) used with permission.

181.   Meyer, Eileen. "Career Counseling: Interviews With Arnold Jacobs and Frank Crisafulli." *Journal of the International Trombone Association* 13, no. 4 (October 1985): 32-33. Used with permission from the *Journal of the International Trombone Association.*

182.   "Arnold Jacobs. Lecture at International Brassfest, Bloomington, Indiana, June 1, 1995." Joe Hughes, transcriber. Brian Frederiksen, editor. Parts 1,2 3. *Atlanta Brass Society Journal*, Volume 7, #1 (Fall, 1995), #2 (Winter,1996), #3 (Spring, 1996). Copyright 1995. Used with permission.

183.   Doherty, Jim, "For All Who Crave a Horn That Thrills, This Bud's for You", *Smithsonian* 25 no. 6, (September 1994): 94-103. reprinted from *Smithsonian*. ©1995 by *Smithsonian*. Used wirh permission.

184.   Bobo, Roger. "Arnold Jacobs [Chicago, December 3, 1979]: Interview with Roger Bobo."
            Parts 1, 2. *Brass Bulletin* 33 (1981): 43-50; 34 (1981): 37, 39, 41, 43-44.
            reprinted from Brass Bulletin. ©1981 by Roger Bobo and Brass Bulletin
            (Jean-Pierre Mathez, CH-1630 Bulle/Switzerland) used with permission.
185.   Schwendener, Peter. "The Best Tuba Player in the World." *Chicago Reader*, June 1, 1984,
            1+. Copyright ©1984 Chicago Reader, Inc. Used with permission.
186.   Bobo, Roger. "Arnold Jacobs [Chicago, December 3, 1979]: Interview with Roger Bobo."
            Parts 1, 2. *Brass Bulletin* 33 (1981): 43-50; 34 (1981): 37, 39, 41, 43-44.
            reprinted from Brass Bulletin. ©1981 by Roger Bobo and Brass Bulletin
            (Jean-Pierre Mathez, CH-1630 Bulle/Switzerland) used with permission.
187.   Haugan, Paul. "TUBA Profile - Arnold M. Jacobs Tubist of the Chicago Symphony
            Orchestra." *TUBA Journal* 4, no. 2 (Winter 1977): 2-10. Used with permission.
188.   Bobo, Roger. "Arnold Jacobs [Chicago, December 3, 1979]: Interview with Roger Bobo."
            Parts 1, 2. *Brass Bulletin* 33 (1981): 43-50; 34 (1981): 37, 39, 41, 43-44.
            reprinted from Brass Bulletin. ©1981 by Roger Bobo and Brass Bulletin
            (Jean-Pierre Mathez, CH-1630 Bulle/Switzerland) used with permission.
189.   Haugan, Paul. "TUBA Profile - Arnold M. Jacobs Tubist of the Chicago Symphony
            Orchestra." *TUBA Journal* 4, no. 2 (Winter 1977): 2-10. Used with permission.
190.   "Arnold Jacobs: Lecture at International Brassfest, Bloomington, Indiana, June 1, 1995."
            Joe Hughes, transcriber. Brian Frederiksen, editor. Parts 1,2 3. *Atlanta Brass
            Society Journal*, Volume 7, #1 (Fall, 1995), #2 (Winter,1996), #3 (Spring,
            1996). Copyright 1995. Used with permission.
191.   Haugan, Paul. "TUBA Profile - Arnold M. Jacobs Tubist of the Chicago Symphony
            Orchestra." *TUBA Journal* 4, no. 2 (Winter 1977): 2-10. Used with permission.

Physical Elements

192.   "Interview with Arnold Jacobs and Jim Unrath." Broadcast on WFMT-FM, Chicago,
            Illinois. 1978. Used with permission from WFMT-FM.
193.   Stewart, M. Dee. "An Arnold Jacobs Biography." *TUBA Journal* 15, no. 4 (May 1988):
            14-17. Used with permission.
194.   "Interview with Arnold Jacobs and Jim Unrath." Broadcast on WFMT-FM, Chicago,
            Illinois. 1978. Used with permission from WFMT-FM.
195.   Stewart, M. Dee. "An Arnold Jacobs Biography." *TUBA Journal* 15, no. 4 (May 1988):
            14-17. Used with permission.
196.   "Arnold Jacobs: Lecture at International Brassfest, Bloomington, Indiana, June 1, 1995."
            Joe Hughes, transcriber. Brian Frederiksen, editor. Parts 1,2 3. *Atlanta Brass
            Society Journal*, Volume 7, #1 (Fall, 1995), #2 (Winter,1996), #3 (Spring,
            1996). Copyright 1995. Used with permission.
197.   "Arnold Jacobs: Lecture at International Brassfest, Bloomington, Indiana, June 1, 1995."
            Joe Hughes, transcriber. Brian Frederiksen, editor. Parts 1,2 3. *Atlanta Brass
            Society Journal*, Volume 7, #1 (Fall, 1995), #2 (Winter,1996), #3 (Spring,
            1996). Copyright 1995. Used with permission.
198.   "Arnold Jacobs: Lecture at International Brassfest, Bloomington, Indiana, June 1, 1995."
            Joe Hughes, transcriber. Brian Frederiksen, editor. Parts 1,2 3. *Atlanta Brass
            Society Journal*, Volume 7, #1 (Fall, 1995), #2 (Winter,1996), #3 (Spring,
            1996). Copyright 1995. Used with permission.
199.   "Arnold Jacobs: Lecture at International Brassfest, Bloomington, Indiana, June 1, 1995."
            Joe Hughes, transcriber. Brian Frederiksen, editor. Parts 1,2 3. *Atlanta Brass
            Society Journal*, Volume 7, #1 (Fall, 1995), #2 (Winter,1996), #3 (Spring,

1996). Copyright 1995. Used with permission.

200. "Arnold Jacobs: Lecture at International Brassfest, Bloomington, Indiana, June 1, 1995." Joe Hughes, transcriber. Brian Frederiksen, editor. Parts 1,2 3. *Atlanta Brass Society Journal.* Volume 7, #1 (Fall, 1995), #2 (Winter,1996), #3 (Spring, 1996). Copyright 1995. Used with permission.

201. "Interview with Arnold Jacobs and Jim Unrath." Broadcast on WFMT-FM, Chicago, Illinois. 1978. Used with permission from WFMT-FM.

202. "Arnold Jacobs: Lecture at International Brassfest, Bloomington, Indiana, June 1, 1995." Joe Hughes, transcriber. Brian Frederiksen, editor. Parts 1,2 3. *Atlanta Brass Society Journal,* Volume 7, #1 (Fall, 1995), #2 (Winter,1996), #3 (Spring, 1996). Copyright 1995. Used with permission.

203. Furlong, William Barry. *Season With Solti: A Year in the Life of the Chicago Symphony.* New York,N.Y.:MacMillan,1974.[267-270, 290-293, 297-307,310-311] reprinted with permission of Simon & Schuster, Inc., from *Season with Solti: A Year in the Life of the Chicago Symphony* by William Barry Furlong. Copyright ©1974 by William Barry Furlong.

204. "Lung Function Testing: Selection of Reference Values and InterpretativeStrategies", *Am Rev Respir Dis 1991*, American Thoracic Society, (March 1991).

205. "Lung Function Testing: Selection of Reference Values and InterpretativeStrategies", *Am Rev Respir Dis 1991*, American Thoracic Society, (March 1991).

206. Furlong, William Barry. *Season With Solti: A Year in the Life of the Chicago Symphony.* New York,N.Y.:MacMillan,1974.[267-270, 290-293, 297-307,310-311] reprinted with permission of Simon & Schuster, Inc., from *Season with Solti: A Year in the Life of the Chicago Symphony* by William Barry Furlong. Copyright ©1974 by William Barry Furlong.

207. "Lung Function Testing: Selection of Reference Values and InterpretativeStrategies", *Am Rev Respir Dis 1991*, American Thoracic Society, (March 1991).

208. "Interview with Arnold Jacobs and Jim Unrath." Broadcast on WFMT-FM, Chicago, Illinois. 1978. Used with permission from WFMT-FM.

209. Furlong, William Barry. *Season With Solti: A Year in the Life of the Chicago Symphony.* New York,N.Y.:MacMillan,1974.[267-270, 290-293, 297-307,310-311] reprinted with permission of Simon & Schuster, Inc., from *Season with Solti: A Year in the Life of the Chicago Symphony* by William Barry Furlong. Copyright ©1974 by William Barry Furlong.

210. Brubeck, David William. "The Pedagogy of Arnold Jacobs." *TUBA Journal* 19, no. 1 (Fall 1991): 54-58. Copyright 1991 David Brubeck. Used with permission.

211. "Interview with Arnold Jacobs and Jim Unrath." Broadcast on WFMT-FM, Chicago, Illinois. 1978. Used with permission from WFMT-FM.

212. "Arnold Jacobs: Lecture at International Brassfest, Bloomington, Indiana, June 1, 1995." Joe Hughes, transcriber. *Atlanta Brass Society Journal* (Fall 1995). Copyright 1995. Used with permission.

213. "Interview with Arnold Jacobs and Bill Russo." Broadcast on WFMT-FM, Chicago, Illinois. Used with permission from WFMT-FM.

214. Rusch, Harold W. and Jacobs, Arnold. *Hal Leonard Advanced Band Method: With Special Studies by Arnold Jacobs.* Winona, Minnesota: Hal Leonard Music, 1963. Used with permission.

215. "Arnold Jacobs: Lecture at International Brassfest, Bloomington, Indiana, June 1, 1995." Joe Hughes, transcriber. Brian Frederiksen, editor. Parts 1,2 3. *Atlanta Brass Society Journal,* Volume 7, #1 (Fall, 1995), #2 (Winter,1996), #3 (Spring, 1996). Copyright 1995. Used with permission.

216.   Furlong, William Barry. *Season With Solti: A Year in the Life of the Chicago Symphony.* New York,N.Y.:MacMillan,1974.[267-270, 290-293, 297-307,310-311] reprinted with permission of Simon & Schuster, Inc., from *Season with Solti: A Year in the Life of the Chicago Symphony* by William Barry Furlong. Copyright ©1974 by William Barry Furlong.

217.   "Interview with Arnold Jacobs and Jim Unrath." Broadcast on WFMT-FM, Chicago, Illinois. 1978. Used with permission from WFMT-FM.

218.   "Arnold Jacobs: Lecture at International Brassfest, Bloomington, Indiana, June 1, 1995." Joe Hughes, transcriber. Brian Frederiksen, editor. Parts 1,2 3. *Atlanta Brass Society Journal.* Volume 7, #1 (Fall, 1995), #2 (Winter,1996), #3 (Spring, 1996). Copyright 1995. Used with permission.

219.   Haugan, Paul. "TUBA Profile - Arnold M. Jacobs Tubist of the Chicago Symphony Orchestra." *TUBA Journal* 4, no. 2 (Winter 1977): 2-10. Used with permission.

220.   Rusch, Harold W. and Jacobs, Arnold. *Hal Leonard Advanced Band Method: With Special Studies by Arnold Jacobs.* Winona, Minnesota: Hal Leonard Music, 1963. Used with permission.

221.   Haugan, Paul. "TUBA Profile - Arnold M. Jacobs Tubist of the Chicago Symphony Orchestra." *TUBA Journal* 4, no. 2 (Winter 1977): 2-10. Used with permission.

222.   "Arnold Jacobs: Lecture at International Brassfest, Bloomington, Indiana, June 1, 1995." Joe Hughes, transcriber. Brian Frederiksen, editor. Parts 1,2 3. *Atlanta Brass Society Journal.* Volume 7, #1 (Fall, 1995), #2 (Winter,1996), #3 (Spring, 1996). Copyright 1995. Used with permission.

223.   Rusch, Harold W. and Jacobs, Arnold. *Hal Leonard Advanced Band Method: With Special Studies by Arnold Jacobs.* Winona, Minnesota: Hal Leonard Music, 1963. Used with permission.

224.   "Arnold Jacobs: Lecture at International Brassfest, Bloomington, Indiana, June 1, 1995." Joe Hughes, transcriber. Brian Frederiksen, editor. Parts 1,2 3. *Atlanta Brass Society Journal.* Volume 7, #1 (Fall, 1995), #2 (Winter,1996), #3 (Spring, 1996). Copyright 1995. Used with permission.

225.   "Daniel Beroulli", *Software Toolworks Multimedia Encyclopedia.* Novato, Ca.: Software Toolworks, Version 5.1, 1992.

226.   Furlong, William Barry. *Season With Solti: A Year in the Life of the Chicago Symphony.* New York,N.Y.:MacMillan,1974.[267-270, 290-293, 297-307,310-311] reprinted with permission of Simon & Schuster, Inc., from *Season with Solti: A Year in the Life of the Chicago Symphony* by William Barry Furlong. Copyright ©1974 by William Barry Furlong.

227.   Rusch, Harold W. and Jacobs, Arnold. *Hal Leonard Advanced Band Method: With Special Studies by Arnold Jacobs.* Winona, Minnesota: Hal Leonard Music, 1963. Used with permission.

228.   Brubeck, David William. "The Pedagogy of Arnold Jacobs." *TUBA Journal* 19, no. 1 (Fall 1991): 54-58. Copyright 1991 David Brubeck. Used with permission.

229.   Rusch, Harold W. and Jacobs, Arnold. *Hal Leonard Advanced Band Method: With Special Studies by Arnold Jacobs.* Winona, Minnesota: Hal Leonard Music, 1963. Used with permission.

230.   Rusch, Harold W. and Jacobs, Arnold. *Hal Leonard Advanced Band Method: With Special Studies by Arnold Jacobs.* Winona, Minnesota: Hal Leonard Music, 1963. Used with permission.

231. Furlong, William Barry. *Season With Solti: A Year in the Life of the Chicago Symphony*. New York,N.Y.:MacMillan,1974.[267-270, 290-293, 297-307,310-311] reprinted with permission of Simon & Schuster, Inc., from *Season with Solti: A Year in the Life of the Chicago Symphony* by William Barry Furlong. Copyright ©1974 by William Barry Furlong.

232. Schwendener, Peter. "The Best Tuba Player in the World." *Chicago Reader*, June 1, 1984, 1+. Copyright ©1984 Chicago Reader, Inc. Used with permission.

233. "Lung Function Testing: Selection of Reference Values and InterpretativeStrategies", *Am Rev Respir Dis 1991*, American Thoracic Society, (March 1991).

234. Furlong, William Barry. *Season With Solti: A Year in the Life of the Chicago Symphony*. New York,N.Y.:MacMillan,1974.[267-270, 290-293, 297-307,310-311] reprinted with permission of Simon & Schuster, Inc., from *Season with Solti: A Year in the Life of the Chicago Symphony* by William Barry Furlong. Copyright ©1974 by William Barry Furlong.

235. Furlong, William Barry. *Season With Solti: A Year in the Life of the Chicago Symphony*. New York,N.Y.:MacMillan,1974.[267-270, 290-293, 297-307,310-311] reprinted with permission of Simon & Schuster, Inc., from *Season with Solti: A Year in the Life of the Chicago Symphony* by William Barry Furlong. Copyright ©1974 by William Barry Furlong.

Mental Elements

236. Bobo, Roger. "Arnold Jacobs [Chicago, December 3, 1979]: Interview with Roger Bobo." Parts 1, 2. *Brass Bulletin* 33 (1981): 43-50; 34 (1981): 37, 39, 41, 43-44. reprinted from Brass Bulletin. ©1981 by Roger Bobo and Brass Bulletin (Jean-Pierre Mathez, CH-1630 Bulle/Switzerland) used with permission.

237. "Arnold Jacobs: Lecture at International Brassfest, Bloomington, Indiana, June 1, 1995." Joe Hughes, transcriber. Brian Frederiksen, editor. Parts 1,2 3. *Atlanta Brass Society Journal*, Volume 7, #1 (Fall, 1995), #2 (Winter,1996), #3 (Spring, 1996). Copyright 1995. Used with permission.

238. Rusch, Harold W. and Jacobs, Arnold. *Hal Leonard Advanced Band Method: With Special Studies by Arnold Jacobs*. Winona, Minnesota: Hal Leonard Music, 1963. Used with permission.

239. Bobo, Roger. "Arnold Jacobs [Chicago, December 3, 1979]: Interview with Roger Bobo." Parts 1, 2. *Brass Bulletin* 33 (1981): 43-50; 34 (1981): 37, 39, 41, 43-44. reprinted from Brass Bulletin. ©1981 by Roger Bobo and Brass Bulletin (Jean-Pierre Mathez, CH-1630 Bulle/Switzerland) used with permission.

240. "Arnold Jacobs: Lecture at International Brassfest, Bloomington, Indiana, June 1, 1995." Joe Hughes, transcriber. Brian Frederiksen, editor. Parts 1,2 3. *Atlanta Brass Society Journal*, Volume 7, #1 (Fall, 1995), #2 (Winter,1996), #3 (Spring, 1996). Copyright 1995. Used with permission.

241. Doherty, Jim, "For All Who Crave a Horn That Thrills, This Bud's for You", *Smithsonian* 25 no. 6, (September 1994): 94-103. reprinted from *Smithsonian*. ©1995 by *Smithsonian*. Used wirh permission.

242. "Arnold Jacobs: Lecture at International Brassfest, Bloomington, Indiana, June 1, 1995." Joe Hughes, transcriber. Brian Frederiksen, editor. Parts 1,2 3. *Atlanta Brass Society Journal*, Volume 7, #1 (Fall, 1995), #2 (Winter,1996), #3 (Spring,

1996). Copyright 1995. Used with permission.

243. Brubeck, David William. "The Pedagogy of Arnold Jacobs." *TUBA Journal* 19, no. 1 (Fall 1991): 54-58. Copyright 1991 David Brubeck. Used with permission.

244. Kohut, Daniel L. "Learning How to Perform Music." *TUBA Journal* 15, no. 4 (May 1988): 18-20. Used with permission.

245. "Arnold Jacobs: Lecture at International Brassfest, Bloomington, Indiana, June 1, 1995." Joe Hughes, transcriber. Brian Frederiksen, editor. Parts 1,2 3. *Atlanta Brass Society Journal.* Volume 7, #1 (Fall, 1995), #2 (Winter,1996), #3 (Spring, 1996). Copyright 1995. Used with permission.

246. Schwendener, Peter. "The Best Tuba Player in the World." *Chicago Reader*, June 1, 1984, 1+. Copyright ©1984 Chicago Reader, Inc. Used with permission.

247. Brubeck, David William. "The Pedagogy of Arnold Jacobs." *TUBA Journal* 19, no. 1 (Fall 1991): 54-58. Copyright 1991 David Brubeck. Used with permission.

248. Haugan, Paul. "TUBA Profile - Arnold M. Jacobs Tubist of the Chicago Symphony Orchestra." *TUBA Journal* 4, no. 2 (Winter 1977): 2-10. Used with permission.

249. Trusheim, William H., *Mental Imagery and Musical Performance: An Inquiry into Imagery Use by Eminent Orchestral Brass Players in the United States,* Rutgers The State University of New Jersey - New Brunswick, 1987 [University Microfilms #8808237]. Used with permission.

250. Haugan, Paul. "TUBA Profile - Arnold M. Jacobs Tubist of the Chicago Symphony Orchestra." *TUBA Journal* 4, no. 2 (Winter 1977): 2-10. Used with permission.

251. Haugan, Paul. "TUBA Profile - Arnold M. Jacobs Tubist of the Chicago Symphony Orchestra." *TUBA Journal* 4, no. 2 (Winter 1977): 2-10. Used with permission.

252. Brubeck, David William. "The Pedagogy of Arnold Jacobs." *TUBA Journal* 19, no. 1 (Fall 1991): 54-58. Copyright 1991 David Brubeck. Used with permission.

253. Ebbers, Paul. "Masterclass Tuba: Arnold Jacobs." *Accent*, Spring 1978.

Performance

254. Haugan, Paul. "TUBA Profile - Arnold M. Jacobs Tubist of the Chicago Symphony Orchestra." *TUBA Journal* 4, no. 2 (Winter 1977): 2-10. Used with permission.

255. Rusch, Harold W. and Jacobs, Arnold. *Hal Leonard Advanced Band Method: With Special Studies by Arnold Jacobs.* Winona, Minnesota: Hal Leonard Music, 1963. Used with permission.

256. "Arnold Jacobs: Lecture at International Brassfest, Bloomington, Indiana, June 1, 1995." Joe Hughes, transcriber. Brian Frederiksen, editor. Parts 1,2 3. *Atlanta Brass Society Journal,* Volume 7, #1 (Fall, 1995), #2 (Winter,1996), #3 (Spring, 1996). Copyright 1995. Used with permission.

257. Haugan, Paul. "TUBA Profile - Arnold M. Jacobs Tubist of the Chicago Symphony Orchestra." *TUBA Journal* 4, no. 2 (Winter 1977): 2-10. Used with permission.

258. Haugan, Paul. "TUBA Profile - Arnold M. Jacobs Tubist of the Chicago Symphony Orchestra." *TUBA Journal* 4, no. 2 (Winter 1977): 2-10. Used with permission.

259. Schwendener, Peter. "The Best Tuba Player in the World." *Chicago Reader*, June 1,

1984, 1+. Copyright ©1984 Chicago Reader, Inc. Used with permission.

260.   Haugan, Paul. "TUBA Profile - Arnold M. Jacobs Tubist of the Chicago Symphony
        Orchestra." *TUBA Journal* 4, no. 2 (Winter 1977): 2-10.
        Used with permission.

261.   Trusheim, William H., *Mental Imagery and Musical Performance: An Inquiry into
        Imagery Use by Eminent Orchestral Brass Players in the United States*,
        Rutgers The State University of New Jersey - New Brunswick, 1987
        [University Microfilms #8808237]. Used with permission.

262.   Schwendener, Peter. "The Best Tuba Player in the World." *Chicago Reader*, June 1,
        1984, 1+. Copyright ©1984 Chicago Reader, Inc. Used with permission.

263.   Haugan, Paul. "TUBA Profile - Arnold M. Jacobs Tubist of the Chicago Symphony
        Orchestra." *TUBA Journal* 4, no. 2 (Winter 1977): 2-10.
        Used with permission.

264.   Haugan, Paul. "TUBA Profile - Arnold M. Jacobs Tubist of the Chicago Symphony
        Orchestra." *TUBA Journal* 4, no. 2 (Winter 1977): 2-10.
        Used with permission.

265.   Haugan, Paul. "TUBA Profile - Arnold M. Jacobs Tubist of the Chicago Symphony
        Orchestra." *TUBA Journal* 4, no. 2 (Winter 1977): 2-10.
        Used with permission.

266.   Furlong, William Barry. *Season With Solti: A Year in the Life of the Chicago Symphony*.
        New York,N.Y.:MacMillan,1974.[267-270, 290-293, 297-307,310-311]
        reprinted with permission of Simon & Schuster, Inc., from *Season with Solti:
        A Year in the Life of the Chicago Symphony* by William Barry Furlong.
        Copyright ©1974 by William Barry Furlong.

267.   Trusheim, William H., *Mental Imagery and Musical Performance: An Inquiry into
        Imagery Use by Eminent Orchestral Brass Players in the United States*,
        Rutgers The State University of New Jersey - New Brunswick, 1987
        [University Microfilms #8808237]. Used with permission.

268.   Meyer, Eileen. "Career Counseling: Interviews With Arnold Jacobs and Frank Crisafulli."
        Journal of the International Trombone Association 13, no. 4 (October 1985): 32-
        33. Used with permission of the *Journal of the International Trombone
        Association*.

269.   Schneider, Richard. "Arnold Jacobs Sounds Off." *Fritz Reiner Society Newsletter*
        No. 4, n.d. Used with permission.

Instruments

270.   Bobo, Roger. "Arnold Jacobs [Chicago, December 3, 1979]: Interview with Roger
        Bobo." Parts 1, 2. *Brass Bulletin* 33 (1981): 43-50; 34 (1981): 37, 39, 41, 43-
        44. reprinted from Brass Bulletin. ©1981 by Roger Bobo and Brass Bulletin
        (Jean-Pierre Mathez, CH-1630 Bulle/Switzerland) used with permission.

271.   "Interview with Arnold Jacobs and Bill Russo." Broadcast on WFMT-FM, Chicago,
        Illinois. 1978. Used with permission from WFMT-FM.

272.   Furlong, William Barry. *Season With Solti: A Year in the Life of the Chicago Symphony*.
        New York,N.Y.:MacMillan,1974.[267-270, 290-293, 297-307,310-311]
        reprinted with permission of Simon & Schuster, Inc., from *Season with Solti:
        A Year in the Life of the Chicago Symphony* by William Barry Furlong.
        Copyright ©1974 by William Barry Furlong.

273.   Bobo, Roger. "Arnold Jacobs [Chicago, December 3, 1979]: Interview with Roger

Bobo." Parts 1, 2. *Brass Bulletin* 33 (1981): 43-50; 34 (1981): 37, 39, 41, 43-44. reprinted from Brass Bulletin. ©1981 by Roger Bobo and Brass Bulletin (Jean-Pierre Mathez, CH-1630 Bulle/Switzerland) used with permission.

274.   von Rhein, John. "Tuba or not Tuba, After 44 Years, Arnold Jacobs is leaving the CSO." *Chicago Tribune*, September 25, 1988. © Copyright Chicago Tribune Company. All rights reserved. Used with permission.

275.   Haugan, Paul. "TUBA Profile - Arnold M. Jacobs Tubist of the Chicago Symphony Orchestra." *TUBA Journal* 4, no. 2 (Winter 1977): 2-10. Used with permission.

276.   Bobo, Roger. "Arnold Jacobs [Chicago, December 3, 1979]: Interview with Roger Bobo." Parts 1, 2. *Brass Bulletin* 33 (1981): 43-50; 34 (1981): 37, 39, 41, 43-44. reprinted from Brass Bulletin. ©1981 by Roger Bobo and Brass Bulletin (Jean-Pierre Mathez, CH-1630 Bulle/Switzerland) used with permission.

277.   Bobo, Roger. "Arnold Jacobs [Chicago, December 3, 1979]: Interview with Roger Bobo." Parts 1, 2. *Brass Bulletin* 33 (1981): 43-50; 34 (1981): 37, 39, 41, 43-44. reprinted from Brass Bulletin. ©1981 by Roger Bobo and Brass Bulletin (Jean-Pierre Mathez, CH-1630 Bulle/Switzerland) used with permission.

278.   Haugan, Paul. "TUBA Profile - Arnold M. Jacobs Tubist of the Chicago Symphony Orchestra." *TUBA Journal* 4, no. 2 (Winter 1977): 2-10. Used with permission.

279.   Furlong, William Barry. *Season With Solti: A Year in the Life of the Chicago Symphony.* New York,N.Y.:MacMillan,1974.[267-270, 290-293, 297-307,310-311] reprinted with permission of Simon & Schuster, Inc., from *Season with Solti: A Year in the Life of the Chicago Symphony* by William Barry Furlong. Copyright ©1974 by William Barry Furlong.

280.   Furlong, William Barry. *Season With Solti: A Year in the Life of the Chicago Symphony.* New York,N.Y.:MacMillan,1974.[267-270, 290-293, 297-307,310-311] reprinted with permission of Simon & Schuster, Inc., from *Season with Solti: A Year in the Life of the Chicago Symphony* by William Barry Furlong. Copyright ©1974 by William Barry Furlong.

281.   Schwendener, Peter. "The Best Tuba Player in the World." *Chicago Reader*, June 1, 1984, 1+. Copyright ©1984 Chicago Reader, Inc. Used with permission.

The Jacobs Studio

282.   Haugan, Paul. "TUBA Profile - Arnold M. Jacobs Tubist of the Chicago Symphony Orchestra." *TUBA Journal* 4, no. 2 (Winter 1977): 2-10. Used with permission.

283.   "Looking Back." *Fine Arts Building Newsletter*, n.d. [History of the Fine Arts Building, 428 S. Michigan, Chicago, Illinois]

York Tuba

284.   Farrar, Lloyd P. "Toward a Schedule of Engraved and / or Stamped Trade Marks, Serial Numbers, Patent Notices, and Dates on Brasswinds Made in Grand Rapids, Michigan by J. W. York and by J. W York & Son(s)." Unpublished manuscript, n.d.
York, J. W. Biographical notes, nd.
Comments from William Scarlett.

285.   Funderburk, Jeffrey L. "The Man and his Horn." *TUBA Journal* 15, no. 4 (May 1988): 43. Used with permission.
286.   Funderburk, Jeffrey L. "The Man and his Horn." *TUBA Journal* 15, no. 4 (May 1988): 43. Used with permission.
        Taylor, John. "Reminiscences of the Man and His Horn." *TUBA Journal* 9, no. 2 (Fall 1981): 20.
        Tucci, Robert. "A Closer Look at the Hirsbrunner York Model CC-Tuba." *TUBA Journal* 17, no. 1 (Fall 1989): 34-37. Used with permission.
287.   Tucci, Robert. "A Closer Look at the Hirsbrunner York Model CC-Tuba." *TUBA Journal* 17, no. 1 (Fall 1989): 34-37. Used with permission.
        Hirsbrunner, Peter. "The History of the Big York-Hirsbrunner Tuba: The Instrument-Maker's Point of View." *Brass Bulletin* 40 (1982): 34-39.
288.   Bishop, Ronald. "Arnold Jacobs on Record: Its Influence on me." *TUBA Journal* 15, no. 4 (May 1988): 27-29. Used with permission.
289.   Schneider, Richard. "Arnold Jacobs Sounds Off." *Fritz Reiner Society Newsletter* No. 4, n.d. Used with permission.
290.   Taylor, John. "Reminiscences of the Man and His Horn." *TUBA Journal* 9, no. 2 (Fall 1981): 20.
291.   Schneider, Richard. "Arnold Jacobs Sounds Off." *Fritz Reiner Society Newsletter* No. 4, n.d. Used with permission.
292.   Taylor, John. "Reminiscences of the Man and His Horn." *TUBA Journal* 9, no. 2 (Fall 1981): 20.

Appendix A: *Arnold Jacobs Discography*

293.   Those that are only released by the CSO are listed as "Chicago Symphony Release"
        There are thousands of recordings of CSO concerts recorded by WFMT-FM and distributed throughout the world.
        Recordings from Arnold Jacobs' collection.
        Daniel, Oliver. *Stokowski: A Counterpoint of View.* New York: Dodd, Mead and Company, 1982.
        Helmbrecht, Arthur. *Fritz Reiner: The Comprehensive Discography of His Recordings.* Novelty, Oh.: Fritz Reiner Society, 1978.
        Opperby, Preben. *Leopold Stokowski.* New York: Hippocrene Books, 1982.
        Chicago Symphony Orchestra Recordings, 1916-1991. Published by the CSO as part of their centennial season index. Used with permission.
        Conversations with Rex Martin, Bob Rusk, Dave Fedderly, Dan Corrigan, John Taylor, Bob Tucci, Charles Guse, Norm Schweikert, Don Little, Gene Pokorny, Wally Horban (CSO Library), Abe Torchinsky

Appendix B: *Brass Personnel*

294.   Indianapolis Symphony Orchestra Programs. Personnel Rosters 1937-1940
295.   Pittsburgh Symphony Orchestra Programs Personnel Listings 1938-1944
        Comments from Norman Schweikert.
296.   All-American Youth Orchestra Programs 1940-41.
297.   Clark, Keith C. "Trumpet Sections of American Symphony Orchestras: The Chicago Symphony Orchestra." *International Trumpet Guild Journal* 8, no. 2 (December 1983): 17-22. Used with permission of the *International Trumpet Guild Journal.*

298.   Tracy, Bruce. "Orchestra Showcase The Chicago Symphony Orchestra. "*International Trombone Association Newsletter* 7, no. 2 (April 1980): 10-15. Used with permission of the *International Trombone Association Journal.*
        Corrections from Norman Schweikert
299.   From Norman Schweikert.

Bibliography

All-American Youth Orchestra Programs 1940-41.

Arado, M., Henderson, E. M. , Robinson, W. , Ward, D. "Orchestra Hall Tours
Fact Sheet." Chicago Symphony Orchestra, October 7, 1985.

"Arnold Jacobs Biography." *Intermezzo*. [Newsletter of the Chicago Federation of Musicians] (April
1988).

"Arnold Jacobs: Lecture at International Brassfest, Bloomington, Indiana,
June 1, 1995." Joe Hughes, transcriber. Brian Frederiksen, editor.
Parts 1,2 3. *Atlanta Brass Society Journal,* Volume 7, #1 (Fall, 1995),
#2 (Winter,1996), #3 (Spring, 1996).

Artner, Alan G. "CSO Shows Talent of Numbers with a Trio of Unusual Works." *Chicago Tribune*,
October 27, 1978, sec. 4, p. 5.

Bannon, Lorraine. "City to Have Traditional 4th of July—on July 5th."
Evanston [Illinois] Review, July 1, 1982.

Bauer, Paul. "Frank Crisafulli." *Journal of the International Trombone Association* 17, no. 4 (Fall
1989): 13-17.

Berkow, Robert, ed. *The Merck Manual*. Rahway, N.J.: Merck Sharp & Dohme Research Laboratories,
1982, 1368.

Bishop, Ronald. "Arnold Jacobs on Record: Its Influence on me." *TUBA Journal* 15, no. 4 (May 1988):
27-29.

Bobo, Roger. "Arnold Jacobs [Chicago, December 3, 1979]: Interview with Roger Bobo." Parts 1, 2.
Brass Bulletin 33 (1981): 43-50; 34 (1981): 37, 39, 41, 43-44.

Bodyworks, Cambridge, Ma.:Softkey Multimedia Inc., a subsidiary of Softkey
International, Inc.(CD-ROM version), 1994.

Brubeck, David William. "The Pedagogy of Arnold Jacobs." *TUBA Journal* 19, no. 1 (Fall 1991): 54-
58.

Brubeck, David and Olah, John. "Connie's Final Toot." *TUBA Journal* 18, no. 1 (Summer 1991): 28-36.

Carter, Elliott. "Letters to the Editor." *Journal of Music Theory* 7, no. 2 (1963): 270-273.

"Chi. Tuba Tooter Files T-H Violahon Rap Vs. Philly Orch, Local 77." *Variety*, April 13, 1949, 51.

Chicago Symphony Orchestra Programs, 1943-1991
    Claudio Abbado, April 1-5, 1988, p. 45-46
    Daniel Barenboim, October 1-8, 1991, p. 32-34
    Frank Brouk, November 23-25, 1967
    Fritz Busch, January 26-27, 1950
    Vincent Cichowicz, January 4-6, 1968
    Frank Crisafulli, January 11-13, 1968
    Frank Crisafulli, April 9, 1987, p. 42-44
    Desire Defauw, November 14-15, 1943, p. 47
    Jay Friedman, September 24, 1987, p. 56
    James Gilbertsen, Youth Concert Program, October 19-25, 1983
    Carlo Maria Giulini, April 1, 1976
    Adolph Herseth, November 24, 1971, p. 27
    Adolph Herseth, November 25, 1987, p. 64
    Arnold Jacobs, January 15, 1948
    Arnold Jacobs, April 20-21, 1967
    Arnold Jacobs, January 27, 1968
        [Performance of Vaughan Williams *Tuba Concerto*]
    Arnold Jacobs, October 26-28,1978
        [Performance of Vaughan Williams *Tuba Concerto*]
    Arnold Jacobs, January 14, 1988, p. 44
    Edward Kleinhammer, March 7-9, 1968, p. 48
    Rafael Kubelik, October 30, 1975
    Jean Martinon, September 28-29, 1967
    Richard Oldberg, April 7, 1988
    Eugene Ormandy, February 18-20, 1971, p. 29
    Personnel, all years
    Gene Pokorny, October 17, 1991, p. 14
    Arthur Rodzinski, October 14, 1947
    Hans Rosbaud, November 8-9, 1962
    William Scarlett, October 13, 1988, p. 8
    Norman Schweikert, January 9-14, 1992
    Sir Georg Solti, November 14, 1974
    Charles Vernon, January 19, 1989, p. 8

Chicago Symphony Orchestra Recordings, 1916-1991
    Published by the CSO as part of their centennial season index

Chicago Symphony Orchestra Repertory. [95th Season] Chicago: Chicago Symphony Orchestra, 1986,
    107.

Clark, Keith C. "Trumpet Sections of American Symphony Orchestras: The Chicago Symphony
    Orchestra." *International Trumpet Guild Journal* 8, no. 2 (December 1983): 17-22.

Clevenger, Dale. "Mentors." *Chicago Tribune Magazine*, January 27, 1985.

Compton's Interactive Encylopedia. Carlsbad, Ca.: Compton's NewMedia, Versions 1.01 VW (1992),
    2.01 VW (1993).
    [Samuel Barber, Leonard Bernstein, Diaphragm, Douglas Fairbanks, Wilhelm
    Furtwangler, Lungs, Gian Carlo Menotti, Orchestra, Respiratory System, George
    Solti, Leopold Stokowski]

Arnold Jacobs: *Song and Wind*

"Cowden, Hugh—In Memoriam." *The Horn Call* 19, no. 2 (April 1989): 110-111.

"Curtis Institute has Second Commencement." *Musical America*, June, 1935, 15.

"Curtis Institute Holds Third Commencement." *Musical America*, June 1936, 31.

"Curtis Institute adds Four to its Faculty." *Musical America*, October 25, 1937, 21.

Daniel, Oliver. *Stokowski: A Counterpoint of View*. New York: Dodd, Mead and Company, 1982.

"Del Segno Brunch." *Intermezzo*. [Newsletter of the Chicago Federation of Musicians] (June 1988):

Doherty, Jim, "For All Who Crave a Horn That Thrills, This Bud's for You",
    Smithsonian 25 no. 6, (September 1994): 94-103

"Donatelli, Philip." Obituary in *Billboard* 66 (April 17, 1954): 34.

"Donatelli, Philip." Obituary in *Variety* 194 (April, 14, 1954): 63.

Ebbers, Paul. "Masterclass Tuba: Arnold Jacobs." *Accent*, Spring 1978.

Farkas, Philip. *The Art of Brass Playing*. Bloomington, Ind.: Wind Music Inc., 1962.

___. "Oral History Project ", *Chicago Symphony Orchestra Program*, January 17-22, 1991.

Farrar, Lloyd P. "Toward a Schedule of Engraved and/or Stamped Trade Marks, Serial Numbers, Patent
    Notices, and Dates on Brasswinds Made in Grand Rapids, Michigan by J. W. York and by
    J. W York & Son(s)." Unpublished manuscript, n.d.

"Four Day Mid-West Band and Orchestra Clinic." *School Musician* 35, no. 3 (November 1963): 72-73.

Frederiksen, Brian. "Arnold Jacobs: A Bibliography." *International Trumpet Guild Journal* 17, no. 4
    (1993): 25-27.

Funderburk, Jeffrey L. "Proper Breath." *TUBA Journal* 14, no. 2 (November 1986): 17-18.

___. "The Man and his Horn." *TUBA Journal* 15, no. 4 (May 1988): 43.

Furlong, William Barry. *Season With Solti: A Year in the Life of the Chicago Symphony*. New York,
    N.Y.: MacMillan, 1974.[267-270, 290-293, 297-307, 310-311]

Haugan, Paul. "TUBA Profile - Arnold M. Jacobs Tubist of the Chicago Symphony Orchestra." *TUBA
    Journal* 4, no. 2 (Winter 1977): 2-10.

Helmbrecht, Arthur. *Fritz Reiner: The Comprehensive Discography of His Recordings*. Novelty, Oh.:
    Fritz Reiner Society, 1978.

Hirsbrunner, Peter. "The History of the Big York-Hirsbrunner Tuba: The Instrument-Maker's Point of
    View." *Brass Bulletin* 40 (1982): 34-39.

Arnold Jacobs: *Song and Wind*

Indianapolis Symphony Orchestra Programs
     Personnel Rosters 1937-1940
     December 11, 1938 [performance of Dubensky Fantasia]

"Interview with Arnold Jacobs and Bill Russo." Broadcast on WFMT-FM,
     Chicago, Illinois.

"Interview with Arnold Jacobs and Jim Unrath." Broadcast on WFMT-FM,
     Chicago, Illinois

Kohut, Daniel L. *Musical Performance: Learning Theory and Pedagogy*. Englewood Cliffs, N.J.:
     Prentice Hall, 1985, 179-181

___. "Learning How to Perform Music." *TUBA Journal* 15, no. 4 (May 1988): 18-20.

Krell, John. *Kincaidiana*.Culver City, Ca.: Trio Associates, 1973

Leff, Rebecca. "Second Lives in the Second Symphony." *Symphony* 42, no. 3
     (May-June 1991): 60.

Leroux, Charles. "Beautiful Music is a Breeze for the Maestro of Breathing." *Chicago Tribune*, June 22,
     1982. Reprinted in *Getzen Gazette*. Elkhorn, Wi., September 1982.

Little, Donald. "A Young Tubist's Guide to the Breath." *TUBA Journal* 8, no. 3 (Winter 1981): 2-7.

___. "An Arnold Jacobs Clinic." *TUBA Journal* 15, no. 4 (May 1988): 21-26.

Lockspeiser, Edward. "Philadelphia Orchestra Tours Britain." *Musical
     America*, July, 1949, 6.

"Longy, Renee." Obituary in *Central Opera Service Bulletin*. 22, no. 1 (1980): 42-43.

"Looking Back." *Fine Arts Building Newsletter*, n.d. [History of the Fine Arts Building, 428 S.
     Michigan, Chicago, Illinois]

"Lung Function Testing: Selection of Reference Values and Interpretative
     Strategies", *Am Rev Respir Dis 1991*, American Thoracic Society,
     (March 1991).

Maldonado, Luis. "A Conversation with Abe Torchinsky." *TUBA Journal* 16, no. 4 (Summer 1989):
     17-21.

Marsch, Robert C. "Kubelik and the Thomas Tradition." Program notes to *Chicago Symphony
     Orchestra: The Kubelik Legacy*. Mercury Records MG 3-4500, 3-4501, 1973.

___. "Solti in Chicago, a Critical Discography." *Ovation* 5 (December 1984): 26-29, 35.

___. "An Illustrated Interlude." In *Ravinia: The Festival at its Half Century*, 43-76. Highland, Il:
     Ravinia Festival Association in conjuction with Rand McNally, 1985.

Arnold Jacobs: *Song and Wind*

Mayo Clinic Family Health Book, Eagan, Mn.: Mayo Foundation for Medical
Education and Research, IVI Publishing (CD-ROM Version), 1993

Meckno, Michael. "Arnold Jacobs." *Twentieth Century Brass Soloists*. Westport, Conn.: Greenwood
Press, 1984, 136-138.

"Meet Your First Desk Players." *International Musician* (November 1957): 10.

Meyer, Eileen. "Career Counseling: Interviews With Arnold Jacobs and Frank Crisafulli." *Journal of
the International Trombone Association* 13, no. 4 (October 1985): 32-33.

Microsoft Cinemania CD ROM. Bellevue, Washington: Microsoft Corporation. "Mary Pickford."

Monfried, Walter. "Tuba Man Arnold Jacobs Enjoys Tilting at Wind Ills."
Milwaukee Journal," March 23, 1975

Murrow, Richard. "August Helleberg, Sr. Part 1." *TUBA Journal* 10, no. 1 (Summer 1982): 2-3.

"News Supplement—World News." *Brass Bulletin* 62, no. 2 (1988): n.p.

Northwestern University. Press Release, "NU School of Music Names Eleven CSO Professors,"
January, 11, 1972.

Opperby, Preben. *Leopold Stokowski*. New York: Hippocrene Books, 1982.

Overtones: 50th Anniversary Edition. Vol. 11, no. 1, (October 1974). Philadelphia, Pa.: Curtis Institute,
1974.

Philadelphia Orchestra Program. Marcel Tabuteau, December 21, 1951, 265.

"Philly Cures Tuba-Culosis." *Billboard*, March 19, 1949, 20.

"Philly Orch, AFM Arbitrate Snarl." *Variety*, March 16, 1949, 38.

"Philly Orch British Tour Pacted in $400,000 Deal." *Variety*, February 5, 1949, 50.

Pittsburgh Symphony Orchestra Programs Personnel Listings 1938-1944

Ravina Festival Programs
Dale Clevenger, June 26-29, 1975
Jay Friedman, June 26-29, 1975
James Levine, 1980 season
Seiji Ozawa, June 16, 1964, p. 57

Ravinia Festival Assocation. *Ravinia: The Festival at its Half Century*. Highland Park, Il: Ravinia
Festival Association in conjuction with Rand McNally, 1985.

"Reiner Conducts Last Concert at Institute." *Musical America*, May 25, 1941, 39.

Reich, Howard. "The Honor is All Theirs." *Chicago Tribune*, September 18, 1994, Section 13, 16-17.

Arnold Jacobs: *Song and Wind*

___. "LAMA Night Made for City's Musicians." *Chicago Tribune*, September
19, 1994, Section 1, back page.

Rusch, Harold W. and Jacobs, Arnold. *Hal Leonard Advanced Band Method: With Special Studies by
Arnold Jacobs*. Winona, Minnesota: Hal Leonard Music, 1963.

Ryan, Nancy. "Orchestra Hall: Crushing Note" *Chicago Tribune*, May 19, 1995.
Section 2, page 1.

Schneider, Richard. "Arnold Jacobs Sounds Off." *Fritz Reiner Society
Newsletter* No. 4, n.d.

Schweikert, Norman. "Frank Brouk Retires from the Chicago Symphony." *The Horn Call* 9, no. 2 (April
1979): 75-78.

Schwendener, Peter. "The Best Tuba Player in the World." *Chicago Reader*, June 1, 1984, 1+.

"Seventieth Birthday Celebration Planned for Arnold Jacobs." *TUBA Journal* 8, no. 3 (February 1985):
17.

"Sevitzky Players in Ninth Symphony." *Musical America*, May 10, 1936, 22.

"Sevitzky to lead Indianapolis Players." *Musical America*, March 25, 1937.

Singer, Joseph. "The Basic Rules of Horn Playing." *Woodwind Magazine* 5, no. 1 (September 1952):
9-14.

Slonimsky, Nicolas, ed. *Baker's Biographical Dictionary of Musicans*. Seventh Edition. New York:
Schirmer Books, 1984.
[Claudio Abbado, Julius Baker, Daniel Barenboim, Leonard Bernstein, Fritz
Busch, Desire Defauw, Carlo Maria Giulini, Josef Hofmann, Raphael Kubelik,
James Levine, Erich Leinsdorf, Jean Martinon, Pierre Monteux, Eugene
Ormandy, Seiji Ozawa, Fritz Reiner, Arthur Rodzinski, Hans Rosbaud, Fabian
Sevitzky, Georg Solti, Leopold Stokowski, Georg Szell,Marcel Tabuteau, Bruno
Walter]

Smith, William Ander, *The Mystery of Leopold Stokowski*,
Associated University Press, 1990, p. 182

Software Toolworks Multimedia Encyclopedia. Novato, Ca.: Software Toolworks, Version 5.1, 1992.
[Claudio Abbado, Samuel Barber, Daniel Barenboim, Leonard Bernstein, Daniel
Beroulli, Robert Boyle, Butler University, Pablo Casals, Chicago Symphony
Orchestra, Curtis Institute of Music, Diaphragm, Carlo Maria Giulini, Josef
Hofmann, Raphael Kubelik, James Levine, Erich Leinsdorf, Gian Carlo Menotti,
Pierre Monteux, Northwestern University, Eugene Ormandy, Seiji Ozawa, Mary
Pickford, Pittsburg Symphony Orchestra, Georg Solti, Leopold Stokowski, Georg
Szell, Bruno Walter, Ralph Vaughan Williams]

Arnold Jacobs: *Song and Wind*

Stewart, M. Dee, ed. *Arnold Jacobs The Legacy of a Master*. Northfield, Il.: The Instrumentalist Company, 1987.

___. "An Arnold Jacobs Biography." *TUBA Journal* 15, no. 4 (May 1988): 14-17.

Stoddard, Hope. "Brass Ensembles—Twentieth Century Specialty." *International Musician* [February, 1958]: cover photo, 22-23, 42-45.

"Stokowski to Gather New Youth Orchestra." *Musical America*, January 10, 1941, 8.

Tabuteau, Marcel. "Marcel Tabuteau of Philadelphia Orchestra Summarizes Training." *Musical America*, November 25, 1944, 29.

"Tabuteau, Marcel." Obituary in *Opera News*, February 19, 1966, 33.

"Tabuteau, Marcel." Obituary in *Variety* (January 19, 1966): 63.

Taylor, John. "Reminiscences of the Man and His Horn." *TUBA Journal* 9, no. 2 (Fall 1981): 20.

Tracy, Bruce. "Orchestra Showcase The Chicago Symphony Orchestra. "*International Trombone Association Newsletter* 7, no. 2 (April 1980): 10-15.

___. "A Conversation with Robert Harper." *Journal of the International Trombone Association* 12, no. 3 (July 1984): 15-16, 18.

Trusheim, William H., *Mental Imagery and Musical Performance: An Inquiry into Imagery Use by Eminent Orchestral Brass Players in the United States*, Rutgers The State University of New Jersey - New Brunswick, 1987 [University Microfilms #8808237]

"Tuba Man Blows Top on Philly's Ork and Union." *Billboard*, April 16, 1949, 33.

Tucci, Robert. "A Closer Look at the Hirsbrunner York Model CC-Tuba." *TUBA Journal* 17, no. 1 (Fall 1989): 34-37.

"Valfy, Tereza M." Obituary in *Chicago Tribune*, December 29, 1985, Sec. 3, p. 7.

von Rhein, John. "Tuba or not Tuba, After 44 Years, Arnold Jacobs is leaving the CSO." *Chicago Tribune*, September 25, 1988.

Walters, Rick. *The Canadian Brass Book*. Milwaukee: Hal Leonard Publishing Corporation, 1992.[: 27-28, 92]

Whitfield, Edward J. "Remembrances and Recollections of Arnold M. Jacobs." *TUBA Journal* 12, no. 4 (May 1985): 7-8.

Whitman, Dale. "In Memoriam: Joseph Singer." *The Horn Call* 9, no. 2 (April 1979): 21-22.

Arnold Jacobs: *Song and Wind*

"Who is Arnold Jacobs?" *TUBA Journal* 15, no. 4 (May 1988): 30-34.
[Comments by: Sir Georg Solti, Volta Andy Anders, Roger Bobo, Chuck Daellenbach & Gene Watts, Eugene Dowling, Richard Frazier, Ralph Hepola, Fritz Kaenzig, Don Little, Dan Perantoni, Gene Pokorny, Chester Roberts, Roger Rocco, Abe Torchinsky, William Winkle.]

Yeo, Douglas. "Edward Kleinhammer: A Tribute." *Journal of the International Trombone Association* 8, no. 3 (July 1985).

Young, Jerry. "A Lecture by Arnold Jacobs." *TUBA Journal* 12, no. 1 (August 1984): 21.

"Youth Orchestra Plays in New York." *Musical America,* May 25, 1941, 12.

Name Index

Subject Index

Notes

Notes

Notes